United Nations Peacekeeping Operations
India's Participation
(Select and Completed Missions: Post-Cold War Period)

United Nations Peacekeeping Operations
India's Participation

(Select and Completed Missions: Post-Cold War Period)

R. Satyanarayana

AKANSHA PUBLISHING HOUSE
NEW DELHI • GUWAHATI • VISAKHAPATNAM

AKANSHA PUBLISHING HOUSE
4649-B/21, Ansari Road
Darya Ganj, New Delhi - 110 002
Ph.: 23263193 / 9811582579 / 09435116718
Fax: 011-23263193
Email: ektabooks@yahoo.com
www.akanshapublishinghouse.com

United Nations Peacekeeping Operations: India's Participation

First Published 2012

ISBN 978-81-8370-328-4

PRINTED IN INDIA

Published by Akansha Publishing House, New Delhi and Printed at Harmain Offset, Delhi.

Contents

	Preface	vii
	Acknowledgements	ix
	List of Acronyms	xiii
1.	Introduction	1
2.	United Nations Iran-Iraq Military Observer Group (UNIIMOG) Aug. 1988-Feb. 1991	30
3.	United Nations Observer Mission in El Salvador (ONUSAL) July 1991–April 1995	54
4.	United Nations Advanced Mission in Cambodia (UNAMIC) March 1992 May 1994	81
5.	United Nations Protection Force (UNPROFOR) March 1992–Dec. 1995	114
6.	United Nations Operation Mission in Mozambique (ONUMOZ) December 1992–November, 1994	146
7.	Conclusion	168
	Appendices	176
	Bibliography	221
	Index	241

Preface

It is said that peace is not merely the avoidance of war, but bringing in a comprehensive prosperity of both the strong and the weak; the strong lending a helping hand to the weak and leading them to prosperity. Without prosperity of all peace eludes but is never achieved.

The scourge of World War I extended far and wide beyond the warring nations and promoted leaders of the world to think of a world body for the prevention of such conflicts and for the founding of global peace and prosperity. This gave birth to the League of Nations, the aim of which as to successfully resolve disputes, promote collective security and tackle the problem of disarmament. As the major powers tried to promote their own interests the League of Nations became less effective resulting in World War II.

The scourge of the World War II was more pronounced than the first one and the gust of the cold war winds necessitated a more powerful world body namely the United Nations. U.S.A., U.S.S.R., U.K., France and China became the permanent members of the United Nations Security Council. The underlying rivalry between the U.S. and the U.S.S.R. camps and the veto power in the Security Council obstructed the effective working of the United Nations.

The end of the Cold War ushered in a new era for the United Nations. With the superpower rivalry removed many of the barriers that had hitherto prevented the United Nations from taking action, especially in the security realm, for example the United Nations support for worldwide military action against Iraq in the Gulf War of 1991, (the first collective security attempt since the Korean War of 1950).

The United Nations also authorized far more peacekeeping operations in the changed environment than in the forty five years of the cold war days.

The concept of peacekeeping changed fundamentally from the enforcement action described in Chapter VII of the United Nations Charter. It was restricted to a non-violent use of military force to preserve peace between two states. Now the post-cold war peace negotiations seemed more of settling intra-state wars. Today societies are going through post – conflict reconstruction. This required the development of an entirely new method of peacekeeping operations by the United Nations. This 'Second Generation' (as they are commonly known as) of peacekeeping operations is multifunctional with political, humanitarian, social and economic components requiring civilian experts to work in collaboration with peacekeeping soldiers. Several of these new operations took on functions such as humanitarian assistance, nation building and election supervision that previously were not within the purview of the UN peacekeeping.

India actively participates in most of the United Nations peacekeeping operations till date. She was one of the first states to answer the call by the then Secretary-General Dag Hamarskjold in 1956, when the United Nations Emergency Force was established. For India the peacekeeping activities of the United Nations is viewed from the point of her foreign policy. This study makes an attempt to understand India's role in the peacekeeping operations of the United Nations during the post-cold war and confines only to the completed missions. The selection of the cases were made such that they reflect one each from all the continents to ensure a global perspective of India's participation. Care has been taken while selecting the cases where the peacekeeping force performed multiple functions.

Author

Acknowledgements

I am deeply beholden to Prof. (Smt. B. Meena Rao), my Research Director for helping me, choose the topic as well as guide me through and through helping me in presenting the study in the way in which I did.

I am equally thankful to all the faculty of the Department of Politics and Public Administration, Prof. K. Sriranjani Subba Rao, H.O.D, Prof. P. Krishna Prasad, Chairman, B.O.S., Prof. M. Nalini, Prof. Madhusudan, Prof.K. Ravi, Prof. D. Syamala Devi, Prof.E.A. Narayana, Prof. K.A.P. Lakshmi, Prof. A. Venkateswara Rao, Dr. Hari, Dr. B. Ch. Appala Raju, Dr. S. Ratna-manikyalu, Dr. Premanandam as well as Messers. A.Sri Rama Murthy, Ch. Viswakala, K.Appala Raju, Appa Rao, L.Savitri of the non-teaching staff of the Department for their valuable cooperation.

I express my sincere gratitude to Prof. A.Prasanna Kumar, Prof. K.Venkateswarulu, Prof. D.Suran Naidu and Prof. B.S.R. Anjaneyulu for providing me useful suggestions whenever I met them.

I am very thankful to the Chief Librarian and other staff of Dr.V.S.Krishna Library, Andhra University for their cooperation.

I am deeply indebted to Jawaharlal Nehru University, United Services of India, United Nations Information Centre, Statistical Data Analysis of India, in Delhi for the assistance they provided me.

I am specially thankful to Prof. C.N. Murty of Jawaharlal Nehru University for providing good guidance to choose the books in their library and supplying me his articles on U.N.Peacekeeping and also Messers Gyan, Saroj and Chandra, who are research scholars in the University.

I'll be failing in my duty if I don't thank my friends Mr.Ganapathi Chanda, Assistant Registrar, Research Scholars, Mr.Niranjan Mahapatro and Behra, University of Hyderabad for their hearty cooperation in my work.

I could make use of the Library of Osmania University U.N. cell in Hyderabad and also the National Library in Calcutta where I enjoyed the sincere cooperation of the Chief Librarians and other staff and I offer my sincere thanks to them.

I express my indebtedness to Sri R.V.G.K. Ranga Rao, Chairmen of Rajah R.S.R.K.Ranga Rao College, R.V.S.K.Ranga Rao, Secretary Correspondent of the Raja College, Sri R. Badari South Eastern Regional Office of the University Grants Commission, Hyderabad and Commissioner of Collegiate Education of Hyderabad and Regional Joint Director, Rajahmundry for sponsoring me for research under F.I.P. in Xth Plan. I am equally thankful to Retired Principals, Sri D.Raghunadha Rao, Sri K. Appala Naidu, K. Lakshun Naidu, P. Satyanarayana and the Present Principal Smt. P. Anjali Devi and the staff, both teaching and non-teaching of my parent college for their undaunted cooperation.

I express my sincere gratitude to Sri A.L.Prasada Rao, E. Vijaya Kumar, J.V.B.Nageswara Rao. A.Subba Rao and B.V. Ramana, K. Eswara Prasad, Ch. Ravi, Smt. B. Gruha Lakshmi, B. Srinivasa Sastry, B. Sailava, R. Ravi Babu for extending their helping hand in finalizing my research work. I would also like to put on record my thanks to Akansha Publishing House, New Delhi.

Last but not the least I am deeply indebted to my mother, wife and children for not burdening me with domestic work and shouldering the complete responsibility and sparing me for my research work during the research period.

I express my gratitude to other relatives and friends for extending cooperation, support and encouragement in the successful fulfillment of my ambition to do research.

R. Satyanarayana

List of Acronyms

ARENA	Alianza Republicana Nacionalista
ASEAN	Association of South East Asian Nations
BLDP	Buddhist Liberal Democratic Party
C.D.	Convergencia Democratica
CCFADM	Joint Commission for the Formation of the Mozambican Defence Force
CMLO	Chief Military Liaison Officer
COMPOL	Police Commission
COPAZ	National Commission for the Consolidation of Peace
CPAF	Cambodian People's Armed Forces
CPP	Cambodian People's Party
CSC	Supervisory and Monitoring Commission
E.U.	European Union
F.M.L.N.	Frente Farabundo Marti para la Liberacion Nacional
FRELIMO	Frent da Libertacao de Mocambique
FUNCINPEC	United National Front for an Independent, Neutral , Peaceful and Cooperative Cambodia
GPA	General Peace Agreement

ICFY	International Conference on the Former Yugoslavia
ICORC	International Committee on the Reconstruction of Cambodia.
JNA	Yugoslav People's Army
KPNLAF	Khmer People's National Liberation Armed Forces
KPNLF	Khmer People's Liberation Front
LCY	League of Communists of Yugoslavia
MAC	Mixed Armistice Commission
MAC	Movimiento Autentico Cristiano
MINUSAL	United Nations Mission in El Salvador
MMWG	Mixed Military Working Group
MNR	Movimiento National Revolucionaria
MSN	Movimiento do Solidaridad Nacional
NADK	National Army of Democratic Kampuchea
OAU	Organization of African Unity
ONUMOZ	United Nations Operation in Mozambique
ONUCA	United Nations Observer Group in Central America.
ONUSAL	United Nations Operation in El Salvador
PAT	Auxiliary Transitory Police
PCN	Partido Conciliacion Nacional
PDC	Partido Democrata Cristiano
PDK	Party of Democratic Kampuchea
PMU	Partido Movimiento de Unided

PNC	National Civil Police
RENAMO	Resistencia Nacional Mocambicana
SNC	Supreme National Council
SOC	State of Cambodia
UD	Uniao Democratica
U.N.	United Nations
UNTSO	United Nations Truce Supervision Organization.
U.S.	United States
USA	United States of America

1

Introduction

Jawaharlal Nehru, in his statement on India's foreign policy made as early as 1946 said "The world, in spite of its rivalries and hatreds and inner conflicts moves inevitably towards closer cooperation and the building up of a world commonwealth. It is for this one world that free India will work, a world in which there is free cooperation of free people and no class or group exploits another".[1]

A long standing foreign-policy goal of India has been the solving of disputes (national or international) through peaceful means. This is very much in line with Chapter VI of the United Nations Charter which is fully devoted to the issue of pacific settlement of disputes in international relations.

India looked to the United Nations as a means to achieve her foreign policy objectives. In Nehru's words "Our basic international policy is that we want to be friendly with all countries. We work for peace in so far as we can...."[2] There is a perfect compatibility between resolving of issues through peaceful means as a goal of India's foreign policy and the maintenance of international peace and security as the goal of the United Nations. Thus to support and actively participate in the working of the United Nations is a fundamental principle of India's foreign policy though India is conscious of the big power domination of the United Nations and is critical of the existing structure of the United Nations because of the inadequate and disproportionately low representation of Asia and Africa in the Security Council, yet it has always tried to uphold the spirit of the United Nations Charter and it accepts its duty to work for it both in and outside the United Nations. India's main objective was to make the United Nations the real instrument of justice and peace."[3]

Even as a colonial state India had a direct linkage with the growth of multilateralism in international politics. India was a participant in the post- World War I Versailles Conference which led to the signing of the Treaty of Versailles in 1919. Though a British colony India was one of the original member of the League of Nations. Even as a subject country, India was committed to the cause of structuring global peace and stability through multilateral cooperation.[4]

In spite of the fact that the League of Nations fell far short of its expectations of maintaining international peace through multilateral cooperation, still that did not deter India's faith in international peace through international cooperation. Thus India was one of the founding members of the United Nations at the end of Second World War. Speaking at the United Nations General Assembly in Paris on 3 November 1948, Jawaharlal Nehru said "We do not think that the problems of the world or India can be solved by thinking in terms of aggression or war or violence. Nehru went on to add: "again I should like to state at this Assembly on behalf of my people and my government that we adhere completely and absolutely to the principles and purposes of the United Nations Charter and that we shall try to the best of our ability to work for the realization of those principles and purposes".[5] This faith in the United Nations remains unaltered even after the passage of 64 years.

The history of United Nations starts with President Roosevelt's Declaration to the Congress of United States of

America on January 6th 1941 embodying the four fundamental freedoms.[6] An agreement of allied nations was signed in London on June 12th 1941, who strongly felt that the only true base for peace is the willing cooperation among free nations of the world. They firmly believed that economic and social security can be enjoyed when they are relieved of the menace of aggression. The Charter was formally signed on 26th June 1945 by 51 states. The United Nations came into force on October 24th 1945, after the Great Powers and a majority of the signatory states had ratified it.

India has been one of the original members of the United Nations Organisation. It participated in the San Fransisco Conference and signed the Charter of the United Nations in 1945. Since that time India has been supporting as well as actively participating in the activities of United Nations and other international agencies.[7]

To support the ideology of the United Nations and to actively and constructively support its activities has been an important principle of India's foreign Policy. In other words India's foreign policy has been firmly committed to the purposes and principles of the United Nations.

To illustrate this view, it is pertinent to make a comparison of the United Nations purposes and principles which have been enumerated in Chapter-I, article 1 of the United Nations Charter and the fundamental principles and objectives of the India's Foreign Policy.

They are

United Nations Charter Principles and Objectives	*India's Foreign Policy Principles and Objectives*
1. To maintain international peace and security and to that end, take effective collective measures for the prevention and removal of threats to	Solving conflicts by peaceful means, adhering to the principle of Panch Sheel i.e.

(Contd...)

	United Nations Charter Principles and Objectives	*India's Foreign Policy Principles and Objectives*
	peace and for the suppression of acts of aggression or other breaches of peace and resolve conflict through peaceful means in conformity with the principles of justice, international law. Adjustment or settlement of international disputes or situations which might lead to a breach of the peace.	i. Mutual respect for each other's territorial integrity and sovereignty. ii. Non-aggression iii. Non-intervention in each other's domestic affairs. iv. Mutual benefits and equality and v. Peaceful – coexistence cooperation with all peace loving nations and the United Nations for promoting for international peace and prosperity.
2)	To develop friendly relations among nations based on respect for the principle of equal rights, and the right of self determination of people and take other appropriate measures to strengthen the Universal Peace.	The opposition to imperialism colonialism and respect equality of all nations.To maintain friendly relations with all and close relations with neighbours, support for world peace.
3)	To achieve international cooperation in solving international problems of economic, social, cultural or humanitarian character and in promoting and encouraging respect for human rights, and for fundamental freedoms for all without distinction to race, sex, language or religion and	Opposition to racial and social discrimination and neocolonialism and maintain good relations and to cooperate with all countries
4)	To be a center for harmonizing the actions of all nations in the attainment of these common ends.	Support for United Nations actions with respect to threats to peace, breaches of peace and acts of aggression.

About the Indian constitution, it is said "that there is hardly a single document in the entire realm of world constitutions, which agrees so scrupulously with the charter of the United Nations."[8] The United Nations charter contains several provisions for the function of maintaining international peace and security. To meet that need two provisions were regarded as imperative; the procedures for the "pacific settlement of disputes" found in Chapter VI and the ability to counter "threats to the peace, breaches of the peace, and acts of aggression" in Chapter VII also known as collective security.

Ironically, the term 'peacekeeping' is not found in the United Nations Charter. Dag Hammarskjold, the second United Nations Secretary-General referred to it as belonging to 'Chapter six and a half' of the Charter, placing it between traditional methods under Chapter VI, and more forceful action as authorized under Chapter VII.[9] But many a times it was felt that there ought to be something between these two chapters which would act as a buffer. This middle path was more to do with peacekeeping in war torn regions. Founders of the United Nations did not foresee anything like peacekeeping. The thought of using neutral international contingent to make possible the establishment of peace was a unique idea. Multilateral diplomatic efforts within the framework of the Security Council, bilateral efforts of member states or the good offices of the Secretary-General were considered as peacemaking efforts. Peacekeeping operations usually come into play when all peacemaking efforts failed to bring about permanent peace. All the peacemaking operations are only temporary measures. Their task is essentially to contain hostilities and help to create conditions and supervise the implementation of or final settlement negotiated between the conflicting parties. Observer missions are sometimes reinforced by infantry and logistic support usually for a specific purpose and for a brief period.

Alternatively peacekeeping forces are assisted in their work by unarmed military observers.[10]

Following the Arab-Israel conflict of 1948 the first United Nations peacekeeping mission which consisted of a team of observers was deployed to the Middle-east. The mission was officially authorized on May 29, 1948. This date is used as a memorial day to all the known as International Day of United Nations Peace-keepers in the memory of those who laid down their lives during their missions. The troop United Nations Truce Supervision Organization (U.N.T.S.O.) as it was named was tasked with monitoring the Armistice Agreement between Israel and its Arab neighbours and continues to monitor the situation and has provided observers for a number of conflicts in the region since then. Ralph Bunche Under Secretary-General for Special Politics. Affairs developed most of the rules for the peacekeeping operations. Peacekeeping normally involved an international effort by offering to place United Nations – authorized observers or military personnel into conflict region as part of an agreement to end hostilities.[11] It was always carried out with the express permission of both sides to the conflict. An interesting feature of the peacekeeping is that only military from small or relatively neutral states were included in the peacekeeping force and neither the superpowers nor any of the other permanent members of the Security Council contributed personnel. Either by virtue of the Security Council resolution or an Emergency Special Session of the General Assembly, a peacekeeping operation was supervised by the Secretary General or his designee. Peacekeepers arrived after both parties had negotiated a settlement, and then they position themselves between the combatants. The sole purpose of early peace-keeping efforts was to supervise the implementation of truce agreements and specifically to verify that both sides took appropriate actions to carryout the agreements already reached. Although military personnel were involved, they carried only light arms. Peacekeepers had no enforcement powers and were directed to use force just to defend themselves. Peacekeepers were sent only after the United Nations Secretariat negotiated a Status of Forces Agreement (SOFA), by which the host state-since it remained a sovereign nation-granted permission to use its territory. The agreement also defined the peace-keepers' powers, their access to facilities, and the specific territory in which they would operate.[12]

On account of the far-reaching changes in the post-war international relations, it became difficult if not impossible to use such measures even against other states for the maintenance of international peace. Neverthless, the United Nations continued to undertake such pacific-settlement activities as establishment of cease-fire lines and demilitarized zones, supervision of cease-fires, withdrawal of combatants from demilitarized areas, interposition of United Nations personnel between the armed forces of the disputant states, border monitoring, civil and military police functions, and observation and fact-finding. These pacific activities cannot be regarded as constituting conciliation or mediation by the United Nations, but they did create the necessary environment for the success of the United Nations mediatory role. The objectives of these pacific activities is to prevent and contain violence or to moderate and, if possible even to secure a termination of hostilities.

In addition to these pacific-settlement activities, the exigencies of the cold-war and specifically the urgency of the Suez Crisis (1956) made it necessary to set up a United Nations forces. In the light of the earlier experiences of United Nations intervention in such areas as Indonesia[13], Greece[14], Kashmir[15], and Palastine.[16] Lester B. Pearson[17], formulated the idea of establishing the United Nations Emergency Force (UNEF). The credit for further development of this idea into the concept of United Nations Peacekeeping operations should go to the political ingenuity and international statesmanship of Dag Hammarskjold. This distinctive and realistic approach to international peace-keeping was further perfected during the United Nations operations in Congo. Dag Hammarskjold made vigorous efforts for several years and evolved new methods and procedures to enable the otherwise-incapacitated principal organs of the organization to act with the help of non-aligned and relatively uncommitted member states as agents of preventive diplomacy.[18]

The authors of the Charter were not precise in their use of the term peace-keeping, and the meaning and scope of that term are still a matter of political and legal controversy. Peacekeeping operations of the United Nations are generally divided into three categories: Patching up (Investigation, mediation, supervision and administration), prophylaxis (accusation, sedation, obstruction and refrigeration), and proselytism (invalidation and coercion). Alan James differentiates between peace-keeping operations and collective security on the basis of "their attitude towards the associated issues of force and consent, collective security relying ultimately, on the mandatory use of force, while peace-keeping eschewed force, except in self-defense, and required the consent of the host state for the addition of United Nations personnel.[19]

Peace-keeping operations are in no way enforcement actions against any specific state or states in "the coercive and punitive sense" understood in Chapter VII of the United Nations Charter. The primary objective of peace-keeping operation which may at times be also called preventive diplomacy. If the essence of such an operation in any given situation consisting in preventing the involvement of the major powers, is to ensure that there is no deterioration in the situation and hence no need for any collective security operation. To quote Professor Inis L. Claude, Jr, "A collective security force in action aims to separate an aggressor, forcibly from the victim. A preventive diplomacy force in action aims to keep competitive powers, by mutual agreement, separated from each other"[20].

India's participation in peace-keeping began when the Indian combat troops were first assigned to Korea in 1950 as the Custodian Force of India. Pandit Jawaharlal Nehru, the first Prime Minister of India, gave the following message to it before its departure to Korea: "You the custodian force of India, deployed for the urgent humanitarian duty in the War-torn peninsula of Korea in the early 1950s, are going on a mission of peace and goodwill... with ill-will to none and categorical friendship to all. India and the Indian Army are honoured by being asked to undertake this task but the responsibility is a heavy one".[21]

The United Nations peacekeeping has gradually grown to meet the demands of different conflicts and changing political landscapes. Post-Cold War gave rise to fierce claims of subnational identity based on ethnicity, religion, culture and language. Thus the strategic context for United Nations peacekeeping, dramatically changed, and it expanded its field operations from "traditional" missions involving strictly military tasks to complex "multidimensional "enterprises, such as 1. monitoring elections 2. protecting inhabitants irrespective of majority or minority from the threat or use of force. 3. protecting designated "Safe areas" 4. ensuring partial demilitarization of particular areas 5. guarding the weapons surrendered by or taken from parties to a conflict. 6. assuring the delivery of humanitarian relief suppliers and the performance of a wide range of other humanitarian tasks during conflicts. 7. assisting in the reconstruction of governmental or police functions. 8. reporting of violations of international humanitarian laws by belligerents.[22] India's participation in the 'second generation' of peacekeeping operations has been as emphatic as the first generation of all developing nations India's participation has been consistent, as she continues to be committed to the peacekeeping missions. Thus since the end of cold war India has been engaged in most of the peacekeeping operations. India has traditionally being keen to contribute peace keeping troops to new situations as they rise. India has been and continues to be major player in United Nations peacekeeping operations.

As the number of peacekeeping operations grew, so did the complexity of situations confronting the Blue Helmets. Failed states presented challenges as governmental functions as well as the police and judiciary collapsed. Infrastructure was destroyed and populations were uprooted. Crimes against humanity, mass killings, massive displacement of populations, banditry and chaos became the order of the day.[23]

Hence peacekeeping operations became multifunctional. Political, humanitarian, social and economic components required civilian experts as well as relief experts to work in tandem with soldiers. Now the, peacekeeping troops or the Blue Helmets had to help regroup and demobilize combatants, destroy weapons, coordinate massive humanitarian assistance as well as programme human rights. Supervise elections in Nicaragua, Eritrea and Cambodia and other parts of the world. They encouraged peace negotiations in El Salvador, Angola, and Western Sahara. They distributed food in Somalia.

The United Nations today has evolved to be a neutral intervening force. Maintaining neutrality, however, poses a big dilemma, especially when confronted with situations where civilians were victimized or when the Blue Helmets themselves are attacked or killed. In some situations some groups play the peacekeepers against their opponents in order to gain advantage or relief, deny access to victims and confiscate relief supplies and equipment. In such situations it is imperative that the United Nations and the international community integrate the relevant dimensions of the problems developing a coherent vision, strategy and plan of action for responding to such situation.

To consider the new opportunities for international peace and security, the Security Council met for the first time at the level of heads of state or government on 31st January 1992. The Council asked the then Secretary General Boutros Boutros Ghali for "analysis and recommendations on ways of strengthening and making more efficiency the capacity of the United Nations for preventive diplomacy for peacemaking within the frame and provisions of the charter." The Secretary-General, in response, submitted a report on 17th June 1992 entitled "An Agenda for Peace", followed by a supplement to the report on 3rd January 1995, which considered the vital role of the United Nations in pursuing and preserving peace. The central theme of this report is that the role of the United Nations must assist in a progressive way from conflict prevention, resolution and emergency assistance to reconstruction and rehabilitation, and then to economic and social development.[24]

The basic features of peacekeeping operations in brief, falls into nine points.

- The first essential one is peacekeeping operations should be undertaken with the consent and tacit approval of the parties to the conflict, their consent about the countries for contributing troops is equally necessary.
- Secondly the operation must not interfere in the internal affairs of the host country and should be strictly impartial. The impartiality is fundamental not only on grounds of principles but also to extract continuing support and cooperation from the conflicting parties.
- Thirdly peacekeepers have no right of enforcement of resolution and the use of force is limited to self defence as a last resort.

- The peacekeeping operations are undertaken by the Security Council specifically authorizing the Secretary-General.
- A broad consensus within the international community is another important factor and the Security Council is responsible to ensure the mandate.
- The next characterize flows from this that is, the Secretary-General receives the necessary support and cooperation from the Security Council to implement the mandate in any ambiguous situations and recurrent and controversial difficulty.
- The military personnel serving on peacekeeping operations are provided by member states on a voluntary basis and they act under the command of the Secretary Council.
- The military observers are almost invariably unarmed. The forces in peacekeeping are armed with light weapons purely in self defence. The right to use force is sparingly exercised as their use obviously affects impartiality and so exceptional restraint is demanded on the part of the soldiers in peacekeeping operations.
- Finally it is essential that the operation should have a sound financial basis. All operations are financed by obligatory contributions levied on member states. In effect, the countries contributing the soldiers must bear an unfairly high share of the cost of the operation too.

The United Nations has been involved in several peace-keeping operations since its establishment. A study of these peace-keeping operations is of great importance because these operations constitute a significant innovation in the activities of the United Nations.

Statement of the Problem

The essence of India's foreign policy lies in the effort of

solving conflicts by peaceful means and cooperation with all peace loving nations, and support for United Nations actions with respect to threats to peace, breaches of peace and acts of aggression. These two are directly associated with the basic principles and objectives of the United Nations Charter that is, to maintain international peace and security through collective measures and resolve conflict through peaceful means in conformity with the principles of justice and international law. India has always supported multilateral cooperation for maintaining international peace. India being one of the founder members of the United Nations actively participated in most of the United Nations peacekeeping missions throughout the world. She is a major contributor to the peacekeeping forces. In this context the scholar has observed that India has worked together with the United Nations towards these endeavours in United Nations peacekeeping operations. Therefore the researcher has specifically undertaken the study of five cases namely:

1. Iran - Iraq (UNIMOG) 1988 – 1991
2. El Salvador (ONUSAL) 1991 – 1995
3. Cambodia (UNAMIC & UNATAC), 1992 -1994
4. Croatia (UNPROFOR & UNCRO) 1992 – 1995
5. Mozambique (ONUMOZ) 1992-1994.

To examine this contention each case has been studied in its entirety. These are the peacekeeping missions of United Nations in which India participated in the aftermath of the cold war. The title of the study is 'Untied Nations Peacekeeping Operations: India's participation (select and completed missions: post cold-war period)'.

Need for the Study

Peacekeeping operations, not foreseen in the United Nations Charter, emerged ad hoc in response to international crisis. During cold-war (1945-1989) a total of forty four years there were a mere thirteen peacekeeping operations worldwide, when compared to the post-cold war period from 1990 to date there is fifty peacekeeping missions globally. India has been an integral part of these missions. Given the significant role of these peacekeeping forces in the changed scenario in the post-cold war period, it would be very valuable to study the United Nations peacekeeping force and their missions. The declining of the use of veto in the post-cold war period is perhaps responsible for this. Another reason is the mood of optimism of the role of United Nations in international security and peacekeeping. The Secretary General Boutros-Boutros Ghali's "An Agenda for Peace" reinforced this optimism. There has been a dramatic expansion in the number and functions of United Nations peacekeeping and observer forces. Hence the need for a study of United Nations Peacekeeping operations and India's commitment to world peace in the post cold war period.

Objectives of the Study

1. To understand the dynamics of the peacekeeping operations.
2. To study the role of United Nations Peacekeeping force in the specific cases under study.
3. To assess India's participation in the United Nations peacekeeping operations in those specific cases.

Scope of the Study

1) The scope of the study is limited to only those peacekeeping operations in which India had a role.
2) The study confines itself to the post-cold war period focusing only on a few selected and completed missions. The selection of cases is on the basis of one each from five continents to reflect and ensure that United Nations peacekeeping operations have a global perspective.

3) The post-cold war peacekeeping operations run into nine different functions. The selection of the cases was made such that taken together all the nine functions are reflected between them.

Methodology

In this study five cases where India was a part of the United Nations peacekeeping operations has been dealt with. The period of study is from 1988 i.e. post-cold war and the choice of cases is confined to those in which India participated. Care was taken to ensure that the cases were completed at the time of doing research to enable the researcher to understand the issue in its totality. To understand the universal characteristic of the working of the peacekeeping operation, the case-studies were deliberately taken one from each continent. On the basis of these criteria, the following instances of United Nations peacekeeping operations were selected for the study. 1. United Nations Iran-Iraq Military Observation Group (UNIMOG) Aug 1988 – February 1991, 2. United Nations Observer Mission in El Salvador (ONUSAL) July 1991 – April 1995, 3. United Nations Advanced Mission in Cambodia (UNAMIC), which merged with the United Nations Transitional Authority in Cambodia (UNATAC), March 1992, May 1994. 4. United Nations Protection Force (UNPROFOR) and United Nations Confidence Restoration Operation in Croatia (UNCRO), March 1992 – Dec. 1995. 5. United Nations Operation Mission in Mozambique (ONUMOZ) December 1992-1994. Each case has been studied in its entirety.

For every case study the background of the issue and under what circumstances it became necessary for the United Nations peacekeeping to intervene was also dwelt with. An attempt was also made to study in detail the Security Council resolutions, the operations carried out by the peacekeeping forces and how peace was restored in these specific cases. In addition to this an attempt is made to assess India's involvement in these cases, even though the United Nations peacekeeping missions are carried out under the common United Nations flag.

For the collection of data both primary and secondary sources have been used in the study.

The primary source comprised of interviews with the defence personnel who participated in peacekeeping operations at the United Service Institution, and the Institute of Defence and Strategic Analysis, New Delhi. The research scholar also interacted with personnel of the Ministry of External Affairs and some diplomats from other countries at the United Nations Information Center, New Delhi. The researcher also held consultations with Mr. Kuldip Nayar former High Commissioner of Great Britain.

Apart from books and journals the secondary source includes documented material and United Nations reports were also consulted. Information available on the internet was used extensively. Numerous newspapers clippings pertaining to the period of study were consulted.

Extensive use of material available at a number of libraries namely Jawaharlal Nehru University, Delhi University, United Services Institution and United Nations Information Center at Delhi, University of Hyderabad, Osmania University and American Studies Research Center at Hyderabad, the Andhra University V.S.K.Library at Visakhapatnam were referred to. Some reports carried out in newspapers pertaining to the period of study were also referred to at the National Library, Kolkata. In addition to this United Nations newsletters, United Nations chronicles, United Nations yearbooks as well as United Nations Peacekeeping resolutions at the United Nations Information Center were referred to. Some documented material available at the Indian Defence and Strategic Analysis were also consulted.

Review of Literature

"Peacekeeping in International Politics" written by Alan James discusses broad political circumstances which have given to rise to peacekeeping operations. The book is set in five parts, and each part is devoted to the different kinds of peacekeeping operations.

The first category outlines the 'backyard operations', i.e. those which take place within the sphere of influence of a major power. The second category deals with peacekeeping operations arranged by a group of states to deal with an 'intra-group problem'. Thirdly comes the category of 'neighbourhood quarrels'. Fourthly, in some cases, the concerned state, instead of resolving the issue internally, takes the matter to the United Nations. Finally there arises the possibility of a minor accident to become a major conflagration.

"The Evolution of United Nations Peacekeeping" is an edited volume by William J.Durch. The author describes peacekeeping through a number of case specific studies and then goes on to do a comparative analysis of the cases. He makes a study of twenty structured operations from 1947 to 1991. Between 1990 and 1992 he conducted nearly a hundred interviews which formed the basis of a policy report which was released in March 1992. This study is closely focused on peacekeeping and does not address peace enforcement;

"Peacekeeping and Public Information" is edited by Ingrid A.Lehmann. This book deals with international communications and conflict management by international organization. The five carefully researched case studies in this book-illustrate the mutually reinforcing relationship between public perceptions of a crisis and the international response to it. Lehmann's analysis concludes that it is only

the operation itself which can be relied upon for accurate reporting about its purposes and activities.

"The Politics of Peacekeeping" written by Alan James. In this book the author gives an in-depth analysis of the concept peacekeeping. He traces the growth of peace-keeping from 1948 (UNEF) to the present. In this course of evolution he draws attention to how peacekeeping falls within a very vide definition as the nature of peacekeeping operations are multifaceted.

'The United Nations and Peacekeeping Results, Limitations and Prospects; The lessons of 40 years of Experience' edited by Indarjit Rikhye and Kill Skjelsbaek. This is a compilation of eleven articles on the potentials and problems of peacekeeping. Some of them are: Henry Wiseman in his article.

'Peacekeeping in the International Political Context (Historical Analysis and Future Directions)', suggests that peacekeeping functions can be grouped into three categories—military, political and civil. He puts emphasis on the principle of consent and argues that with consent, peacekeeping operations have proved more successful.

Kjett Skjelsbaek's work *'United Nations Peacekeeping: Expectations Limitations and Results: 40 years of Mixed Experience'*, brings to light the political controversialist surrounding the peacekeeping operations. He notes that United Nations peacekeeping represents the concerns of the international community and argues that the United Nations Blue Berets carry an international stamp of legitimacy.

In *'Peacekeeping and peacemaking. The need for patience'* by Gunther G.Greindl makes a study of the peace-keeping operations in Cyprus in 1964. In this work Greindl suggests ways to minimize the loopholes in peace-keeping operations.

'The Management of United Nations peacekeeping by James O.C. Jonah deals with the structural changes in peacekeeping force. For a better understanding Jonah traces the peacekeeping force from the United Nations Emergency Force 1956 the first peacekeeping force upto 1988.

'The Financing of United Nations peacekeeping operations The need for a Sound Financial Basis' by Susan R. Mills, Deputy Controller of the United Nations makes a presentation in her paper, discusses the financial aspects of peacekeeping. Having first hand experience with the system she provides a summary of financing methods.

'Peacekeeping and the Parties' written by Alan M. James in his paper states that the success of the operations rests on certain factors. He opines that peacekeeping firstly rests on the consent of the state or states on whose territory the peacekeepers operate, secondly that it must have the cooperation of relevant disputants whether or not they happen to be host states and thirdly providing personnel and finances by the contributing states, and finally he says there must be complete and unquestioned respect for the principle that a peacekeeping body operates on the basis of impartiality.

'Peace-building in Post-conflict Societies: strategy and process' by HO-Won Jeong offers a systematic approach to strategies and processes for long-term social, political and economic transformation, on a case specific basis. The focuss in this book is on the psychological trauma which the victims are scarred with, sometimes for life.

'Introduction to International relations' of Pierre Marie Martin in French translated by Arti Sharma and edited by J.C. Johari. He discusses the cooperation in international organizations, the characteristics of the United Nations and maintenance of peace through United Nations Organization.

'The United Nations' by Prem Arora dealt with practical working of the peace keeping operations in many countries.

'The Untied Nations and Collective Security' by K.P. Saksena pointed out the challenges to peace force, the response, assessment and conclusion.

'Building Peace', 'An Agend for Peace', by Boutros - Ghali clearly distinguishes between the concepts of peace making, peacekeeping, peace building operations and the procedures.

In *'Cooperating for peace'* Gareth Evans wrote about maintenance, peace by restoring peace, enforcing peace, and cooperation for peace in his book.

'Dag Hammerskjold's memorial lectures' edited by Andrew W Cordier and Wilderfoot published under the titles *'The Quest for peace'* gives a graphic picture of the efforts of the international organizations for international peace and security only.

'The United Nations in the 1990's: A Second Chance by Max Jakobson gives a detailed narrative of the birth of peace-keeping, an overview is also given in this book regarding the dynamics of international securing in the post-cold war. Jakobson also clearly defines the concepts of peace-keeping and peace-making. The book traces the traditional peace-keeping developed into peace-making in the twenty first century.

'View from the U.N.' by U.Thant former Secretary General of United Nations focused the key role of the Secretary-General as a mediator and his efforts for peace.

'The Blue Helmets: A Review of United Nations peacekeeping' published by the Department of Public Information of United Nations gives comprehensive account of the peacekeeping operations of the United Nations from 1984-1990 as well as the role of the Blue Helmets.

Steven Ratner (Member of the United Nations Secretary-General's three person group of experts for Cambodia) in his book *"The New UNITED NATIONS Peacekeeping: Building Peace in Lands of Conflict after the cold war"* describes the different roles of peace-keeping. At one stage the functions were mainly military, which later on were more politically focused. The author has made multiple case studies. Steven Ranter gives a detail account of the peace-keeping operation in Cambodia, which was by and large a political function.

'New Dimension of Peace-keeping' edited by Daniel Warner is a collection of papers from convention held in Geneva March 1994. The papers presented dealt with military and humanitarian aspects of peace-keeping in former Yugoslavia, Cambodia and Somalia. In addition a critical analysis of peace-keeping as a whole is also dealt with.

'Keeping the peace: multidimensional United Nations Operations in Cambodia and El Salvador' edited by Michael W.Doyle, Ian Johnstone and Robert Carr, discusses at length the peace-keeping operations in Cambodia and El Salvador. Critical assessment is made of these two operations which not only established after cold war but also played multiple roles.

'Peace-keeping and Peace making towards effective intervention in the post-cold war conflicts 1998 by Tom Woodhouse, Robert Bruce, Malcolm Dando, *1998*. The papers presented at the conference distinguished between the changing nature of conflicts. They hold the view that international conflicts are divided between interstate conflicts and intrastate conflicts. Therefore it is vital for the United Nations to first to make the distinction and then deploy peace-keeping force.

'A future for peace-keeping' edited by Edward Moxon Browne, *1998*. The authors of the different papers had distinctive perspectives. Some were of that view the peace-keeping in its traditional function is valid even today, even though the nature of peace-keeping functions has changed.

Some papers presented the opposite view that deploying armed force at a short notice only increase the risk. For them sending a peace-keeping force had to be done after a lot of contemplation regarding the time and resources were taken into considerations.

'The Politics and Practice of United Nations Peacekeeping: past present and future' is written by Indrajit Rikhye, Climentsfort, Canada, published by the Canadian peace-keeping press. The book is divided into five chapters, beginning with that overview of the evaluation of peace-keeping operations. The book deals with theoretical and practical dimensions of peace-keeping. It also describes the changing nature of peace-keeping operations before and after cold war.

REFERENCES

1. Nanda, B.R., *Indian Foreign Policy: The Nehru Years,* Vikas Publishing House, New Delhi, 1976, p.280.
2. *Indian Foreign Policy Affairs, Volume VII,* No.6, 1964, p.38.
3. Parkatil Francis, *India and United Nations Peace–Keeping Operations,* S. Chand & Co. Pvt. Ltd., 1997, p.175.
4. http: Fletcher, tufts, ed/multilaterals, html.
5. Nehru, Jawaharlal, India's Foreign Policy Selected Speeches, September 1946 – April 960, The Publication Division, Ministry of Information and Broadcasting Government of India, 1961, pp.162-163.
6. Freedom of religion

   Freedom of Speech and Expression.

   Freedom from want

   Freedom from fear.
7. Clark Grenuille and Sofa B. Lavis, (Second edition revised), *World Peace through world Law',* Harvard University Press, 1962, pp.5-11.
8. Francis Parkatil, *op.cit,* p.181.

9. See Appendix No. I.
10. Alan James, *The Politics of peace-keeping,* Chatto and Vindus Ltd., London, pp.3,45.
11. Higgins Rosalyn, *United Nations peacekeeping 1946-1967,* New York, Oxford University Press, 1980.
12. Bloomfield, Lincoln P.etal., *International Military Force,* Boston: Little Brown, 1964.
13. Negotiations between the Netherlands government and Indonesian leaders, begun in 1945, led to the Linggadjati Agreement, formally signed on March 25, 1947. For the establishment of a United States of Indonesia within the framework of the Kingdom of the Netherlands. Each side soon charged that the other had violated this agreement, and on July 20, 1947, Dutch troops began military action against the so-called Indonesian Republic. This action was immediately brought to the attention of the Security Council by Australia and India, and on August 1, 1947, the Council called on both parties to cease hostilities and to settle their differences by peaceful means.

    To assist in the settlement the Council set up a Committee of Good Offices, composed of representatives of Australila, Belgium, and the United States, with Dr. Frank P. Graham as the first American member. After negotiations aboard the U.S.S. Renville under the auspices of the UN committee, Dutch and Indonesian negotiators signed, on January 17, 1948, a truce plan and a set of principles to serve as a basis for settlement. Despite the strenuous efforts of the committee, negotiations for the political implementation of the Renville agreement dragged on through the rest of 1948.

    In December Dutch troops resumed military operations. The United States formally requested an emergency session of the Security Council to deal with the new situation. The Council issued a cease-fire order and passed several resolutions; but for weeks the Dutch government refused to comply with these resolutions, even re-enforced as they were by pressure of world public opinion, by official remonstrance's from several nations and by the resolutions of an Asian conference convened in New Delhi by the Indian Prime Minister, Jawaharlal Nehru.

    The United Nations Commission for Indonesia, which had replaced the Committee of Good Offices, was finally able to effect an agreement under which Dutch troops evacuated Jogjakarta, leaders of the Indonesian Republic were released from their confinement, and hostilities were brought to a halt. In July, 1949, the Indonesian government returned to Jogjakarta, and on the twenty-third of that month Republican and Federalist leaders announced that they had reached an agreement on the creation of a United States of Indonesia. A round-table conference at The Hague, held shortly after wards and attended by representatives of the Dutch government, Indonesian Republicans and Federalists, and the UN Commission for Indonesia, confirmed the general terms of the understanding and outlined the steps by which the transfer of sovereignty should be effected. Both Dutch and Indonesians, encouraged by the UN commission, implemented these far-reaching agreements in good faith. As a result, a new state – the Republic of Indonesia – was born.

Palmer and Perkins: 'International Relations', CBS Publishers and Distributors, Delhi, 1985, p.328.

14. Cases involving the political independence and territorial integrity of Greece were on the agenda of the Security Council almost continuously from 1946 to 1951. In January, 1946, the Soviet Union charged that the presence of British troops in Greece constituted a threat to peace. After some debate the Council adopted a resolution saying that it had heard the statements in the matter and considered the incident closed.

    In August, 1946, the UIkrainjan Soviet Socialist Republic complained of internal conditions in Greece and of incidents along the Greek-Albanian frontier, allegedly provoked by Greek troops. A proposal that the Council establish a commission to investigate the facts relating to the alleged border incidents was vetoed by the Soviet member.

    On December 3, 1946, Greece contended that her neighbours to the north were aiding Greek guerrillas and were, in fact, promoting civil war, and asked the Council to order an on-the-spot investigation. The Council unanimously voted to create a Commission of Investigation. On May 27, 1947, eight of the eleven members of the commission reported to the Security Council that "Yugoslavia, and to a lesser extent, Albania, and Bulgaria" had "supported the guerrilla warfare in Greece". With only the Soviet and Polish members dissenting, the commission proposed the establishment of a new "watchdog" commission. With the Council's approval the commission thereupon appointed a Subsidiary Group to keep the Council informed of activities along the Greek border.

in Palestine, and concluded its report in Geneva on August 31. Its report to the General Assembly contained eleven general principles unanimously agreed upon by the committee, a majority plan for the partition of Palestine, with economic union, and a minority plan for a federal state. On November 29, in a tense plenary session, the General Assembly adopted by the required two-thirds vote the plan for the partition of Palestine, with economic union, and an international area for Jerusalem. It then named a commission to implement the recommendations.

For once the United States and Russia had agreed on a major political issue. Both supported the partition plan, and the United States was largely responsible for its adoption by the General Assembly. Jewish leaders hailed the action of the Assembly as a great victory; but Arab spokesmen warned that such a plan would never be accepted, and the increasing tempo of violence in the Holy Land gave weight to their warnings. The Palestine Commission soon reported to the Security Council that it could not "discharge its responsibilities on the termination of the Mandate" unless assisted by armed force. Until early March, 1948, the United States continued its firm support of the partition proposal; then, on March 19. Warren R. Austin, the American representative in the Security Council, without previous warning to the British or any other government, formally proposed that the Security Council instruct the Palestine Commission to suspend its efforts to implement the partition plan. He urged, instead that a temporary trusteeship for Palestine under the Trusteeship Council of the United Nations be established and that a special session of the General Assembly be called to consider this new proposal.

Although Secretary-General Trygve Lie pointed out that a trusteeship for Palestine might be even more difficult to implement peacefully than the partition plan, he issued a call for a special session of the Genera] Assembly, to meet on April 16. On April 17 the Security Council requested· all groups in Pakstine to desist from acts of violence, and on April 23 it established a Truce Commission. The special session of the Assembly - the second special session to consider the Palestine problem - showed little enthusiasm for the "Draft Trusteeship Agreement' for Palestine" which the United States submitted on April 20. Instead it passed an innocuous resolution, instructed UNSCOP to terminate its activities, established the office of United Nations Mediator for Palestine, and appointed Count Folke Bernadotte of Sweden to that office.

At midnight on May 14, 1948, at the expiration of the British mandate, the new state of Israel was proclaimed. This action, plus other developments of April and May, led to renewed hostilities in Palestine and to attempted invasion of the Holy Land by Egyptian troops. A cease-fire order of the Security Council, issued on May 29 and vigilantly supervised by Count Bernadotte and military observers from Belgium, France, and the United States, produced a truce of four weeks. Thereafter fighting resumed, with the armed forces of Israel quickly gaining the advantage over the combined Arab armies. In mid-July a stronger cease-fire order of the Security Council was generally observed, except in the Jerusalem area, until well into October, when serious fighting broke out in the Negev in southern Palestine. On September 16 Count Bernadotte finished his last and most definite plan for a settlement in Palestine. Two days later he was murdered in Jerusalem Dr. Ralph Bunche, an American who had been Count Bernadotte's chief assistant, was named acting mediator. His efforts, reinforced by two strong resolutions of the Security Council in November, met with only partial success throughout the remainder of 1948, but early in 1949 Egypt and Israel agreed to suspend hostilities and to undertake armistice negotiations.

On December 11, 1948, the General Assembly voted to establish a Conciliation Commission to assume the functions of the mediator and the Truce Commission. At the second part of the Third Session, held in the spring of 1949, Israel was admitted to the United Nations as the fifty-ninth member, in spite of the bitter opposition of the Arab states. Lengthy negotiations between Israel and the Arab states, conducted by Dr. Bunche mostly on the island of Rhodes, resulted in four general armistice agreements being signed between February 24 and July 20, 1949. On August 11, the Council declared that these superseded the truce directed by the Council on July 15, 1948, and it relieved the mediator of further responsibility to the Council. Later negotiations at Lausanne failed to bring agreement on final terms of peace.

Twice in succeeding years the uneasy truce forged by United Nations efforts dissolved into warfare. The crises of 1956 and 1967 were so significant, and the role of the United Nations in relation to them so important, that they are given separate consideration in this chapter.

Palmer and Perkins: *'International Relations'*, CBS Publishers and Distributors, Delhi, 1985, p.332.

17. A strong advocate of the United Nations role in peacekeeping. He won the Nobel Peace Prize in 1957 for organizing the United Nations Emergency Force to resolve the Suez Canal Crisis. http://www.an.org/en/peacekeeping.

18. *Op.cit.,* Palmer & Perkins.

19. Alan James, *The Politics of Peacekeeping.*

20. Professor Ihis L. Claude Jr.

21. Mr.Rajan, *United Nations and World Politics* Har, Anand Publications, 1995, pp.87,237.

22. Gareth Evans, *Co-operating for Peace,* Allen & Unwin, Australia, p.99.

23. *The Blue Helmets, A Review of the United Nations Peace-Keeping*, U.N. Publication DPI/80, 1990.

24. See Appendix No.IV.

2

United Nations Iran-Iraq Military Observer Group (UNIIMOG)

Iran and Iraq are two neighbouring countries in South West Asia. Afghanistan and Pakistan are to the east of Iran, while Arabian Sea and Persian Gulf were to the South and South west and Iraq is to the west of Iran with Caspian Sea and Turkmenistan to the north of Iran. Turkey is to the northwest and Syria is to the west, Zordan to South West and Saudi Arabia to the South of Iraq.[1]

There is a historical legacy for vulnerability and aggression in the region. Iraq claims a long historical ancestry from the ancient Mesopotamian Kingdoms.[2] Iraq began to be drawn into a messy conflict with Iran-first, over the boundary along with Shatt-Al-Arab water way in the South and then, vie for support for ethnic and political dissidents in each other side, into sporadic armed conflict.[3] Encouraged by America and Israel, Iran shah waged a covert war against Baghdad manipulating the kurds in 1970.[4] Algeers agreement in 1975 defined the frontiers of Iran and Iraq.[5] Iraq then appeared to find peace with Iran. Less than four years later the Shah was overthrown and a new militant regime was in power in Tehran. It called for the overthrow of the Baathist government in Iraq which was considered the second apostate regime doomed to follow Shah's into oblivion.[6] Iran supported

UNIIMOG Deployment as of June 1990

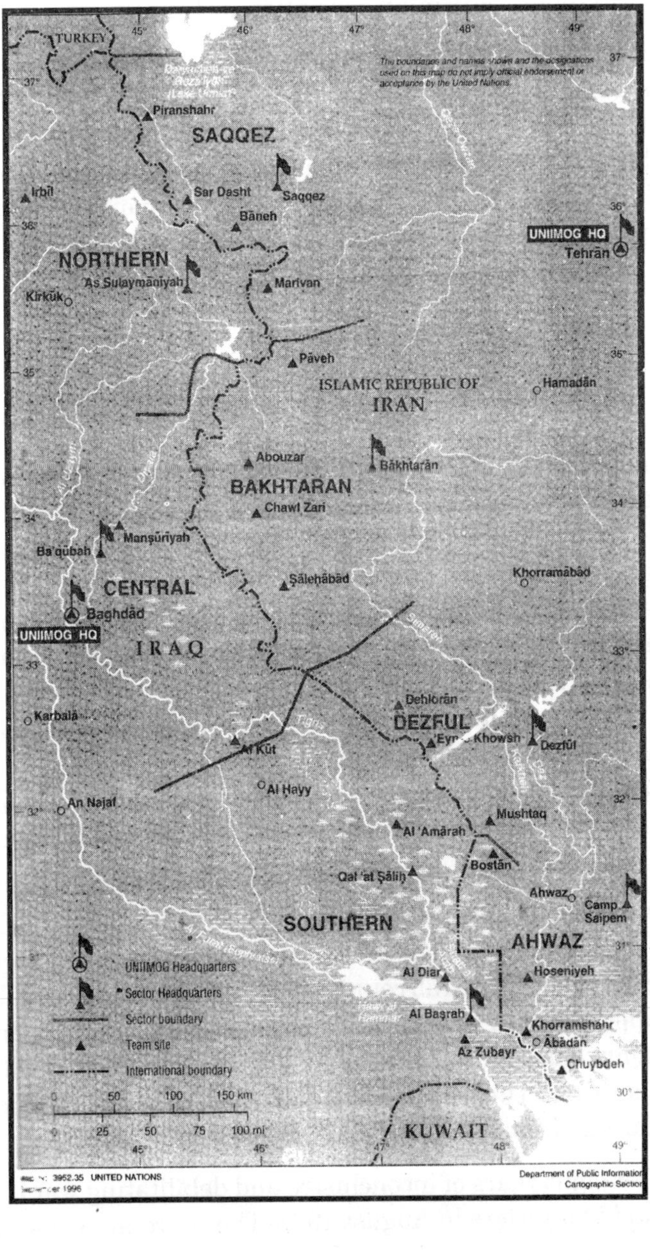

the urban guerrillas of the Iraqi Shiite Dawn party which hoped to replicate Iranian revelation in Iraq.[7]

Shias are the dominant sect in Iran while Sunnis are the dominant sect in Iraq, although Shias are also in good number besides Kurds. However it is not a war between two sects of Muslims. The main reason for the war is border dispute. There are differences with regard to the area on the banks of Shatt–Al-Arab river.[8] Iraq contended that Kurdistan under the occupation of Iran should naturally belong to Iraq. Similarly Iran too claimed certain areas under Iraq's occupation.[9]

Iraq is economically vulnerable because of its geographical position. Its access to the Persian Gulf from its only port of Basra was liable to Iranian interruption. Its oil pipelines ran through states that could, if political relations worsened, interrupt the flow. The Iranians used the Kurdhs before 1975 and again during the latest war.[10] This is Iraqees sense of anxiety on one side. Iraq too was feared and suspected. Iraq refused to recognize the frontiers of its neighbours. In spite of 1975 treaty Iran renounced it and played the Shatt-Al-Arab card once again.[11] The Kuwait dispute, dormant for some time was focused on a few Islands at the mouth of Shatt-Al-Arab. Iraq's aspirations for hegemony in the region were also feared. Saddham was lucky to survive the war with Iran inspite of Iranian denunciation of his regime.[12]

The eight year war between Iran and Iraq started in 1979. Ayathulla Khomeni was a fundamentalist to the core. So the neighbouring Arab countries with liberal outlook could not support him. Iraq was ruled by the socialist government of Saddam Hussain.[13] U.S. and its allies supported Iraq with arms against the fundamentalists of Iran for fear of domination of fundamentalists in the region.[14]

After eight years of inconclusive and debilitating war the U.N. had to interfere in August 1988. The Secretary General

Kurt Waldheim authorized by Security-Council started intensive negotiations between the two foreign ministers of the Islamic republic of Iran and Republic of Iraq. Both accepted the suggestion of the secretary-general for immediate cease-fire and direct talks between the two foreign ministers under the auspices of the Secretary-General of the United Nations. Attempts by the United Nations to seek an end to the war dated back to 1980 with the outbreak of armed conflict between Iran and Iraq. The Secretary General of U.N. Kurt Waldheim offered his good offices to work for a peaceful settlement of the conflict. He brought the threat to the international peace and security to the attention of the Security Council on 23rd September 1980 in accordance with article 9 of the United Nations charter. In the resolution of 479 of 28th September 1980 the Council, among other things, called upon both Iran and Iraq to immediately refrain from any further use of force and settle their dispute through peaceful means. It had little effect.

Mr. Olof Palme, the former Prime Minister of Sweden was appointed as the special representative of Secretary-General to Iran and Iraq on 11th November 1980.[15] Shortly thereafter he undertook a mission to the region. Some progress was made on the freeing of merchant shipping caught in the hostilities in Shatt-Al-Arab water way. A limited number of prisoners of war were exchanged in 1981 and 1982. Yet a settlement remained elusive.

The efforts were stalled on the issues of the responsibility for the war and control of Shatt-Al-Arab. The United Nations was able to play a role on the issue of the bombing of purely civilian population centers of both countries. For that missions despatched by the Secretary-General confirmed the use of chemical weapons and investigated the situation of prisoners of war in both countries. The year 1984 saw the establishment of the first United Nations' presence in the area. On June 1984 the Secretary-General Javier-Perez-de-cullar appealed to both the sides to refrain from deliberate military attacks on purely civilian centres of population.[16] Iran and Iraq agreed to this. The Security Council, on receiving information from the Secretary-General took a decision to deploy inspection teams in the region. Their main task would be to investigate alleged attack on civilian population. This truce in the "War of the cities" lasted for some nine months. Two teams each composed of three officers selected from the military personnel of the United Nations Truce Supervision Organisation (UNTSO) and one senior official of the United Nations Secretariat were installed in Baghdad and Tehran.[17] Their presence in the capitals helped to expedite the establishment of UNIIMOG (United Nations Iran and Iraq Monitoring Group).

Iran's military successes between 1982-1986 were ephemeral and costly with long gaps between major offensives from 1984-86.[18] The problem was as much due to deficiencies in strategies as to logistics. Iraq was unwilling to resort to counter-offensives or to take casualities. Saddham confined its troops more to defensive strategy. However, he flagrantly violated the prohibition of the use of chemical weapons. Though successive U.N. investigations had verified and found the mustard gas and tabun nerve gas since 1984 only March 1986 did the U.N. Security Council explicitly named Iraq as the culprit.[19] Iran and Iraq had been trading attacks on each other city centres since 1984. Iraq used its air superiority to take the war home to Iran by bombing Tehran in the spring of 1985.

The escalation of the war had increasing international repercussions. Attacks on merchant shipping in the Persian Gulf including repeated strikes against commercial oil tankers became more frequent.[20] In response, several countries dispatched mine sweeping vessels and air crafts in an effort to facilitate safe commercial passage through international waters.[21] The Secretary General undertook a new diplomatic initiatives to reach a settlement between the two in January 1987.[22] Enlisting the cooperation of all the members of the council at a meeting in his office on 23rd January 1987, he suggested a number of proposals for their consideration. After extensive consultations, the council adopted the resolution 598 of 20th July 1987 accepting[23] propose. The Secretary-General's endeavours more fruit because of the readiness of all the five permanent members to work together to put an end to this long standing conflict between Iran and Iraq.

The Council requested the Secretary General to explore, in consultation with Iran and Iraq, the question of entrusting an impartial body with enquiring into the responsibility for the conflict and to report to the council as soon as possible. A team of experts were to be assigned the study of the question of reconstruction of destructed areas. He was also asked to explore measures to enhance the stability of the region in consultation with not only with Iran and Iraq but also with the other states in the region. He was further asked to keep the Security Council informed on the implementation of the resolution.

Iraq welcomed the resolution and informed the Secretary-General of its readiness to cooperate in the implementation of the resolution. However, Iran, while not rejecting the resolution, criticized fundamental defects and incongruities in the resolution.

The Secretary-General travelled to Tehran and Baghdad in September 1989 and intensive diplomatic activity ensured.[24] Negotiations took place in the region as well as at U.N. Head Quarters in New York. The Secretary General tabled the implementation plan of the resolution in October 1987. It contained his original plan presented to the council in September 1987. He repeatedly met the representatives of both the countries in the Spring of 1988 in an attempt to reach an accord with both on the implementation of the resolution 598. The Secretary General invited both sides in March 1988 to send special representatives to New York for consultations in April 1988.

Meanwhile the war continued with the ever present risk of widening of the hostilities. Naval vessels sent by a number of countries to escort merchant shipping in the Persian Gulf were involved in incidents with one or the other of the combatants. In July 1988 the U.S. Vincennes, a United States cruiser, mistakenly shot down an Iranian commercial air lines killing all Two Hundred and Ninety passengers and the crew on board.[25] On 17th July 1988 Iran notified the Secretary-General of its formal acceptance of the resolution 598. It expressed the need to save life and to establish justice and regional and international peace and security. The following day Iraq also reaffirmed its agreement with the principles embodied in the resolution.

The Secretary-General met the foreign ministers of Iran nine times and the representative of Iraq six times between 26th July and 7th August 1988. The talks aimed at steps to be taken to the implementation of the resolution. After intensive efforts and with the assistance of regional diplomacy, the president of Iraq declared his readiness for a cease-fire to be followed by direct talks on 6th August 1988. The Secretary-General, in his letter dated 8th August 1988, informed the permanent representatives in Iran and Iraq that both governments agreed for direct talks between their foreign ministers to be held under his auspicies immediately after the implementation of the cease-fire. The talks were meant to reach a common understanding of the other provisions of the Security Council's resolution 598 (1987), and the procedures and timing for their implementation. With the formal agreement insight, the Secretary-General sent a technical mission to Iran and Iraq to workout the modalities for the dispatch of United Nations observer group. Lieutenant General Martin Vadsat of Norway, Chief of Staff U.N.T.S.O.

led the mission which included a senior political adviser, a civilian logistics expert and four military observers from United Nations Truce Supervision Organizaion (U.N.T.S.O) led the mission which included a senior political adviser, a civilian logistics expert and four military observers from U.N.T.S.O. It was assisted by the small teams which had been stationed in Baghdad and Tehran since 1984. In the course of three working days in Tehran and three in Baghdad, the mission held detailed discussions with the political and military authorities in both capitals about the method of operation of the military observer group called for in the resolution 598, its deployment in each of the two countries and the cooperation and facilities it would require from both parties.

The information furnished by the technical mission was used in defining the terms of reference and the concept of operations of UNIIMOG. The Secretary-General presented a report to the Security Council containing his proposals for the composition and the precise mandate of the UNIIMOG. Once a date for the cease-fire had been agreed. This was achieved on 8th August 1988 when he announced the agreement of both Iran and Iraq to a cease-fire from 0300 GMT on 20th August 1988. Direct talks between the two countries would begin under his auspices on 25th August 1988 in Geneeva.[26]

UNIIMOG's mandate in accordance with the resolution 598 was to verify, confirm and supervise the cease-fire and withdrawal. Its terms of reference were set out in the Secretary-General's report of 7th August 1988.[27] They are (a) to establish agreed cease-fire lines on the basis of the forward defence locations occupied by both the sides on the D-day but adjusting these, as may be agreed, when the position of the two sides were adjudged to be dangerously very close to each other; (b) to monitor complaints of the cease-fire; (c) to investigate any alleged violation of the cease-fire and restore the situation anti to the violation; (d) to prevent through negotiations, an other change in the status quo, pending withdrawal of all forces to the internationally recognized boundaries; (e) to supervise, verify and confirm the withdrawal of all forces to the internationally recognized boundaries; (f) to monitor thereafter the cease-fire on the internationally recognized boundaries, investigate alleged violations and prevent through negotiations, any other change in the status quo pending negotiations of a comprehensive settlement, and (g) to obtain the agreement of the parties to other arrangements pending negotiation of a comprehensive settlement which could help to reduce tension and build confidence between them in such matters as the establishment of areas of separation of forces on either side of the international border, limitation on the number and category of weapons to be deployed in areas close to the international border, and patrolling the United Nations naval personnel of certain sensitive areas in or near the Shatt-Al-Arab. The Secretary-General also drew attention, in his report on 7th August 1988, to four essential conditions to be met for UNIIMOG to be effective.[28] 1. It should have at all times the full confidence and backing of the Security Council; 2. It had to enjoy the full cooperation of the two parties; 3. It should be able to function as an integrate and efficient military unit; 4. adequate financial arrangements were to be made to cover all costs.

The Secretary-General further recommended that the guidelines which had been in vogue to the peacekeeping forces in general since 1973, should be applied mutatis mutandis to UNIIMOG. The group would be under the command of the United Nations, vested in the Secretary-General under the authority of the Security Council which the Secretary General would keep fully informed. UNIIMOG would act with complete impartiality. It would proceed on the assumption that the parties would take all necessary steps to comply with the decisions of the Security Council, including giving it the freedom of movement and communication and other facilities that would be necessary for the performance of its tasks. It would be composed of a number of military contingents to be provided by the member states at the request of the Secretary-General. The contingent would be selected in consultation with the two parties as well as the Security Council, bearing in mind the accepted principle of equitable geographical representation.

The Security Council approved the Secretary General's report in its resolution 619 of August 1988 and decided to establish UNIIMOG immediately for a period of six months.[29] Major General Salvko Jovic of Yugoslavia was appointed to the post of Chief Military observer and Brigadier General S. Anam Khan of Bangladesh took command on Jovics departure in November 1990. At its peak the total military strength of UNIIMOG was approximately 400 of all ranks including some 350 military observers. The military observes were contributed by Argentina, Australia, Bangladesh, Canada, Denmark, Finland, Ghana, Hungary, India, Indonesia, Ireland, Italy, Kenya, Malaysia, New Zealand, Nizeria, Norway, Peru, Poland, Senegal, Sweden, Turkey, Uruguay, Yugoslavia and Zambia. New Zealand operated an air unit and the observer group also included military police provided by Ireland and medical orderlies from Austria. At the beginning of the operation and pending the establishment of a civilian operated communication system, a signal unit from Canada ensured the vital communications which UNIIMOG needed. As in other peacekeeping operations UNIIMOG also included international and locally recruited civilian staff.

One day after the enabling resolution of the security council i.e. 10th August 1988, the first of UNIIMOG two advance parties arrived in Iran and Iraq.[30] Each group consisted of 12 military observers (9 of whom were temporarily drawn from U.N.T.S.O.) in addition to the team leaders and a civilian component. In the days before the arrival of the main body of military observes, the advance parties established liaison with Iranian and Iraqi authorities and conducted reconnaissance of the forward locations where UNIIMOG would be deployed. The cease-fire came into effect as stipulated in the agreement. By that time three hundred and seven military observers and the main elements of the Canadian signals unit were present in Iran and Iraq and 51 patrols were deployed on the very first day. These patrols had the double task of establishing the forward defence locations occupied by the two sides when the cease-fire came into the effect and of defusing confrontations resulting from actual or alleged breaches of cease-fire. In some areas there existed disagreement between the two sides over the precise positions of both held on 20th August 1980. This became one of the principal causes of tension at certain points.

On 1st September 1988, the Secretary-General appointed Jan Eliasson of Sweden as his personal representative on issues pertaining to the implementation of Security Council resolution 598. Preliminary Agreements concerning the status of UNIIMOG were conducted with the governments of Iraq and the Islamic of Republic of Iran. They embodied the principles of the charter of the United Nations as well as the convention on the privileges and immunities of the United Nations based on the experience of previous United Nations peacekeeping operations. They were intended to ensure UNIIMOG's ability to function independently and, in particular, the freedom of movement and communications and other facilities that were necessary for the performance of its tasks.

It was originally envisaged that UNIIMOG group Head Quarters would be divided between Baghdad and Tehran, with its Iran detachment Head Quarters at Bakhtaran, and Iraq detachment head quarters along side group head quarters at Baghdad. However the group and detachment head quarters were merged into a single UNIIMOG head quarters one in Baghdad and another in Tehran to increase efficiency and to release more military observers for patrol duty on the cease-fire lines.[31] The chief military observer and his senior staff, known as "Command group" spent alternate weeks at each headquarter. An assistant Chief Military observer was permanently stationed in each capital and directed UNIIMOG's operation in the country and concerned under the overall command of the Chief Military observer.

Originally, the military observers were deployed in four sectors on the Iranian side with the sectors head quarters at Saqquer, Bakhtaran, Dezful, and Ahwaz and three on the Iraqi side with sectors head quarters at Sulaymaniyah, Baqubah, and Basra. Each sector controlled a number of team sites which were located as forward as possible in order to minimize the time spent by military observes travelling between team site and cease-fire line. The length of the cease-fire line was monitored by a team site varied from 70 km. in the South to 250 km. in the north.[32] The air wing of UNIIMOG consisted of three fixed wing aircraft for communication, observation, and freight and passenger duties. It was also envisaged that UNIIMOG would also operate a squadron of United Nations helicopters for observation of no man's land and cease-fire lines but one of the parties did not agree to that arrangement each at a particular place. As a result UNIIMOG military observers had to use helicopters provided by the parties themselves and which could therefore fly only behind the respective cease-fire lines. This inhibited UNIIMOG's ability to maintain close observation of the cease-fire line.

The cease-fire lines extended approximately fourteen hundred kilometres. It covered a wide variety of terrain. UNIIMOG had to adopt the method of patrolling according to the terrain. Teams of two or more military observers conducted mobile patrols by vehicles, by helicopters, by boats in the southern marshes and on mule back or on foot in the mountain terrains of the north. UNIIMOG deployed a daily average of 64 patrols around the clock. The patrols' primary task was to check that the side to which they were assigned was complying with the cease-fire. They did this through their own regular observation of the forward defence locations and by verifying complaints received from the other side. They also transmitted complaints to their counter parts on the opposite side of the cease-fire lines. Wherever necessary, they negotiated a return to the statusquo with the commanders on the spot. Where this was not possible, the matter was referred to the relevant sector headquarters so that it could be taken up with the liaison authorities of the side concerned. Besides investigating alleged violations, the military observers engaged themselves in such humanitarian and confidence-building measures as they exchanged the dead found on the battlefield. Observers from both the sides of the cease-fire lines maintained radio communication across no man's land and also met regularly in it. Both Iran and Iraq established interdepartmental groups to coordinate cooperation with UNIIMOG. Both provided liaison officers and logistic facilities required of them.

UNIIMOG received frequent complaints of alleged cease-fire violations throughout the mission. During the first nine weeks one thousand and seventy two (1072) such complaints were recorded. The number, however, declined steadily as cease-fire stabilized. All complaints were thoroughly investigated. Some of them were confirmed, but many were minor in nature. However, more significant violations did occur on 23rd and 24th August 1988 shortly after the commencement of the cease-fire. Several hundred Iranian soldiers were taken as prisoners in a serious incident near Eyn-E-Khowsh. Another serious violation was on 13th September 1988 when Iran started flooding an area of no man's land in the Khusk region. This created a water obstacle between the forward position occupied by the two armies which in this area lay, immediately to the east of the internationally recognized water. The area under flooding was the scene of several military confrontations. The flooding ceased to affect Iraqi positions after the withdrawal of Iranian forces in 1990. There were also some firing incidents. Other violations included the movement of troops, the establishment of new observation posts or other positions in the forward defence locations and the reinforcement of defensive positions was by wiring, mining, improving bunkers and general engineering works. In all such cases UNIIMOG endeavored successfully to persuade the side concern to restore the status quo.

The situation in the region worsened significantly following the Iraqi invasion and occupation of Kuwait in August 1990.[33] Although this development complicated the work of UNIIMOG, the Iran-Iraq border remained significantly calm. In spite of the continuing cease-fire violations of the nature described above, the overall implementation of UNIIMOG's mandate proceeded without major hindrance. By the end of September 1990, the withdrawal of all forces of both the sides to the internationally recognized boundaries had been almost completed. There were however, a few locations where, in UNIIMOG's view, the forces of each side remained on the wrong side of the borders. Under these circumstances, the Secretary-General recommended to the Security Council to extend the mandate of UNIIMOG for a limited period of only two months instead of six months as had been done on three previous occasions. This, the Secretary-General opined, would permit UNIIMOG to complete its tasks relating to the withdrawal of forces and would also allow time to both the parties and the security council whether there was continuing requirement for an impartial third party to monitor the cease-fire.

During this period, it was suggested that UNIIMOG would concentrate on (a) verifying confirming and supervising the stages of the withdrawal, (b) help the parties to resolve any local tensions that might arise as a result of differences about the exact line of the border, forward moves, accidental firing etc and (c) assist the parties in establishing an area of separation, an area on either side of the borders into which each party would agree not to deploy any military forces. It was also judged that only 60 percent UNIIMOG's existing strength would be required to perform these tasks.[34]

The Security Council concurred with the recommendations of the Secretary-General and adopted the resolution 671 of 27th September 1990. The strength of UNIIMOG was reduced to two hundred and thirty in all ranks including One hundred and eighty military observers. In the course of such reduction, the military observers were redeployed in the three sectors on the Iranian side with the sector headquarters at Saqqez, Bakhtaran and Dezful, and three on the Iraqi side with sector head-quarters at Sulaymaniyah, Mansuriyah and Basra.

In the following two months both sides continued the process of withdrawal of their forces to the internationally recognized boundaries.[35] Both sides, however, continued to occupy or reoccupy positions in the proposed area of separation. In some cases local tensions rose high when the two sides established positions in close proximity or even co-located with each other. But there were no series of incident. Difficulties also occurred because of the presence of unmarked minefields in area from which the forces were withdrawing, especially on the Iranian side of the border.

In the meantime the Secretary-General held consultation with the two parties about the future of UNIIMOG after the expiry of the two months mandated period. The Secretary-General opined that after the with-drawl of the forces had been completed, UNIIMOG would still have continuing role of play in facilitating the early solution of residual problems arising out of the withdrawl of the forces, and in helping the parties negotiate and implement agreements on areas of separation as well as in the area of limitation of armaments.[36] The Secretary-General felt that the mandate should extended for a longer period than two months and that the strength of UNIIMOG could be reduced to fifty to sixty observers on each side.

The parties had divergent views on these issues. The Iraqi side expressed a strong preference for the mandate to be renewed for a full period of six months without reducing UNIIMOG's existing remaining strength. The Iranian authorities refused to accept the extension of the mandate for more than two months although they did not rule out the possibility of a further extension there after and also insisted on the reduction of UNIIMOG's strength from fifty to sixty observes on each side. Under the circumstances, the Secretary-General had no choice but to recommend to the Security Council to extend the mandate of UNIIMOG for a period of two months with the strength not exceeding one hundred and twenty military observers, plus the necessary support personnel. The Security Council adopted a resolution 676 of 28th November 1990 accepting the Secretary General's proposals. As agreed with the parties, UNIIMOG, during that period was mandated to resolve the remaining problems on the border, try to arrange an exchange of information between the parties about unmarked minefields and also to help in the negotiation and implementation of the area of separation and subsequently arrange limitation of armaments too. The number of military observers were reduced to sixty on the Iranian side and fifty six on the Iraqi side and three in the command group. This necessitated a further reorganization of deployment of UNIIMOG's observers. On each side a small number of observers were deployed in the headquarters with approximately fifteen military observers in each of the three sectors. All previous team sites were closed on permanently manned locations and became forward patrol basis which were manned as the situation demanded.

In January 1991 the two parties agreed to conduct a technical meeting of military experts to discuss and resolve the question of relating to the UNIIMOG's mandate about still outstanding issues.[37] An agreement was reached bilaterally and the meeting itself was organized outside the frame work of the mixed military working group that UNIIMOG had previously tried to establish. The meeting was attended by the acting Chief Military observer of UNIIMOG. The two sides also reached agreement on the question of disputed positions along the internationally recognized borders, in the area of separation along those boundaries and the exchange of information on minefields. These agreements were fully consistent with UNIIMOG's mandate. The agreements also provided for UNIIMOG to monitor the implementation within a specified time frame.

The disputed positions were all to be removed by 22nd January 1991.[38] UNIIMOG was then to verify and confirm the completion of the withdrawal of all forces to the internationally recognized border described in the 1975 treaty. concerning the state frontier and neighbourly relations between Iran and Iraq. The agreements in the area of separation provided for one kilometer withdrawal on both sides along the entire length of the recognized borders. This was to take place between 10th and 27th January 1991 with UNIIMOG helping in the implementation.

Due to the outbreak of the hostilities in the area in mid-January 1991 the implementation of the agreement, however, could not proceed fully according to the schedule by the end of January 1991 Iran had withdrawn thirteen out of the seventeen disputed positions and Iraq had withdrawn twenty three out of twenty nine such positions. There was a little progress made in relation to mine-cleaning also.

UNIIMOG's capacity to fulfil the role assigned to it was seriously affected after the adoption of the Security Council's resolution 678 of 29th November 1990, authorizing the use of all necessary means by a multi national coalition of Iraq did not withdraw from Kuwait by 15th January 1991. UNIIMOG undertook detailed planning to ensure the security of its personnel without compromising operational efficiency. With the deterioration of the situation in the second week of January 1991, it was decided to thin out both military and civilian staff in Baghdad. Following the Secretary-General's visit to Baghdad on 12th – 13th January 1999, a decision was taken to relocate UNIIMOG's personnel temporarily from Baghdad to the sectors closer to the border. The command group moved to Tehran on 14th January 1991. After the outbreak of hostilities on 16th January 1991, all remaining UNIIMOG staff in Iraq was also moved either to Cyprus or Iran.[39]

In spite of these difficulties the Secretary-General again recommended to the Security Council that the mandate of UNIIMOG, set to expire at the end of January 1991, be extended for another month so that the group may fullfil completely its important responsibilities. He stated that the implementation of the Security-Council's resolution 598 of 1987 as related to UNIIMOG was very close to completion. To implement what still remained to be done, the role required of the Secretary-General was mainly political and, he intended to recommend how that could be achieved. The Security Council unanimously adopted the resolution 685 of 31st January 1991 extending the mandate of UNIIMOG to 28th February 1991.

In the following months as a result of continuing hostilities in Persian Gulf region, UNIIMOG continue to operate in the Iranian part of the area only but maintained regular contacts with Iraqi authorities through meetings on the borders. At the beginning of February 1991, some twenty military observers from Iraq side whose duty tours were due to expire, returned home. The balance of the observers who had come from Iraq were temporarily relocated in Cyprus to await a possible return to Iraq as circumstances demanded.

During the period, UNIIMOG continued to assist the parties in the implementation of the bilateral agreement of January 1991. The group reported on 20th February 1991 that the last of the disputed positions along the internationally recognized boundaries had been withdrawn. UNIIMOG thus completed verification and confirmation of the withdrawal of all forces in accordance with the resolution 598 of 1987. Both the sides informed UNIIMOG of their compliance. However, in the case of Iraq, UNIIMOG was not in a position to verify its compliance. However, the parties continued their cooperation with regard to the exchange of information about unmarked minefields.

The Secretary-General, reporting to the Security Council on 27th February 1991, described the general situation along the Iran-Iraq borders as very calm. He also reported, with considerable satisfaction that the forces of two sides had withdrawn fully to the internationally recognized borders and that military component of the resolution 598 of 1987 could thus be considered completely implemented. The remaining tasks under that resolution were essentially political in nature and therefore the Secretary-General recommended to replace UNIIMOG with small civilian offices in Baghdad and Tehran. Accordingly the Secretary-General recommended that the council take no action to further extend the mandate of UNIIMOG. The Security Council informed the Secretary-General of its concurrence with his proposals. Thus UNIIMOG completed its mandate on 28th February 1991. At the time of the withdrawal UNIIMOG consisted of ninety six military observers from Austria (1), Bangladesh (1), Canada (4), Denmark (3), Finland (9), Hungary (15), India (11), Ireland (1), Italy (9), Malaysia (10), New Zealand

(1), Norway (1), Poland (1), Sweeden (7), Turkey (1), Uruguay (9), Yugoslavia (11), and Zambia (1). The group also included military police provided by Ireland (60) and a medical unit from Austria (2).[40]

The civilian officers were appointed in February 1991. A few military officers attached to them were allowed by the United Nations to continue to respond promptly to the requests by either of the governments to investigate and help resolve matters for which military expertise was required. These officers were also important in the Secretary General's efforts to complete the implementation of the resolution 598 of 1987. The resolution also referred to fixing of the responsibility for the conflict. The Secretary-General, in his report in December 1991 added that no useful purpose would be served in pursuing the matter. He suggested, in the interests of peace it would be rather imperative to move on with the settlement process. The offices in Baghdad and Tehran were phased out by the end of 1992. The permanent missions of Iran and Iraq became the channels of communication between the two countries and the United Nations on matters related to resolution 598 of 1987.

The Secretary General originally recommended to the Security-Council that the cost of UNIIMOG should be considered as expenses of the organization to be borne by members in accordance with article 70 of Paragraph 2 of the U.N. Charter. He further informed the council that he intended to recommend to the General Assembly that the assessments to be levied on the member states should be credited to a special account which should be established for this purpose. General Assembly duly accepted this recommendation in its resolution 42/233 as early as 17th August 1988. The total financial commitment of UNIIMOG came up to $ 177,895,000.

The Iran-Iraq war was completely something unusual among the conflicts in the third world. The most commonly cited are the costs in human life, the economic resources and the inordinate length. Even according to Rafsanjani the total Iranians killed were 1,33,000. The deaths were attributed to missile and air attacks on cities. The battle of Huweiza marshes resulted in at least 20,000 estimated causalities on the Iranian side even according to Iraqi officer corps. The evidence suggests that the Iranian offensive too inflicted a sizahle Iraqi causality as many as 7,500 to 10,000. Iraq spent more than Iran every year between 1981 to 1985 in ratios between 6:1, and 3:1 in terms of arms purchase. Iraq maintained the constant annual rate of $ 12 to 14 billions while Iran's expenditure dipped from $ 14 billions to 5.89 billions almost during the same period. Thus it was one of the costliest wars with limited resources. The war continued for nearly eight years. The advent of a cataclysmic change in Iran replacing the Shah of Iran by a revolutionary order that made claims on its neighbours was the principal reason for the instability in the region. Iran's rhetorical excesses and claims and inattention to the military balance were matched on the Iraq side by compound of fear about Iran's goals if the revolutionaries were to become entrenched in ambition to achieve regional supremacy on Iraq was relatively un-matched in military and economic strength. The revolutionary régime in Iran eagerly embraced the war as a "Blessing", labeling it as a struggle between "Islam and Blashemy". It defined its war aims as the overthrow of the Baathist regime in Baghdad. Rafsanjani wanted to use the war to suppress his enemies at home. The war thus came to represent a test for the revolution. Iraq relied on superior weapon system because of its continued access to friendly governments especially USSR and France after 1982. Iran by contrast relied heavily on the superior commitment of its forces. They believed in the faith of Islamic troops stronger than Iraq's superior fire power". Iran fought the war with both hands tied; without dependable or rich allies, without access to weapons system compatible with those in its inventory. Iran for a time seemed to be winning the war. The breakthrough at Fao in February 1986 seemed to confirm that Iranian victory was only a matter of time. By February 1986 it was felt that peace was only possible with the removal or disappearance of one of the two leaders Saddham Hussain or Ayatallah Khomeini. Compromise seemed unimaginable. Iran could not loose the war nor Iraq win it. The instruments of war were dwindling. Iran's much vaunted numerical advantage of 3:1 in terms of population was not much in evidence on the battle field. Iraq was able to increase its man power by some 150,000 men and expand its forces from 30 to 39 infantry divisions. The war became harder for Iran. The Iran's strategy of internationalising the conflict began to bear fruit. The internationalization of war, regional isolation and the threat of future comprehensive arms embargo increased psychological pressure on Iran. By the end of 1987 Iran's leadership had begun to despair a military solution to the conflict. The U.S. Naval vessel destruction of Iran-Air bus compelled Khomeini's approval for accepting cease-fire.

The determined effort of International community, the Secretary General's personal visits to Baghdad and Tehran, the special representatives uncompromising and unstinted efforts to bring both parties to the conference table and the realization on both sides, Iran and Iraq, are all responsible for the success of UNIIMOG. UNIIMOG conformed closely to the traditional concept of United Nations peacekeeping. The United Nations military observers were effectively deployed on the cease-fire between the hostile parties. Diplomatic initiatives were pursued to reach a comprehensive settlement. By the time UNIIMOG completely withdrew, the military component of the resolution 598 of 1987 was successfully completed. UNIIMOG succeeded in separating the hostile parties along the internationally recognized border. The non-pursuit of fixing of the responsibility for the conflict too was a wise decision.

U.N. efforts to end the eight year long war (1980-88) between Iran and Iraq led to the establishment of UNIIMOG. Its mandate was to verify, confirm and supervise the cease-fire and withdrawal of the troops behind the internationally recognized borders. The terms of reference were: (a) establish agreed cease-fire lines between the hostile parties. (b) monitor the compliance of the cease-fire, investigating any alleged violations and restoring status quo; (c) to prevent through negotiations, any other required changes in status quo pending withdrawal of all forces to the internationally recognized boundaries; (d) thereafter effectively monitor the cease-fire obtaining the agreement of the parties for a comprehensive settlement of all affairs. At its peak the total military strength of UNIIMOG was approximately four hundred of all ranks including three hundred and fifty military observers. Brigadier V.M. Patil from India was appointed as Assistant Chief Military observer (Iraq). India contributed second largest contingent besides Hungary. The Indian Military observers performed their tasks in difficult areas with admirable dedication, professionalism and impartiality.

REFERENCES

1. *The World Book of Encyclopedia,* World Book Incorporation, Ascott Setzer Company, pp.318, 327
2. Fred Halliday, Iraq And Its Neighbours: The Cycle of in Security, *The World Today,* June 1990, p.104.
3. *Op cit.,* The World Book of Encyclopedia, p.323.
4. Claudia Wright, Religion and Strategy in the Iraq – Iran War, *Third World Quarterly,* 7(4) October 1985, p.839.
5. *Op cit.,* The World Book of Encyclopedia, p.326.
6. *Ibid.,* p.327.
7. *Op cit.,* Fred Halliday, p.104.
8. *Op cit.,* Claudia Wright p.842.
9. *Op cit.,* The World Book of Encyclopedia, p.329.
10. *Op cit.,* Claudia Wright, p.842.

11. *Op cit.,* The World Book of Encyclopedia, p.329.
12. *Op cit.,* Fred Halliday, p.105.
13. *Op cit.,* The World Book of Encyclopedia, pp.323,329
14. Shahram Chubin, The Last Phase of the Iran-Iraq War: from Statement to Cease-fire, *Third World Quarterly,* (11)2 April 1989, p.3.
15. The Blue Helmets, A Review of United Nations Peace-keeping, The United Nations Department of Public Information, New York, 1996, p.669.
16. *Ibid.,* p.669
17. *Ibid.,* p.670.
18. Michael Sterner, 'The Iran – Iraq War', *Foreign Affairs – 1984.* p.131.
19. *Op cit.,* The Blue Helmets; p.670.
20. *Op. cit.,* The Blue Helmets; p.670.
21. 'Attrition in the Gulf', *Editorial Page of Third World Quarterly 10(3)* July 1988, p.vii.
22. *Op cit.,* The Blue Helmets; p.30
23. *Ibid.,* p. 670.
24. *Ibid.,* p.671.
25. *Ibid.,* p.671.
26. *Ibid.,* p.672.
27. *Ibid.,* p.672.
28. *Ibid.,* p.672.
29. *Ibid.,* p.672.
30. *Ibid.,* p.673.
31. *Ibid.,* p.673.
32. *Ibid.,* p.673.
33. *Ibid.,* p.675.
34. *Ibid.,* p.676.
35. *Ibid.,* p.676.
36. *Ibid.,* p.676.
37. *Ibid.,* p.676.
38. *Ibid.,* p.676.
39. *Ibid.,* p.677.
40. *Ibid.,* p.678

3

United Nations Observer Mission in El Salvador (ONUSAL) July 1991–April 1995

El Salvador is the smallest Central American country lying to the north of Pacific Ocean, Gwatemala to its North-West and Honduras to its Northeast.[1] It is more densely populated nation in the region. Nahua Indians were the earliest settlers and the ruins of limestone pyramids of Maya kings built between the 1st and 10th century A.D. stands as historical evidence. The Pupil tribe controlled the land to the west of the river Lampa during the 10th century. They built cities, grew crops and some of them were skillful weavers.

Spanish soldiers invaded El Salvador under the leadership of Pedro-de-Alvarado in 1524 and made it a Spanish Colony for almost three hundred years.[2] The first revolt against the Spanish rule in Central American Colonies in 1821, resulted in the birth of United Provinces of Central America in 1823.[3] Jose Matias Delgado, a catholic priest headed the convention that drafted the constitution, but the union slowly disintegrated in 1838. El Salvador withdrew from the union in 1840 and formally declared independence in 1841.[4] The turbulance did not end with the independence. Five of the country's presidents were overthrown and two of

ONUSAL, Deployment as of April, 1992

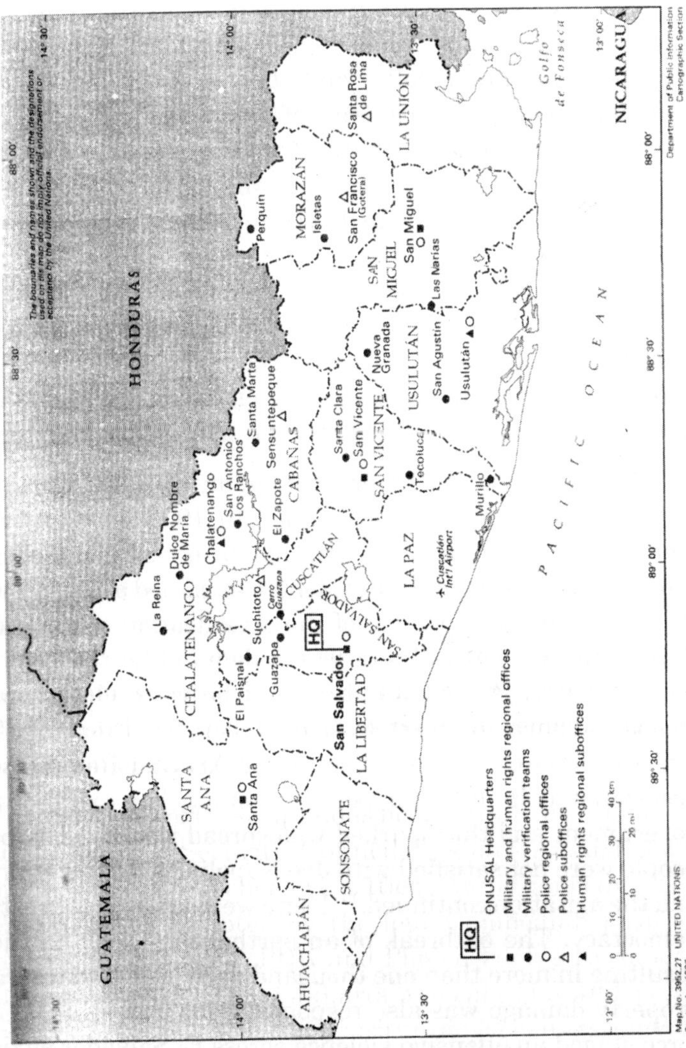

them were executed for corrupt practices. The strong dictators of the neighbouring countries, especially from Gwatemala indirectly made the presidents puppets. However the early 20th century saw stability in the country as the presidents were mostly wealthy landowners.[5] The country prospered with the cultivation, coffee and other farm-products which they exported. This prosperity of a few resulted in a great disparity between the rich and the poor and also the great rural and urban divide. General Maximiliane Hernandez Martiner Sceased power in 1931 providing a stable rule for 12 years. He built state run schools, expanded social service programmes and introduced labour reforms. The craze for fertile land led to migration in sparcely populated neighbouring Honduras. This sparked a brief war in 1969.[6] People became more and more conscious of their rights and the state was again in turbulance overthrowing Martiner.

During 1952 – 1969 there were many disputed elections, military coups, new constitutions.[7] In 1969 tensions were created between Elsavadors and Honduras on account of land reform laws. Elsalvadars and Honduras signed an agreement of ceasfire at the initiation of the organization of American States. In late 1970's there was a demand by the poor for land and jobs. A civil war brokeout between Government troops and Farbindo Marti National Liberation Front (a leftist guerilla force).[8] Archibishop Oscar Arnuflo Romero was assassinated in 1980 for being an outspoken critic of the government and this sparked widespread rioting.[9] The poor people were not satisfied with Joe Napolian Jurate's reforms and the agitation continued.[10] There were attempts to restore democracy. The outbreak of an earthquake in El Salvador resulting in more than one thousand deaths and widespread property damage was also responsible for unrest. F.M.L.N. force staged an offensive violence across El Salvador against Alfredo Christian an elected president. This was the worst fighting of the civil war, when the United Nation had to interfere.[11]

The initiatives of the United Nations brought the warring factions of El Salvador to the negotiation table. The Secretary-General of the United Nations played crucial part and his efforts were fully supported by all the members of the Security Council. The main objectives of the negotiations were to achieve ceasfire, a series of political agreements resolving the prolonged armed conflict, promoting democratization in the country, guaranteeing unrestricted respect for human rights and reunifying Salvodorian society.[12]

The first substantive agreement was on 26th July 1990 agreeing on human rights.[13] Both sides pledged unrestricted respect for the laws and standards of International Human rights. It also ensured a verification mission by United Nations. This would (1) to receive communication on human right violations from any individual or group or organizations in Elsalvador: (2) Interview any one freely and privately; (3) visit any place or establishment freely and without prior notice (4) to carryout an educational and informational campaign on human rights and on the functions of the mission; and (5) take legal action, it deemed appropriate to promote and defend human rights and fundamental freedoms. This is signed by all at Sanjose, Costorica.

The Secretary-General Javier Perez De Cuellar obtained the approval of Security Council for all his initiatives for the political agreements to halt the armed confrontation, for the verification of the rights of the civilian population and the verification of the same by the United Nations. The agreed issues relate to 1. Armed forces 2. Human rights 3. Judicial System 4. Electoral system 5. Constitutional reform 6. Economic and Social issues and verification by the United Nations.

The Secretary-General Javier Perez De Cuellar sought and received the concurrence of the Security Council for his broad concept of operational plan, which included the verification of cease-fire, the monitoring of the electoral process, respect for human rights and verification. He got the concurrence of the Council for the establishment of a small preparatory office in El Salvador at an appropriate time. He informed the Security Council that the two parties, namely Government of El Salvador and the FMLN in the presence of the Secretary-General's Representative, Alvaro De Sorto, Asst. Secretary-General, agreed at the meeting held on 31st October 1990 at Mexico city on the mechanics of negotiations and played an active role as the representative of the U.N. The Secretary-General was for an integrated and coordinated U.N. verification operation.

The Sanjose agreement envisaged for the verification operation to begin after the ceasation of armed conflict and both parties wanted the human rights mechanism to be in place as soon as possible without waiting for further agreements. This would be in keeping with the Esquipular-II agreement.[14] As a first step he sought the establishment of an integrated operation and to put in place the human rights verification component. A preliminary mission was sent in March 1991 to help the Secretary-General to determine the feasibility of acceding to the request. The mission was supported by a small preparatory office which had been established in San Salvador in January 1991.[15] The Secretary-General reported to the council on 16th April 1991 that preliminary mission had found a strong, widespread desire in all sectors in El Salvador that the United Nations should commence, at the earliest, the verification of the agreements without waiting for a ceasefire. There was an assured support from the Military, Security and Judicial authorities as well as FMNL for such an action. Inspite of the possible intimidation by certain extremist groups the establishment of human rights component in advance of ceasefire agreement was recommended.

Negotiations between the parties in the presence of the U.N. representative made good progress and finally an agreement (A/46/553-S/23130) was signed in Mexico City.[16] On 27th April 1991 a number of constitutional reforms had to be presented to the legislative assembly of El Salvador before its term expired at the end of the month. This requires an action by two successive legislative assemblies with a 2/3 majority in the latter one. The agreement mainly focused on the armed forces, the judicial system, the human rights, and the electoral systems. There was also an agreement on the creation of a three member commission on Truce. There was provision to investigate serious acts of violence since 1990. The commission was to submit its report with its conclusions and necessary recommendations to the parties as well as the Secretary-General. The Secretary - General would make this public and would take the necessary decisions and initiatives, he deemed appropriate. The parties avowed to carryout the commission's recommendations. The Secretary - General, after extensive consultations, appointed Mr. Belibario Betancur, former president of Cambodia, Mr. Renaldo, Figueredo Planchart, former foreign minister of Venezuela and Mr. Thomas Buergenthal, former president of the Inter-American Court of Human Rights as members of the Commission on Truce on 10th December 1991.

The Security Council decided to establish United Nations Observer mission (ONUSAL) in El Salvador (Resolution 693-1991).[17] It was to be an integrated peacekeeping operation, monitoring all agreements concluded between the government of El Salvador and FMLN. The mission's initial mandate was to verify the compliance of the Sanjose agreement on human rights by both the parties. It was the duty of the mission to actively monitor the human rights situation in El Salvador, investigate specific cases of alleged Human rights violations, promote human rights in the country, make recommendations for the elimination of violence and report to the U.N. General Assembly and the Security Council through the General Secretary.

This observer mission (ONUSAL) was launched on 26th July 1991 absorbing in it the small preparatory office earlier established.[18] Mr.Iqbal Riza, a member of the United Nations Secretariat was appointed as the Chief of the Mission ranked as Assistant Secretary-General. The mission adopted a two-phase approach. In the first phase a regional office was set up and the operational and conceptual basis for its future work was finalized between July and September 1991. It entered into a second phase of operations on 1st October 1991. It began to investigate cases and situations involving allegations of violations of human rights and followed them up systematically with the competent state organs as well as with FMLN. The purpose of these activities was to establish the varacity of such allegations and followup the actions, wherever required and to identify and punish those responsible with a view to such violations in future. There was a significant expansion of ONUSAL contacts with the parties coordinating the mechanisms with both the parties. At the same time the mission initiated a campaign on human rights education and information on human rights.

A steady progress was also made in the negotiations on other political agreements aimed at ending the armed conflict in El Salvador. All the parties namely the extreme Conservative National Republican Alliance. The Conservative National Conciliation Party, the moderate Christian Democratic Party, the Leftist FMLN and the Leftist Democratic Convergence, a group of rebels after the civil war, agreed, during their meeting in New York between 16-25th September 1991.[19] On a compressed agenda for negotiations covering all outstanding matters and signed what is known as the New York agreement. They decided to create a National Commission for the consolidation of peace to oversee the implementation of all political agreements to purify the armed forces and reduce their size, to redefine the doctrine of the armed forces with regard to their functions and to begin immediately the organization of the new National Civil Police. All the parties signed the New York agreement after weeks of intensive negotiations. This agreement endorsed all the previous agreements, Sanjose (26th July 1990), Mexico-City (27th April 1991) and New York (25th September 1991). Thus there was good progress on all the substantive issues of the peace process.

Before all the agreements were formalized in a Peace agreement in New York, the newly elected Secretary-General Mr. Boutros Boutros Ghali wanted substantial increase in the strength of ONUSAL.[20] The agreement on the ceasation of the armed conflict needs ONUSAL's verification of all aspects of the cease-fire and the separation of forces. The agreement on P and C requires ONUSUAL to monitor the maintenance of public order during the transition period till the P and C was constituted. The creation of two new ONUSAL divisions was also necessitated to deal separately with military and Police affairs.[21] The military division would be commanded by an officer in the rank of Brigadier General. The Security Council by its resolution 729 on 14th January 1992, unanimously decided to enlarge both the mandate and the strength of ONUSAL as per the recommendations of Secretary-General. Two new divisions (Military and Police) in addition to the existing Human Rights division were established. All the three would function under the overall control of a chief of the mission who is responsible for monitoring and implementing the peace agreement.

This peace agreement consists of nine chapters and several annexures and it was the result of Complex negotiations and persuasive persistence over a prolonged period.[22] The agreement conceived the ceasation of the armed conflict, the separation of forces, the end of the military structure of FMLN and the reintegration of its members into society and the United Nations had to verify all these activities. This was a dynamic and irreversible process which must be implemented throughout the national territory of El Salvador within a pre-determined duration.

The human rights division consisted of thirty human rights observers and legal advisors.[23] In addition, the Mission's Regional Coordinators also dealt with all human rights aspects and reported directly to the director of the division. During the course of the mission, the Director of Human Rights Division prepared thirteen periodic reports reflecting the situation of Human Rights in the country. These were submitted to the Security Council through the Secretary-General. They traced a slow improvement but a steady one which led to an overall transformation of the situation of Human rights. An effective enjoyment of Human rights depended primarily on strengthening the National Institutions which were responsible for protecting and defending these rights. The proper functioning of the institutional frame-work provided for in the peace agreements ensured that the state's activities in respect of human rights were in keeping with the law of the land. Human Rights Division's active verification included an objective recording of facts as well as in exercising its good offices at the efforts of Salvadorians to find a remedy to the violations. It also cooperated with Salvadorian institutions to strengthening their ability to work in promoting Human rights. The divisions cooperation with the National Council for Defence of Human rights and also with non-governmental human rights organizations was of particular importance. It contributed to the training of the personnel and increasing their leadership capacity. According to the final submission of the Director of Human rights Division to the Secretary - General in April 1995, this was "The most extensive human rights verification operation ever undertaken in any country with the support of the international community and a process unprecedented in the history of United Nations Peacekeeping operations."

The Military Division was one of the most important constituents established by ONUSAL. It was established on

20th January 1992 after the Peace agreement was signed. Fifteen military officers from Canada, Brazil, Spain, Venezuela and Equador and an authorized strength of 388 U.N. military observers constitute the Division. It maintained liaison with the Military Chiefs of the two parties. Infact, the Military Division escorted F.M.L.N. Commanders from their respective conflict zones to Mexico and New York for negotiations and back to their places. The Division verified the ceasation of the armed conflict, the re-deployment of armed forces of El Salvador to positions to maintain normal peace and concentration of FMLN. forces in agreed designated locations in the areas of conflict. It also monitored the troops of both the parties in the respective locations, verified the inventories of weapons and personnel, authorized and accompanied the movements of both the forces and received and investigated complaints of violations. The Division coordinated the plan for the prevention of accidents from mines and helped control and co-ordinate the clearing of four hundred and twenty five – minefields. The Military Division began its verification activities on 1st Feb. 1992 and the first stage of separation of forces had been successfully completed without any major incident. However it could not be reduced after June 1st according to the original plan as the process of ending a twelve year old civil war, consolidating peace and returning El Salvador politics to normality was not an easy one. With the successful implementation of cease-fire agreement by 15th December 1992, the Military Division was substantially reduced. It was further reduced after 31st May 1993 and again in December 1994. In the final phase the number of military observes dropped to three.

The Police Division of ONUSAL with sixteen police officials from Spain, France and Italy participated in the Mission's work at its inception. It was later expanded to include a police division following the signing of the peace agreement. One of the components of the agreement was the creation of a new Salvadorian Police Force (P.N.C.) to replace the old public security structure. The police division of ONUSAL consisting mostly of specialists in the organization and operation of civilian police force was constituted to monitor national police activities during the transition from armed conflict to national reconciliation. This provided the Salvadorian people with a sense of security as the police had been one of the primary factors in human rights abuses. Although, the strength of the division was 631, it had never reached. The deployment of the observer through the length and breadth of El Salvador began on 7th February 1992.

The ONUSAL police observers supervised and provided instruction to the Auxilary Transitory police (PAT). PAT was responsible for maintaining public order and security in the former zones of conflict until it is substituted by the P.N.C. PAT was made up of recruits from the National Public Security Academy which began its activities on 1st September 1992. ONUSAL monitored the admission and examination to the academy and recommended necessary improvements. The presence of an ONUSAL observer in the Academic Council greatly strengthened its ability for effectively monitoring. ONUSAL also provided support to the Academy to strengthen its training courses on human rights.

The Police Division assumed additional functions in March 1993. The Division carried out, in response to the Government's request and in close coordination with the International Technical Team providing advice to the Director General of P.N.C. and evaluation of the performance of the new police force and provided it technical advice and logistic support. PNC and ONUSAL signed a framework agreement on 27th July 1994.[24] PNC also had memoranda of understanding on technical cooperation with the police division on one hand and Human Rights Division on the other. The Division assisted in locating illegal arms caches and supported the Human Rights Division. The observers conducted special enquiry whenever required and ensured appropriate security measures for FMLN leaders as per the peace accords. Support was also provided to the Electoral Division when it was established later.

While both the Government and FMLN were to be commended for not breaking the cease-fire and for not threatening fragile first phase of national reconciliation, there were serious delays in implementing the various provisions of the agreements. This had "undermined each sides confidence in others good faith" in the implementation of the agreements. Both sides had failed to concentrate their forces in the designated locations. Doubts were expressed about the inventories of arms by FMLN. Suspicion that FMLN was keeping clandestine arms caches persisted. The Government had failed to establish the National Public Security Academy and to begin recruitment for PNC by 1st May 1992. It had also not begun the process of legislation to legalise FMLN as a political party. While the breach of one part of the agreement on the part of one, could not be an excuse on the part of the other to break another part. Hence the peace agreement could not be a haphazard sequence of actions that can easily be altered. It is on the contrary an intricately designed and carefully negotiated mechanism. The purpose of it is to synchronise, the reintegration of FMLN's ex-combatants into the civilian life and the measures the Government had committed itself to undertake to facilitate that process, especially, as regards to agriculture, political activity and recruitments to the National civil police.

The ONUSAL was operating in an atmosphere of deep distrust. The impartiality of ONUSAL was some time misperceived, each side accusing the ONUSAL that it was partial to the other. However, the Secretary-General was successful in extracting renewed assurance for putting back the peace agreement on the rails. There was an agreement to resolve the issues that had delayed the implementation of the peace process and a new revised time table was agreed upon. The forces of both sides would be fully concentrated in the designated locations by 25th June 1992.[25] The first contingent of former FMLN combatants would commence their reintegration into civilian life by 30th June 1992 and the process for all those in that category would be completed by 31st October 1992. The National Academy for Public Security would begun its first course of training for PNC recruits, including personnel from the existing National Police and FMLN combatants in agreed proportion by 15th July 1992. The Government would present in the legislature for the definite abolition of National Guard and the treasury police and establish a special Brigade for military security with no Civil Security responsibilities. Similarly, the Government would propose reforms to the Electoral code to facilitate legalization of FMLN and take steps related to land reforms.

Despite this agreed time table, difficulties continued in ensuring the implementation of the political agreements along with the agreements related to the demobilization of FMLN forces. The FMLN informed the United Nations on 30th September 1992 that in order to maintain the link in the original time table about the key understandings between the two parties, it would suspend demobilization until new dates were set for the start of the transfer of the land and other aspects that had fallen behind schedule.

While an agreement on the land issue was reached, it became evident that complete dismantling of FMLN military structure was impossible by 31st October 1992. The Secretary-General successfully negotiated for the ceasation of armed conflict by 15th December 1992. FMLN accepted the proposal contingent upon the acceptance by the Government. The Government reserved its position on some aspects of the proposal and suspended the restructuring, reduction and demobilization of its armed forces.

Mr. Marrack Goulding, the Under Secretary-General for peacekeeping operations and Assistant Secretary-General Alvaro-de-Soto were deputed to Salvador to help resolve the situation.[26] The consultations that followed led to the arrangement for the formal ending of the armed conflict on 15th December 1992. There was also an arrangement that president of El Salvador, Mr. Alfredo Christiani to complete implementation of the recommendations of the Adhoc commissions on the purification of the armed forces. A commission was set up and its confidential report was submitted to President Christiani as well as the Secretary-General on 22nd September 1992. It recommended the dismissal of transfer of one hundred and three officers including several very senior officers. ONUSAL closely followed all issues related to the creation of the new PNC, the political participation of FMLN, the restoration of public administration in former zones of conflict and reform of judicial and electoral systems besides participating as an observer in COPAZ.

The armed conflict between the Government of El Salvador and FMLN had been brought formally to an end on the 15th December 1992.[27] Legislation recognizing FMLN as a political party was marked as a ceremony presided over by president Christiani and attended by the Secretary-General Boutros Boutros-Ghali and a number of international statesmen. The Secretary-General described the event "a defining moment in the history of El Salvador—whose suffering people can now look forward to a future in which political, economic and social arrangement will be settled through the process of democracy and not by war".[28] At the same time, he stressed that it did not mark the end of the peace process in El Salvador. It was important that both parties and the international community should persevere in their efforts to ensure implementation of their remaining provisions of peace agreements.

The Government of El Salvador on 8th Jan 1993 formally requested United Nations observation of the elections for the president, the legislative assembly, mayors, and municipal councils, all set for March 1994. A technical mission visited El Salvador from 18th-28th April 1993 to define the terms of reference, concept of operations and financial implications of expanding the ONUSAL mandate.[29] On the basis of the findings of the mission in its report of 21st May 1993 and on the recommendation of the Secretary-General's report that the elections were likely to be the culminating point of the entire peace process. The Security Council approved that the mission was to be authorized to observe the electoral process and the Salvador supreme Electoral. Tribunal would receive full cooperation from ONUSAL. Hence, the mandate of ONUSAL was enlarged a second time.

The Electoral Division was to establish in five stages. The preparatory stage from 1st to 30th June 1993 was devoted to organization at the centre and regional levels. The main task would be to verify citizen's registration and followed political activities. Efforts would be concentrated on the observation of electoral campaign from December 1993. The Division would then observed the elections stated for 20th March 1994, the counting of votes and the announcement of the results, should the first round yield a definite results should be concluded on the same day and the activities of the division would also conclude on the same day. However, if a second round of elections for the president was necessary the observation of the ONUSAL would continue up to 30th April 1994. The Security Council approved this time table enlarging ONUSAL's mandate in its resolution 832 of 27th May 1992.

The peace process in El Salvador had been successfully advanced to a stage where the priority assigned to military aspects could be shifted to other provisions of the agreement. Several key commitments except the deployment of PNC made a good progress. Difficulties continue to plague the transfer of the land essential to the reintegration of former combatants on both sides.

The commission for Truth had been originally installed in the presence of Secretary-General at UN Head Quarters in New York on 13th July 1992. The members of the commission which travelled to El Salvador, received over twenty two thousand complaints of serious acts of violence that had taken place between January 1980 and July 1991.[30] These were violence by the agents of the state, massacres of peasants by the armed forces, assassination by death squads, violence by FMLN and assassination of Judges. The report of the commission entitled "from madness to hope the twelve year war in El Salvador" was submitted to the Secretary-General on 15th March 1993.[31]

The Secretary-General instructed a detailed analysis of the commission's recommendations, examining whether they were within the mandate of the commission and also to identify the action required by the Government, FMLN and COPAZ. After an active exchange of views and communications, the government and FMLN at a high level meeting on 8th September 1993 in the presence of ONUSAL, agreed to implement the recommendations with a view to "sweeping the table clear" before the electoral campaign begun.

An illegal arms cache belonging to FMLN was discovered in Nicaragua on 23rd May 1993.[32] Subsequently FMLN admitted that it had maintained large quantities of weapons both within and outside El Salvador. The continuous efforts of the Secretary-General directly and through ONUSAL ensured that all remaining clandestine caches were declared and destroyed. In spite of serious threats to the right of FMLN to its status as a political party, nothing was done to up set the apple cart of the peace process. The complete disarmament of FMLN and the reintegration of its members into the civil, political, and institutional life of the country formed the essential part of the peace process. The strength and irreversibility of the peace process was made to be taken note of and the derailment of the peace agreement was not allowed.

The Secretary-General confirmed that the government had taken steps, it had promised for the broad compliance with the recommendations on the purification of the armed forces. The Secretary-General was satisfied with the measures adopted and implemented by the government in respect of eighty seven of one hundred and two officers. Another was no longer in service while the action on fifteen others was not in conformity with peace accord. President Christiani was insisted on taking early action in this regard. The action taken by the government was a significant achievement in the consolidation of the peace process. The Supreme Electoral Tribunal of El Salvador was also informed, as per its request, that the residual arms deposits by the FMLN had been verified and destroyed and this would enable FMLN to continue as a legally recognized political party. On 5th September 1993 FMLN held its national convention at which it decided to participate in the elections and chose its candidates.

The Election Division of ONUSAL was established in September 1993 with a mandate to observe the electoral process in consonance with the terms of reference.[33]

(a) The measures and decisions made by all electoral authorities should be impartial and consistent with the holding free and fair elections.

(b) Appropriate steps should be taken to ensure that all eligible voters were included in the electoral rolls enabling them to exercise their right to vote.

(c) Mechanisms should be in place effectively to prevent multiple voting as a complete screening of the electoral rolls prior to the elections was not feasible

(d) Freedom of expression, organization, movement and assembly should be respected without restrictions.

(e) Potential voters had sufficient knowledge of the mechanisms for participating in the election.

(f) Examine, analyse, and assess criticism made, objections raised and attempts undertaken to delegitimise the electoral process and, if required, to convey such information to the Supreme Electoral Tribunal.

(g) Inform the Supreme Electoral Tribunal of complaint received regarding irregularities in electoral advertising or possible interference with electoral process with a request for information on corrective measures taken.

(h) Place observers on polling sites on election day to verify that the right to vote was fully respected.

The Division functioned with thirty six professionals deployed throughout the mission's six regional offices. Despite a small number of staff, the division performed its duties on the basis of coordination with and collaboration of other components of ONUSAL. The Division's chief task in its initial phase was to verify the registration of citizens of the electoral rolls and to observe the political activities of the period preceding the electoral campaign and to start the institutional framework for the electoral process.[34] All this began in October 1993. The election time table was scheduled for the 20th March 1994. The election for the president with a second round if no candidate had obtained an absolute majority was to be completed within the next 30 days. Simultaneously, parliamentary elections for eighty four seats in the National Assembly on the basis of proportional representation; Municipal elections for two hundred sixty two mayoral districts on the basis of a simple majority; and for the Central Parliament, treated as a single National District for which twenty deputies would be elected on the basis of proportional representation were also scheduled. Offices were set up in all departments and the municipalities of the country. Board of vigilance with representatives of all the twelve political parties with authority to supervise the work of all electoral tribunal offices was also set up.

The election campaign officially should open on 20th November 1993 for the election of president and the legislative assembly on 20th January 1994 and for the municipality on 20th February 1994. During the period from November 1993 to January 1994 attention was focused on observing voters registration, monitoring the election campaign and providing assistance for drawing up electoral rolls. Joint meetings with the Supreme Electoral Tribunal, the Board of Vigilance and the campaign managers were regularly held to solve problems during the electoral process mechanism was set up to receive and process allegation of violation of the electoral roll and follow up the actions taken.

ONUSAL teams made an average of nine observation visits to each of the two hundred and sixty two towns and despatched a total of three thousand seven hundred patrols.[35] The code of conduct was prepared through discussion and signed by all the contending parties in each of the fourteen departments of El Salvador and in a number of municipalities. All the presidential candidates are made to sign a declaration abjuring violence with a commitment to respect the results as well as to comply with peace accord on 10th March 1994. Periodic meetings at both central and local levels helped in finding solutions to problems and to find technical methodology to improve the registration process. ONUSAL team monitored political meetings and demonstrations, advertising through mass media, complaints of irregularities and transmission of the same to the Supreme Electoral Tribunal for timely action. Complaints from the different sources mostly from the political parties and also problems identified in the field by the ONUSAL observers were promptly solved. The complaints consisted of twenty three percent arbitrary or illegimate action by public authorities, twenty one percent actions of intimidation, eighteen percent destruction of propaganda materials and percent miscellaneous out of three hundred presented to ONUSAL.

ONUSAL monitored the proceedings from the time the polling stations were set up until the completion of the counting deploying nearly nine hundred observers of fifty six Nationalities, covering all polling centres by teams of two to thirty observers. This massive presence of ONUSAL enabled smooth conduct on the election day, resolving countless practical problems collecting information on more than seven thousand forms from all the polling centers. All this was subsequently compiled by the electoral division and this was the basic documentary source for evaluating the conduct of elections. 1.5 million voters constituting fifty five percent on the electoral rolls participated. The quick count based on a random sample of two hundred and ninety polling stations by ONUSAL afforded a reliable projection of the outcome of presidential election two hours after the poll. It is worthy to note that the difference between the quick count and the provisional results announced by the Tribunal was barely 0.5 per cent. The information gathered by the observers on the election day, and in view of the systematic observation of the electoral process during the preceding six months and the stupendous work of ONUSAL vouch. Safe that the elections were held under ideal appropriate conditions in respect of freedom, competitiveness, transparency and security in spite of serious organizational difficulties.

According to the official results of the first round of the presidential elections ARENA secured 49.03 per cent, coalition Convergencia Democratica (C.D.) FMLN – Moveimiento National Revolucionaria (MNR) secured 24.9 percent, Partido Democratica Cristiano (PDC) secured 17.87 parent, Partido Movimiento De Unidad (P.M.U.) secured 2.41

percent, Movimiento De Solidaridad Nacional (MSN) secured 1.06 percent and Movimiento Autntico Cristiano (MAC) secured 0.83 percent.[36]

The eighty four seats of the legislative assembly were shared thirty nine seats by ARENA, twenty one seats by FMLN, eighteen seats by PDC, four seats by PCN, one seat by CD and one by PMU. The two hundred and sixty two mayoralities went to ARENA-206, PDC-29, FMLN-16, PCN-10 and MAC-1. The official counting of votes was monitored by forty specialized observers of ONUSAL. The security council congratulated the people of El Salvador on their exemplary behaviour during the historical elections based on the Secretary-General's letter and report. However, it called for the correction of shortcomings in the first round of voting and also for the full implementation of the peace accord.

Since no candidate obtained the required absolute majority in the first round of presidential elections, a second round was scheduled on 24th April 1994 between the two candidates with highest number of votes namely Mr. Armando Calderol Soil of ARENA and Mr Ruben Zamora of the CD-FMLN-MNR coalition. The anamolies recorded in the first round were eliminated by the tribunal taking appropriate measures in regard to discrepancies in the electoral rolls, the reform of the electoral code, the number of polling centres and training of the electoral personnel. The electoral division posted observers in five areas of work, registration, computation, printing, electoral project unit and training. ONUSAL observers also were present at campaign activities during the two week campaign up to 18th April 1994.[37] The tone of the campaign improved after the two presidential candidates signed a joint statement expressing their commitment to the future governance of El Salvador, their determination to conduct a decent campaign and pledge to make every effort to overhaul the electoral system during the following two years.

ONUSAL deployed nine hundred observers in all the voting centres on 24th April 1994, the polling day. They were present from the opening of the polling stations to the completion of first count of the votes. The elections proceeded without any serious incidents affecting the public order or ballot tampering. There were signs of improvement in the conduct of elections in every sphere. The joint efforts of the two presidential candidates, the political institutions and the supreme electoral tribunal and the donor countries made it possible to have free and fair elections accepted by every body.

The results of the second round of presidential elections gave a clear majority to ARENA with a vote count of 818264 votes constituting 68.35 percent and coalition 378980 votes constituting 31.65 percent out of a total valid votes 1,197, 244. The total number of votes cast were 1,246,220 of which 3,467 were challenged, 40,048 were invalid and 5,461 abstentions. Mr. Ruben Zamero acknowledged the victory of adversory even on the preliminary count on 24th April 1994 while the president elect reaffirmed his commitment to the peace process and reconciliation in El Salvador. Thus persuasiveness, perseverance, and persistence on the part of all concern as well as the international community enabled the successful completion of the election process.

It was presumed that all aspects of the Peace Agreement would almost be implement by Ist June 1994 when the new government would assume office and a vestigial presence of ONUSAL would be enough to monitor any shortcomings in the implementation. However, the deployment of PNC, the demobilization of National Police, the land transfer programme had to make substantial progress. The Secretary-General who believed that United Nations had a continuing responsibility to honour its undertaking for the compliance of the peace accords felt that the ONUSAL mandate should further be extended. He could extract a commitment from all Salvadorian parties an agreement on a new time table.

Further the president elect Mr. Calderon reiterated his personal commitment to the terms of the peace accord. On the recommendations of the Secretary-General on 11th May 1994 and again on 30th November 1994 the mandate was extended twice by its resolution 920 of 26th May 1994 and 961 of 23rd November 1994 and the final period lasted till 30th April 1994.

ONUSAL emphasized institution building and strengthening them with great persuasion both directly and through his special representative by the Secretary-General. He remanded the parties of international communities expectation that each would honour its commitment in full and promptly. The assuming of the power by the new president made a good progress in the implementation of the new time table particularly in those areas that would strengthen and modernize democratic institution. There was a decision to establish firmly the rule of law in the country. The high level Government team responsible to follow up activities at the political level was maintained. Fortnightly tripartite meetings were held regularly. Joint working groups on various outstanding issues continued to function. The Government expressed its determination to take decisive action against all criminal activities within public security apparatus. COPAZ as well as its sub-commissions continued to function. The election by consensus of the new Supreme Court of Justice was also laudable decision. The Vice Minister for public security and the new Director General of P.N.C. were appointed. The Salvadorian legislative assembly began functioning with the participation of FMLN as the Country's second political force as well as other political parties on 1st May 1994.

The Secretary-General was able to report to the Security Council on 24th March 1995 the fact of the Demobilization of the National Police and the complete taking over of all security functions by P.N.C. The P.N.C. had strength of more than seven thousand and approximately two hundred and twenty middle and higher level officers all of whom were graduates from the National Public Security Academy. The New Supreme Court made up of eminent professionals busied itself in the adoption of a new criminal code and a new criminal procedure, decentralization of functions, elimination of extra judicial confessions and the felicitation of Habeas Corpus proceedings. The National Council for the Defence of Human Rights established its offices in all departments with the efforts for strengthening them. The economy of the Nation continued to recover with political stability.

The Secretary - General recommended that COPAZ as the national institution for the verifying of implementation of Peace Accord would take responsibility of all the remaining aspects of the peace accord such as the control of the intelligence activity by certain members of the armed forces, speeding of the programme of transfer of land to former combatants; the dismantling of old military command structure, strengthening of defence of Human rights institutions, purification and modernization of Judiciary and ensuring pending reforms and electoral legislation. In view of this he reduced the military component of the mission to twelve military observers and seven medical personnel from a total of thirty. He intended to reduce the size of Police Division excluding fifteen police instructors posted in the National Police Academy. Progressive phasing out of substantive civil staff of ONUSAL was also intended. He could report to the Security Council on 24th March 1995[38] that preparations for dismantling of ONUSAL were well underway. After the closure of ONUSAL officially at the end of April 1995, a small team of civilian personnel remained to deal with the outstanding claims and handle the final disposal of property and equipment.

The United Nations Mission in El Salvador (MINUSAL) started its work on 1st May 1995 led by the Secretary-

General's Special Representative Mr. Enriqueter Horst.[39] A Trust fund for MINUSAL for supporting the mission's activity was established ONUCA, ONUSAL, MINUSAL each on it. Suit of the previous one successfully concluded the United Nation's mission for not only peace keeping but also in establishing a democratic government honouring the International code of Human rights. Peristant persuasive skills of the Secretary-General, unflinching support of the International Community, the absence of enlightened self-interest of any of the big powers, unrelenting, though a little grudging, support of all political parties in El Salvador as well as very staunch rock-like assistance of the people of El Salvador, tired by twelve year civil war in the country were all helpful in the great mission of the United Nations.

India's participation in ONUCA as well as ONUSAL was laudable. The very nature of the terrain in the region made the operations Herculean. ONUCA's operations involved mobile teams of military observers, patrolling from verification centres and smaller operational posts in the forward areas. Patrols had to be carried out by land, by air, and by river. ONUCA vividly illustrated the complex demands made of the organization in peace making and peace keeping skills. It had to play varied roles in advancing the peace process in Central America, assisting the parties to control and resolve the conflict in the region. India provided four military observers for U.N. Observer mission in El Salvador. The Secretary-General laid rich tributes to military and civilian personnel of ONUCA and ONUSAL which included Indians too for their great success in restoring peace.

REFERENCES

1. *The World Book of Encyclopedia,* World Book Incorporation, Ascott Setzer Company, p.196.
2. *Ibid.,* p.196
3. *Ibid.,* p.200.

4. *Ibid.,* p.200.
5. *Ibid.,* p.200.
6. Alan Riding, "The Central American Quagmire", *Foreign Affairs,* 1982 (Vol.61), pp. 3, 648-649,
7. James Le Moyne, 'El Salvador's Forgotten War', *Foreign Affairs Summer,* 1989, p.105.
8. *Ibid.,* p.106.
9. James John Guy, 'El Salvador Another Domino?', *The World Today,* August 1980, p.329.
10. *Op. cit., The World Book of Encyclopedia,* p.200.
11. Cathy McIlwaine, 'Contesting Civil Society: reflections from El Salvador', *Third World Quarterly,* Volume 19, 1998, p.658.
12. Peter Frisk, 'Displaced Persons and Human Rights: The Crisis in El Salvador', *Third World Quarterly* 2(3) July 1990, p.40.
13. The Blue Helmets, A Review of United Nations Peace-keeping, The United Nations Department of Public Information, New York, 1996, p.426.
14. *Ibid.,* p.426.
15. *Ibid.,* p.426.
16. *Ibid.,* p.426.
17. See Appendix No. VI.
18. *Op cit.,* The Blue Helmets, p.427.
19. *Ibid.,* p.427.
20. *Ibid.,* p.427.
21. *Ibid.,* p.427.
22. *Ibid.,* p.428.
23. *Ibid.,* p.429.
24. *Ibid.,* p.431.
25. *Ibid.,* p.432.
26. *Ibid.,* p.432.
27. *Ibid.,* p.432.
28. *Ibid.,* p.432.
29. *Ibid.,* p.433.
30. *Ibid.,* p.433.
31. *Ibid.,* p.433.
32. *Ibid.,* p.434.

33. *Ibid.*, p.435.
34. *Ibid.*, p.435.
35. *Ibid.*, p.438.
36. *Ibid.*, p.439.
37. *Ibid.*, p.440.
38. *Ibid.*, p.442.
39. *Ibid.*, p.443.

4

United Nations Advanced Mission in Cambodia (UNAMIC) March 1992 May 1994

Cambodia is a South East Asian country that borders on Thailand on North West, Laos on the North and Vietnam on the East and South China Sea on South and South West. It is also known as Campuchea. The Government changed the name to Cambodia in 1989.[1]

It is an ancient country dating back to first century A.D. when the Kingdom of Funan was one of the greatest early powers in the region. A new power had arisen in the sixth century A.D. From 800 to 1400 A.D. the Khmer controlled a great Hindu, Buddhist kingdom in Cambodia and it reached its peak in 1100 A.D., when it took over much of the land that is now Laos, Thailand and Vietnam.[2] Internal quarrels within the royal family and wars with Thailand weakened the Empire and the capital city was lost to Thailand forces. An independent Khmer Kingdom survived until mid 1800's with its new capital near what is now known as Phnom Penh. In 1863, the French occupied the southern part of Vietnam and made Cambodia a protectorate.[3]

The Japanees forces occupied Cambodia from 1941-45 during World War – II. The French colonialism had given

UNTAC Military Deployment for Electoral Support

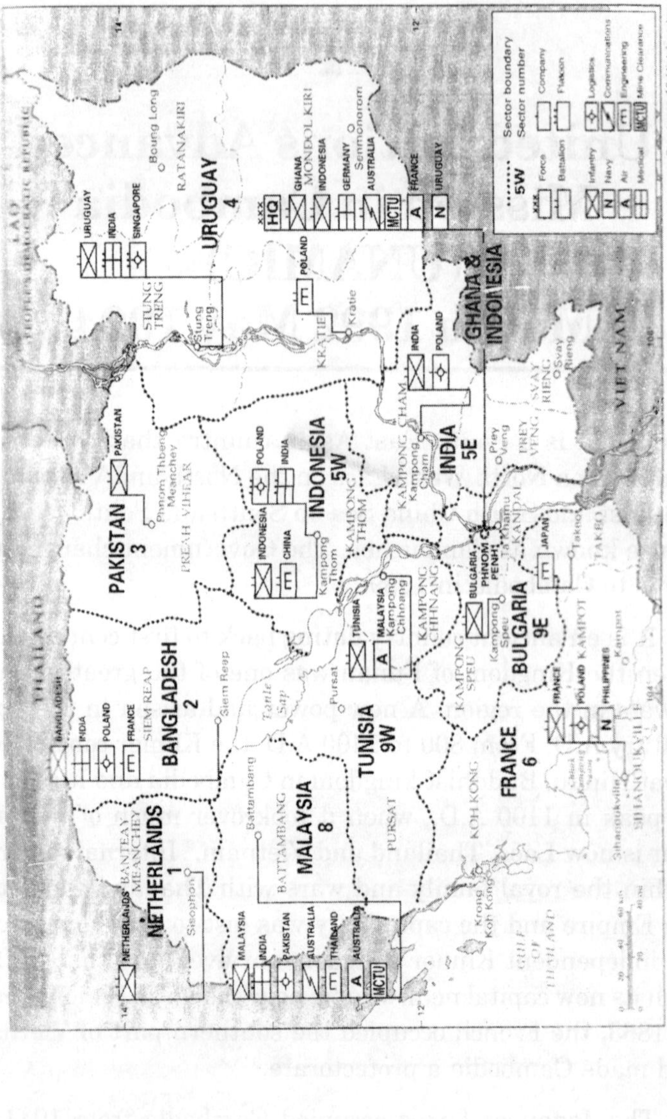

way to a period of political instability in 1950.[4] Civil conflict exacerbated in the 60s and 70s. On account of this spillover of the war in Vietnam including bombardment by United States forces. France recognized Cambodia's independence in 1953, and in 1955 Nordom Shehanouk became the prime minister and head of the state in 1960. United States poured millions of dollars in aid during 1955-63.[5] However, Shehanouk cut off U.S.aid on the plea that it supported attempts to overthrow him. In 1970, the members of Shehanouk's government Lieutenant General Lon Non prince Sisowath Sirik Matak overthrew Shehanouk, while he was out of the country. After Shehanouk's overthrow, the U.S. and South Vietnamese troops entered Cambodia in 1970 April to clear out the communist supply bases. With the clearance, the troops of U.S. left Cambodia at the end of June. But the Vietnamese' communists went deeper into Cambodia 'by the end of 1970. The whole of Cambodia became a war-torn country. [6]

The Cambodian communists of Khmer Rouge organization were engaged in full scale war against the non-communist government. In April 1975, they took over control of Cambodia. Neighbouring South Vietnam and Laos fell into the hands of Communist forces. [7]

Cambodia suffered greatly under the destructive regime of Pol Pot who led the Khmer Communist party from 1975-79.[8] The cities were emptied and general mass of people were subjected to harsh labour and political education.[9] It is estimated that more than one million people died in the brutal process of "Social reconstruction" of Pol Pot's regime.[10] Vietnam which is on the whole of eastern border of Cambodia had to take initiative and influence Cambodia. It began to support a new government in Phnom Penh in later 1978.[11] The battle for the control continued between Pol Pot regime and the one supported by Vietnam. The United National Front consisting of FUNCINPEC led by prince Norodom Shehanouk, Peoples Liberation front (K.P.N.L.F.) and the Party of

Democratic Campuchea (PDK) also known as Khmer Rouge stood for an independent, neutral, peaceful and cooperative Cambodia. The three factions formed a coalition party called coalition Government of democratic Campuchea, which later became National Government of Cambodia. It was backed by China and U.S.A. Democratic Compuchea was recognized by the United Nations as the authentic one representing the people of Cambodia. The Phnom Penh Government, the people's Republic of Campuchea was backed by Vietnam and Soviet Union. Its army approximately consisting of 50,000 soldier controlled some 80-90 percent of the Country.[12] The National Government of Cambodia, backed by China, the United States and the AS.O.Ciation of South East Asian Nations (ASEAN), had a combined force between 50,000 to 60,000 and operated from the areas along the border, and north western Cambodia with Thailand.[13]

The Security Council first considered the question of Cambodia (IS/PV 2108) in early 1979 following the intervention of Vietnam. However, it could take no action for lack of agreement among the permanent members, namely China, France, Soviet Union, United Kingdom and United States. The General Assembly then took up the matter and in November 1979, as it did annually for most of the period, called for withdrawal of foreign forces from Cambodia in its resolution (2A/RES/34/22) as well as self determination for its people. It also supported the efforts of the Secretary-General Javier Perez De Cuellar to coordinate relief assistance to the Cambodian people who fled their country in large number during the turbulent period. There were more than three thousand refugees in Thailand. The situation continued till July 1981. An International Conference was convened in July 1981 (3A/RES/35/6), but Vietnam did not attend.[14] Nevertheless it did accept the offer of good offices of the Secretary-General: Mr. Rafee Uddin Ahmed the Special Representative for humanitarian affairs in South East Asia, visited the area many a time. This helped a set of objectives to be achieved through negotiations. These were included as proposals for action following December 1987 meeting between prince Shehanouk and the Prime Minister of Phnom Penh Government Mr. Hunsen at Paris. At the invitation of the Government of France, Indonesia too played a meaningful good role to end the war in Cambodia. The representatives of Phnom Penh Government and three Cambodian opposition parties, FUNCINPEC, KPNLF, and PDK informally met in Indonesia in July 1988. This first direct contact was followed by another in February 1989 laid the ground for the Paris Conference on Cambodia, held from 30th July to 30th August 1989 attended by the conflicting parties on Cambodia and 18 other states,[11] Australia, Brunei Darussalam, Canada, China, France, India, Indonesia, Japan, Laos, Malayasia, Philippines, Singapore, Soviet Union, Thailand, United Kingdom, United States,[15] Vietnam, and Zimbabwe as well as the Secretary-General with his representative for human affairs. France and Indonesia co-chaired the conference. In spite of a broad strategy to move towards peace a comprehensive settlement could not be agreed upon. The main issues were the power sharing in the transition period before the elections, the drafting of a new constitution and the role of PDK. The conference was suspended without any agreement on International Mechanism to verify the wihdrawal of Vietnamese troops from Cambodia. However, the withdrawal, as announced by Vietnam (A/40/759) was undertaken without international verification in September 1989. The Phnom Penh government of Mr. Hun Sen continued in power.

There was intense diplomatic activity for the establishment of peace and coexistence in the place of instability and civil war continued. The Cambodian parties met in Indonesia in February 1990 and in Tokyo in June 1990. A series of consultations were also continued by the five permanent members of the Security Council beginning in January 1990, besides the meetings in Indonesia and Tokyo. The five countries issued a summary of their conclusions (65/210/89). They all agreed to be guided by the following principles.[16]

1. No acceptable solution could be achieved by force of arms.
2. An enduring peace could only be achieved through a comprehensive political settlement including a verified withdrawal of foreign forces, a cease-fire and a ceasation of outside military assistance.
3. The goal should be self-determination for the Cambodian people through free, fair and democratic elections.
4. An enhanced United Nations role in the resolution of the Cambodian problem.
5. An urgent need to speed up diplomatic efforts to achieve a settlement.
6. The withdrawal of foreign force must be verified by the U.N.
7. An early resumption of a constructive dialogue among all the Cambodian factions to facilitate the transition process without anyone dominating the other.
8. An effective United Nations presence to ensure internal security.
9. A special Representative would supervise the United Nations activities ending in the inauguration of a democratically elected government.
10. The U.N. operations should be consistent with the successful implementation of Cambodian settlement and its planning and execution should take into account the heavy financial burden on member states.

11. Free and fair elections under the direct control of U.N. administration.
12. The elections must be conducted in a neutral political environment with equal advantage to all parties.
13. The five permanent members should commit themselves to honour the results of the elections.
14. All Cambodians should enjoy equal right of freedom and opportunity to participate in the elections.
15. A Supreme National Council might be the repository of Cambodian Sovereignty during the transition period.
16. Questions involving Cambodian sovereignty should be resolved with the agreement of all the Cambodian parties.
17. All the five permanent members would initiate efforts to achieve a comprehensive political settlement and would remain in close touch with all the regional parties as well as themselves.

The United Nations sent several fact finding missions to study – Cambodia's devastated administrative, economic and S.O.Cial infrastructure as well as the requirements for the repatriation of refugees.

The findings of these missions helped the five permanent members of the Security Council to share August 1990 proposals for a comprehensive settlement in Cambodia. The proposals were accepted by the four Cambodian parties, FUNCINPEC, KPNLF, PDK and Phnom Penh government at an informal meeting in Jakarta, the capital of Indonesia on September 10th 1990. The Security Council in its resolution 668 of 20th September 1990 endorsed the proposals. Indonesia and France took charge to negotiate the framework of proposals into a peace agreement. A draft agreement (A/46/61-S/22059) on a comprehensive political settlement was presented to the twelve members of Supreme National Council. After a discussion and an explanatory note A/46/61-S/22059 of the five permanent members was accepted by S.N.C. and it was then presented to Thailand and Vietnam in February, 1991. They, being the border countries were entrusted with peace in Cambodia.

The Secretary-General jointly with France and India appealed for a temporary ceasation of hostilities as a gesture of good faith in his communication A/46/161-S/22552. The ceasefire was effective on a voluntary basis over the next several months as negotiations continued. The S.N.C. elected prince Shehanouk as its Chairman. He signed a letter asking the United Nations to dispatch a survey mission to Cambodia. Prince Shehanouk asked the General Secretary, "to have atleast 200 United Nations observes in order to assist S.N.C. in controlling the cease-fire and the ceasation of foreign military assistance as a first step within the framework of a comprehensive political settlement".

The Security Council deployed a small advance mission consisting mainly of military liaison officers to help the parties to observe the Cease-fire and resolve any alleged violations on either side. The United Nations Advance Mission in Cambodia (UNAMIC)[17] became operational as soon as the peace agreement was signed and the budget was adopted by the General Assembly. The mission was led in the field by a civilian Chief Liaison Officer with responsibility for maintaining contact with S.N.C. on preparations for the deployment of UNTAC as well as other matters related to the role of U.N. A senior military Liaison officer was also appointed. The Secretary-General would report regularly to the Security Council on the operations of UNAMIC on receipt of reports from the Liaison officer.

UNAMIC would deploy small teams of military personnel with experience in training civilian population to avoid injury from mines or booby traps. The team was expected to give priority to populations living in or close to areas of recent military confrontation. The expansion of the programme would eventually take place in consultation with the United Nations High Commission for Refugees (UNHCR) for designing repatriation routes, reception centres and resettlement of the refugees.[18] The UNAMIC was estimated to require eight civil liaison staff. Fifteen military liaison officers, twenty other military personnel to form the mine awareness unit. It is also necessary to have approximately seventy five international and seventy five local civilian support staff.[19] Besides there would be a military communications unit of some forty persons provided by Australia on a voluntary contribution. An air unit of four utility helicopters and one fixed wing aircraft would also be needed. In the first phase the head of the mission accompanied by the Chief Aids, would arrive in Phnom Penh within ten days of the signing of the agreement on comprehensive political settlement. The second phase would begin as soon as the necessary vehicles, generators, accommodation and other items were procured and delivered at the military head quarters of the Cambodian parties. The UNAMIC would function from Phnom Penh as its head quarters. It would deploy military liaison units to the head quarters of each of the Cambodian parties. Teams would also be sent to forward positions, Battambang and Siem Reap which would also be the main bases for mine awareness programme. Effective and independent round-the-clock communication system open to the Cambodian parties also was required to facilitate communication and help resolve problems in the maintenance of cease-fire. It was estimated, it would all cost $ 19.9 million.[20]

The Second Paris Conference on Cambodia met from 1st to 23rd October 1991.[21] Cambodia was represented by Prince Shehanouk as Chairman of S.N.C. The five permanent members of the Security Council, the six members of ASEAN, Australia, Canada, India, Japan and Vietnam. Yugoslavia attended in its capacity as Chairman of Non Aligned movement. The agreements on a comprehensive political settlement of the Cambodian conflict were signed on 23rd October 1991.[22] This Paris agreement invited the Security Council to establish the United Nations Transitional Authority in Cambodia (UNTAC) and to provide it with a mandate set out in the agreement.[23] The Council fully supported the Paris agreement in its resolution 718 on 31st October 1991 and requested the Secretary - General to prepare a detailed plan of implementation.

The Agreement consisted of a comprehensive political settlement of the Cambodian conflict, a final act and three instruments. The agreement is concerning sovereignty, independence, territorial integrity, and inviolability, invetrality and national unity of Cambodia. The declaration also stated the process of rehabilitation and reconstruction of Cambodia.

The first instrument consisted of nine parts with thirty two articles and five detailed annexures one of which set out the mandate of UNTAC.[24] The transitional period would begin on 23rd October 1991 with the signing of Paris Agreement and would end with the formation of constituent assembly duly elected and transformed itself into a legislative assembly. The S.N.C. would be the legitimate body occupying the seat of Cambodia at the U.N. and would be vested with a power to safe guard the sovereignty, independence and unity of Cambodia. They would be responsible and committed to holding free and fair elections under U.N. control as the basis for forming a new and a legitimate government. It would delegate all powers necessary to ensure the implementation of the agreement to the special representative of the Secretary-General. He would seek consensusness of all the members of S.N.C. and in the absence of it, the Chairman of S.N.C. would be entitled to make the decision on the advice to be offered to UNTAC as per the views expressed in S.N.C. The final decision would, however, would rest with Special Representative of the Secretary-General. Similarly, in all cases the Secretary-General's Special Representative or his delegate would determine whether the advice or action of S.N.C. was consistent with the agreement. He would attend the meetings of the S.N.C. as well as the subsidiary bodies and provide all necessary information on UNTAC's decisions. All administrative bodies and officers would be under United Nations Supervision or control. Special attention would be to foreign affairs, National Defence, finance, public Security and information. The representative was given power to issue directives and to install U.N. personnel with unrestricted access to information and administrative operations. Even the civil police was to operate under UNTAC's supervision. UNTAC would supervise other law enforcement and judicial process throughout Cambodia, of course, in consultation with S.N.C. UNTAC was empowered to investigate and take remedial actions in case of complaints.

The cease-fire and disengagement of forces would come into effect immediately. UNTAC should be informed about the total strength of forces, their deployment, armaments, and locations, including a detailed record of minefields and booby troops. All forces would refrain from all hostilities and any form of deployment of forces to extend their territorial control. All foreign forces and military personnel with all their equipment should be withdrawn under UNTAC's verification.[25] The forces of the Cambodian parties would be regrouped and restricted in cantonment areas. The weapons and ammunition would be subjected to the verification and investigation of violation by UNTAC. The agreement called for the release of all prisoners of war and political prisoners and resettlement of the displaced. A mixed military working group with representatives of all the Cambodian parties would ensure the smooth performance of all these functions.

UNTAC, in consultation with S.N.C. would establish a system of laws, procedures and administrative structure necessary for holding free and fair elections. The electoral law and a code of conduct would prohibit all coercion or financial inducements. UNTAC would design and implement a system of registering individual voters and parties and balloting to ensure free and fair elections. It would investigate into complaints of electoral irregularities and take appropriate and corrective action. The duration of this process should not exceed nine months from the beginning of registering voters. All the campaign would be in the presence of foreign observers.[26]

The agreement further ensured respect for Human Rights and fundamental freedoms in Cambodia. UNTAC would develop and implement a programme of education to promote understanding of Human Rights in the transitional period. All complaints of abuse would be investigated and appropriate corrective action would be taken. The agreement set out the right of Cambodian refugees and displaced persons to return to their homes. The two Co-chairmen of Paris Conference as well as all the signatories of the agreement were committed to the implementation of the agreement.

In the second of the three instruments, Cambodia undertook to refrain from any action that might affect the sovereignty, independence, territorial integrity and inviolability, neutrality and national unity.[27] It would also refrain from entering into military alliances and agreements inconsistent with neutratity. It would not permit the introduction or stationing of foreign military personnel except in pursuance of United Nations Authorisation for the implementation of political settlement.

There was also an agreement on the rehabilitation and reconstruction of Cambodia. An international aid effort would have to be phased over a period that would acknowledge realistically the political and technical imperatives. In the first phase the Secretary-General would appoint a coordinator to meet immediate needs and lay the ground-work for further action. Long term priorities for reconstruction were left to the Government of Cambodia after the elections. The Paris Conference suggested the formation of an International Committee on the reconstruction of Cambodia (ICORC) with an eye on harmonization and monitoring the contributions. The Secretary-General was asked to make special arrangements to support I.C.O.R.C.

UNAMIC became operational on 9th November 1991. Mr. A.H.S. Ataul Karim of Bangladesh assumed functions as Chief Liaison Officer of UNAMIC in Phnom Penh.[28] Brigadier-General Michel Lordidon of France assumed command of the military elements of UNAMIC on the same day. An air operation unit was contributed by France while officers and other military personnel were contributed by Algeria, Argentina Australia, Austria, Belgium, Canada, China, France, Germany Ghana, India, Indonesia, Ireland, Malayasia, New Zealand, Pakistan, Poland, Senegal, Tunisia, Soviet Union, United Kingdom, United States, and Uruguay.

The Party of Democratic Campuchea (PDK) delegation arrived in Phnom Penh on 27th November 1991. However it was forced to flee when demonstrations against the delegation became violent. On 3rd December 1991 S.N.C. held an emergency meeting in Pataya, Thailand to discuss among other things, the security measures for S.N.C. members. Demonstrations against corruption in the Phnom Penh administration started around 17th December 1991 also became violent. The security situation in the city deteriorated during the next few days. The S.N.C. meeting scheduled on 21st December 1991 could not materialize. Still, Prince Shehanouk chaired a special meeting of the S.N.C. Secretariat to assess the situation. They also discussed the deployment of UNAMIC liaison teams to the parties headquarters and to activate the military working group (MMWG) as stipulated in the Paris agreement. The deployment of the liaison teams was completed on 22nd December 1991. The first meeting of MMWG was held with the participation of all the four parties on 28th December 1991. The meeting appealed to the Secretary-General for an early deployment of UNTAC and the appointment of his special representative.

The mandate of UNAMIC was expanded on 8th January 1992 by its resolution 728 to undertake on an urgent basis a major demining effort even before the establishment of UNTAC and its work to prepare the ground for safe and orderly repatriation of Cambodian refugees and displaced persons. It added 1090 military personnel on the recommendation of the Secretary-General. Forty of these would work with national mine clearance commission established by S.N.C. as well as with UNHCR and other international agencies. It would gather all information on mine fields and would organize a training programme for Cambodians in mine detection and clearance.[29] It would establish priorities for action and allocate work among different units. It added a field engineering battalion of seven hundred personnel for clearing repatriation routes, reception centres and resettlement areas. It would carry out emergency repair and rehabilitation work on roads and bridges already cleared. Two hundred personnel comprising expert teams to train local military personnel were made available by four Cambodian parties. Another one hundred and fifty logistic support personnel were also made available. The cost of the expansion was estimated at 24.7 millions. It deployed an engineering battalion from Thailand in Sisophon/Battambang area on 21-22 February 1992.

Mr. Boutros Boutros-Ghali succeeded Mr. Javier Perez De Cuellar as Secretary-General on January 1992. He appointed under Secretary-General Yasushi Akashi of Japan as Special Representative for Cambodia.[30] The Security Council approved the action plan of UNTAC indicating administrative and financial aspects (S/23613 and add1) of 19th February 1992. It consisted of seven distinct components, namely Human Rights, electoral military, Civil Administration, Civilian Police, repatriation and rehabilitation.

The Human Right Component concentrated its efforts in encouraging S.N.C. to ratify relevant international human rights instruments, conducted an extensive campaign of human rights education, investigated allegations of human rights abuses and exercised general oversight of human rights aspects of every component of UNTAC.

The Special Representative was assisted in organizing and carrying out free and fair elections in Cambodia by a Chief Electoral officer. Other needed personnel included one hundred and ninety eight international staff operating from headquarters and from twenty one provincial and municipal centres.[31] Some four hundred United Nations Volunteers operating from each of the district undertook duties related to electoral operations, information, training, communication, compliance and co-ordination. Four thousand Cambodian personnel took part during the registration process. One thousand international supervisors, 56,000 Cambodians assisted in the polling process.[32]

The Secretary-General visited Cambodia from 18-20th in April 1992. He attended a meeting of S.N.C. on 20th April. The members signed International Covenants on Civil and Political Rights and also Economic, Social and Cultural Rights. The Secretary-General formally launched an appeal for an international aid of $ 593 millions to fund rehabilitation efforts, food, health services, shelter, education, training and restoration of country's basic infrastructure, public utilities and support institutions to initiate the process of rehabilitation during the transition period. It included the aid figure of $ 116 millions to be the cost of repatriating refugees from Thailand. The Secretary-General could report to the Security Council on 1st May 1992, the generally good start of UNTAC.

UNTAC announced on 9th May 1992 that the phase-I of the cease-fire was in effect since the signing of Paris agreement.[33] It would be followed on 13th June 1992 by Phase-II.[34] The force Commander took the step in consultation with the four Cambodian parties and after obtaining their assurances that it would grant freedom of movement to UNTAC personnel, vehicles and air craft. They would mark mine fields in their areas and provide UNTAC by 20th May 1992, information on troops, arms, ammunition and equipment. They promised to adhere to Paris agreement and particularly not to interfere with troops moving to regrouping and cantonment areas. However, PDK, a signatory to the assurances given did not cooperate. The Special Representative called on all the parties on 26th May 1992 and the meeting of S.N.C. to show their readiness to comply with their assurances especially in respect of permitting full and unrestricted freedom of movement to UNTAC, marking mine fields, providing detailed information about the military to be confined to cantonments and an undertaking for a phased and balanced demobilization of atleast 70 percent of their forces. Three of the parties responded positively. But PDK not only failed to comply with all these but also prevented senior UNTAC officials including the special representative to enter into its area. On 30th May even a personal appeal to Mr.Khieu Samphan, President of PDK by the Secretary-General failed to get any response. Further appeals of the Special Representative too were invain. PDK, in explanation, asserted that foreign military personnel still remained in Cambodia and wanted deferring the commencement of Phase II until the withdrawl and nonreturn of foreign forces was verified and certified by UNTAC. It also raised concern regarding the effective control of existing administrative structure.

UNTAC rejected PDK's view point but took steps to meet PDK's concern to an extent. It established a total of ten check points[35] – one more than foreseen – on the Cambodian border with Vietnam at an earlier date than originally planned. It also wanted all the four parties to participate in manning the check posts. Mobile teams were launched and empowered to carryout investigations, including allegations of the presence of armed forces. In spite of providing a list of allegations in writing, PDK failed to provide personnel to accompany UNTAC's investigation. Vietnam gave its assurance in writing on 30th May 1992 (S/24082) that its forces, volunteers and all equipment had been completely withdrawn from Cambodia even by 26th September 1989 and it did not reintroduce any of them. All its military assistance ended and no other country was allowed to use its territory to provide military assistance to any of the Cambodian parties.

Despite the lack of cooperation from PDK the Secretary-General concluded that Phase II should commence on 13th June and any delay would result in loss of momentum gained. It would also geoparadise UNTAC's ability to organize and conduct elections by April or May 1993.[36] The Special Representative, in consultation with the other three parties ensured that the process of regrouping and confinement of forces to cantonment would minimize any military disadvantage on account of PDK's noncompliance. This, however, would only be a short term solution and PDK would be persuaded to join the other parties in good faith for the comprehensive political agreement. The Statement of the President of the Security Council (S/24091) reaffirmed the importance of the full and timely implementation of all the agreements and the necessity to begin the second phase on 13th June 1992.[37]

The Tokyo Conference from 20th to 22nd June 1992 of all the four parties drew up informal proposals and measures (S/24286) designed to meet some of the Concerns of PDK.[38] At an extraordinary meeting of S.N.C. on 22nd June the four Cambodian parties were asked to respond to the proposals. Three of them accepted immediately while PDK promissed to consider the proposals and respond at a later date.

At a working of session of S.N.C. on 2nd July 1992 PDK introduced its own proposals regarding the role and powers of S.N.C. and the administrative structures under the control of S.O.C. On 7th July the Secretary-General addressed a letter to Mr Khieu Samphan assuring him that the Special Representative would pursue his efforts to attend to the legitimate concern expressed by PDK as well as those of the other three parties on the basis of the Tokyo proposals. The special representative Mr. Rafee Uddin Ahmed met Mr. Khieu Samphan thrice in addition to S.N.C. meetings to secure his agreement to the Tokyo proposals and comply with the Paris agreement. PDK elaborated its positions and particularly called for the dissolution of the main institutions and structures in the state of Cambodia control. The Special Representative, referring to the Paris Agreement, asserted that UNTAC's control should be exercised through the existing administrative structure in each of the four zones of Cambodian Parties, which Phnom Penh formed a part.

UNTAC accelerated its efforts to recruit and deploy its civil administrative staff to exercise its authority under the mandate given by the agreements for direct control over foreign affairs, national defence, finance, public security and information along with supervision of other areas in the existing administrative structures. A comprehensive plan to introduce this control throughout the territory of Cambodia, was announced by the special representative on 26th, June 1992. A control over the administrative structures of S.O.C. (State of Cambodia) dealing with foreign affairs and national defence was established on 1st July 1992. A progressive introduction of control over finance was planned between Ist July 1992 and 1st September 1992. A media working group composed of representatives of the four parties was established as early as on 10th June 1992).

UNTAC's military component was fully deployed by July 1992 with 14,300 troops in the country and the remainder enroute. There were 1,780 UNTAC civilian police monitors deployed throughout the country to supervise a fair and impartial enforcement of law and order. About hundred cases of violations were investigated in S.O.C zones and investigation in other zones were in progress. An estimated two hundred thousand troops confined to cantonment by 10th July 1992 were as follows. Cambodian peoples armed forces (CPAF) – 9003; National Army of independent Kampuchea (NAKI)–3187;[39] Khmer people National Liberation Armed Forces (KPNLAF) – 1,322. However no National Army of Democratic Kampuchea (NADK) of PDK was incomplete on account of PDK's non-cooperation. The U.N. was left with only two possible courses of action either to suspend the operation until all parties complied with agreements, or to pursue the process, demonstrating the international communities determination to assist the Cambodian people, despite the non-cooperation of PDK. The Special Representative Rufee Uddin Ahmed was advised to press forward with the regrouping and confinement to the cantonment process with caution and selectivity with an eye on the security in the countryside. The main question of persuading PDK to comply with its agreement still remained. The Security Council in its resolution 766 of 21st July 1992 demanded the PDK to permit the deployment of UNTAC in areas under its control to implement cease-fire as well as other aspects of the agreement. The Secretary-General was also asked to ensure international assistance to the rehabilitation and reconstruction of Cambodia in areas as per the agreements in Tokyo Conference where Australia Austria, Belgium, Brunei, Darussalam, Cambodia, Canada, China, Denmark, Finland, France, Germany, India, Indonesia, Ireland, Italy, Japan, Laos, Malaysia, Netherland, New Zealand, Norway, Philippines, Portugal, Republic of Korea, Russian Federation, Singapore, Spain, Sweden, Switzerland, Thailand, United Kingdom, United States and Vietnam attended. This should be in the areas where parties cooperated and fulfilled their obligations. An international committee under the Chairmanship of Japan was to coordinate the mechanism of International Community with democratically elected Government of Cambodia on medium and long-term plans of reconstruction of the country. Pledges of aid amounted to $ 880 millions surpassing $ 593 millions as per the appeal.

However, some other problems also came up. The security situation in the countryside worsened. The economic situation was precarious with imminent hyper inflation. UNTAC was grappling with task of keeping the country afloat and having Cambodians focus on their common national priorities. The prospects were daunting. Still the Special Representative was quite optimistic. There was substantial reservoir of resources and goodwill besides unanimous support of the entire international community. A great majority of Cambodians too wanted to build a new and peaceful country.

The Special Representative decided to exercise his power under the Paris Agreement and the draft of the electoral law as amended and was adopted at the S.N.C. meeting in spite of the objections of PDK. All Cambodian persons with right of voting were:

(a) A person born in Cambodia atleast one of whose parents was born in Cambodia.

(b) A person, wherever born, atleast one of whose parents was a Cambodian within the meaning of "a".

(c) The Draft was also amended to permit overseas Cambodians to vote in one polling station in Europe, one in North America, and one in Australia. It was decided that the electoral process should be carried out in accordance with implementation time table as per the agreement.

The UNTAC acquired a powerful momentum by 21st September 1992 despite PDK's refusal to grant UNTAC access to the zones under its control. It achieved a profound and lasting impact on Cambodia. Full control over the administration up to the village level was established and strengthened with a strong police presence. The Cambodians continued to be informed and educated on human rights. More than hundred and fifteen thousand refugees and displaced persons had been repatriated.

The Security Council, as per the recommendations of Secretary-General in his report on 21st September 1992 confirmed that the electoral process should proceed according to the time table agreed upon in its resolution 783 of 13th October 1992.[40] The Council further demanded the PDK to immediately to fulfill its obligations and invited Japan and Thailand, actively involved in finding solutions, to continue their efforts and report the results to the Secretary-General as well as the Co-chairmen of the Paris Agreement. It became clear that consultations would be of no value to address the impass. The Co-chairmen met in Beijing with Prince Shehanouk, Members of the S.N.C. representing the four Cambodian parties and the representatives of the five permanent members of the Security Council as well as Germany, Japan and Thailand on 7th November 1992. The Special Representative also participated. PDK was obstinate and refused to take part in the electoral process till a neutral political condition was ensured.

Voters registration opened in Phnom Penh on 5th October 1992 and in four other provinces on 19th October, progressively extending to other provinces. About a million Cambodians registered their names to vote in the first week. UNTAC broadcasts concentrated on information regarding voters registration and election process.

The confinement of troops to cantonment, disarmament and demobilization process was only to a quarter of the estimated total number of troops handing over the weapons was also to a quarter and PDK non-complied any of these. However, cease-fire was effective by 15th November 1992. It was being that the process of the reduction of the strength of the military component was not feasible until after the elections. The issue of foreign residents and immigrants also disturbed many Cambodians. Killing of Vietnamese speaking villagers aroused serious concern. UNTAC's investigation revealed the responsibility of the units of NADK.

The Security Council, in its Resolution 792 of 30th November 1992 confirmed the elections to the constituent assembly to be concluded by May 1993 and instructed the Secretary–General to make contingency plans for presidential elections too.[42] It also condemned PDK for its failure and demanded that it immediately fulfil and oblige to facilitate full deployment of UNTAC in areas under its control and not to obstruct voter registration and activities of other political parties. It also requested the Secretary-General to take all appropriate steps to ensure the successful implementation of the process of election.

With the onset of the dry season, cease-fire violations increased mostly in Kompong, Thon, Siem Reap and Battam Bang provinces in Central and North West Cambodia. The violations typically took the form of artillery duels which drove among villages from their homes without causing extensive casuality. UNTAC military observers indicated that CPAF was attempting to recover territories over which NADK had extended its influence during the rainy season while NADK was attempting to consolidate its gains and interrupt CPAF's Communication. Frequent exchanges of fire took place between NADK and CPAF throughout the month of December in the Bevel area of Battam-long province and 15000 residents fled from their homes. NADK's artillery shells landed near a location occupied by UNTAC troops. In Sim Reap province on 24th and 25th and again on 31st December, several incidents of temporary detention of UNTAC personnel by NADK units also took place. UNTAC was warned not to enter PDK control zones without prior authorities. However, the Special Representative as well as the president of the Security Council strongly condemned the illegal detention of UNTAC personnel by NADK.

Other problems surfaced. The inability of UNTAC to gain access to the administrative structure of PDK gave rise to a hardening of S.O.C's position regarding supervision and control of its administrative structure. Further, more a spate of violent incidents hightened a sense of insecurity among Cambodians. UNTAC's civil police, military and civil administration components together with the Human Rights components developed measures to prevent and deal with threats to public order besides investigating the incidents reported by KPNLF and FUNCINPEC. It promised to ensure freedom from intimidation, freedom of party affiliations and freedom of action for political parties. The Prince Shehanouk increased the S.N.C. membership to allow FUNCINPEC representative. He informed the special representative on 4th January 1993 that he could no longer cooperate with UNTAC or S.O.C. Citing persistent violent attack on FUNCINPEC staff, the Special Representative issued a directions on 6th Jan. 1993 to process for the prosecution all violations. Thus UNTAC assumed powers to arrest and detain and prosecute suspects of serious violations and the office of special prosecutor (S/25124) was established.

The Special Representative met both Prince Norodom Shehanouk, and Prince Norodom Ranaridh and assured measures to promote a neutral political environment. Both leaders showed understanding. Prince Ranaridh subsequently expressed gratitude for the efforts of UNTAC and assured FUNCINPEC would continue its cooperation. A special S.N.C. meeting on 28th January 1993 in Beijing ensured continued cooperation with the United Nations in implementation of the Paris Agreement. At the same meeting Prince Shehanouk retracked his decision of 4th January to be a candidate in the presidential elections and promissed to wait until the new constitution was adopted before holding the elections. The S.N.C. meeting set the dates for the election of constituent assembly. The dates were 23 to 25 May 1993 and at the mobile stations on 27th and 28th of May. Prince Shehanouk issued, in his own name and in the name of S.N.C. members belonging to FUNCINPEC, KPNF, and S.O.C, a statement condemning violence against Cambodians and foreign persons in Cambodia and any act which would threaten the dignity, fundamental freedoms, rights, security and personal safety of any member of UNTAC.

Cease-fire violations including artillery and mortar fire continued in January and February 1993 between CPAF and NADK. UNTAC protested the moves as exceeding the bounds of self defence. S.O.C was called upon to desist from violating cease-fire and exercise self-restraint. The incidents of violence and intimidation which peaked in December 1992, however, significantly came down in the later months and were concentrated in the provinces of Battambang and Kompongchan and a vast majority of victims were members of FUNCINPEC. While PDK radio had attacked UNTAC and had become increasingly hostile, the Phnom Penh authorities also undertook a media campaign asserting that only S.O.C could defend the country against PDK deserving the electoral support and UNTAC could not be trusted for the protection of Cambodians.

The Special Representative extended the registration of voters till 31st January. At its completion, over 4.6 million people are some 96 percent of the estimated eligible population registered their names for voting. Returnees were given opportunity for registration of their names on their return either in their final destination or in six reception centres. As the end of registration period approached, special arrangement was made between UNTAC's repatriation and electoral components to enable the registration of remaining eligible population in border camps.

Twenty out of the twenty two provisionally registered political parties had applied for official registration, in accordance with the electoral law by 27th January 1993. Neither PDK nor the National Unity of Cambodia, its political wing filed for official registration in the election. The UNTAC announced its decision on 10th February 1993 at a meeting of S.N.C. that the electoral campaign would begin on 7th April 1993 and end on 19th May. It would be followed by a four day cooling off period before polling. During the campaign UNTAC would make its information and broadcasting facilities available to all political parties in order to ensure fair access to the media. The special Representative met the leaders of twenty Political parties on 11th March 1993 to inform them of their rights and responsibilities as party leaders under the electoral law.

All the twenty political parties participated actually in the electoral campaign on 7th April. The Secretary-General, during his visit to Cambodia on 7th and 8th of April 1993, told S.N.C. that the basic acceptable conditions for the conduct of an electoral campaign did exist as per his judgement and felt the electoral campaign would be conducted peacefully with the participation of tens of thousands of Cambodians. He also appealed for an end to violence. Prince Shehanouk also instructed that his armed components refrain from acts of violence which was endorsed by S.O.C, KPNLF and FUNC INPEC (S/25784). All Units of UNTAC's military components were directed to increase vigilance and enhance security measures and procedures. It further refined and strengthened measures to ensure the security of the electoral process and the safety of the Cambodian political parties.

The elections were the focal point of the comprehensive settlement. The election of One hundred and twenty members to the constituent assembly as stipulated in the agreement was held throughout Cambodia on provincial basis in accordance with a system of proportional representation. Every Cambodian of eighteen years or above was eligible to vote. The agreement provided for a multi-party electoral system. Voting was for political parties registered by UNTAC. A list of party candidates for each province was published before the election. The Special Representative promulgated a number of minor amendements to the electoral law in order to ensure security or other consideration as they arose or anticipated. The campaign, scores of political meetings and rally were held daily and peacefully with the participation of tens of thousands of people in all parts of Cambodia. UNTAC organized multi-party meetings.

The election took place from 23rd to 28th May 1993. During the first three days of elections some 1,400 large, medium, and small fixed polling stations operated throughout the country. Two hundred mobile teams went into remote and difficult areas. A Cambodian presiding officer was incharge of each station with support and assistance from polling station officers from international community. Some fixed stations were converted to mobile operations on 26th May and worked as mobile teams on 27th and 28th May. Mobile teams operated for the entire six day period. Counting by UNTAC began on May 29th morning. The Special Representative on behalf of the Secretary-General and the United Nations declared at a meeting of S.N.C. on 29th May that the polling was free and fair. The Security Council endorsed this declaration in Resolution 835 of 2nd June 1993 and called upon all parties to stand by their obligation to respect fully the results.

A total of 4,267,192 voters representing 89.56 percent of the registered voters had turned out to vote. The count of 4,011,631 valid votes indicated that nation wide FUNCINPEC had won 1,84,182 votes or 45.47 percent, CPP – 1,533,471 votes or 38.23 percent. BLDP won 152,764 votes or 3.81 percent and all the other seventeen political parties won the remaining votes. The number of seats won in the constituent assembly was 58 for FUNCINPEC, 51 for CPP, 10 for BLDP and one for fourth political party MOLINAKA. The U.N. expressed its full support to the constituent assembly which would draw up a constitution and transformed itself into a legislative assembly to establish new government for all Cambodians. The Council wanted the assembly to complete its work within three months as stipulated. It also requested UNTAC to continue to play its role inconjunction with S.N.C. during the transitional period.

The post-election hurdles were promptly handled. UNTAC conducted intensive discussion with CPP which raised some allegations of electoral irregularities. The allegations were promptly investigated and any anamolies that would affect the outcome were immediately attended to and could convince the president of CPP Mr. Chea Sim, that the election were impartial and free and fair. Similarly the Caasationists of east provinces which held anti UNTAC demonstrations could also be convinced. Prince Nordom Shehanouk cooperated with UNTAC in calming the situation, contacting the leaders of CPP and FUNCINPEC. The special Representative also encouraged dialogue between S.O.C and FUNCINPEC.

Duly elected constituent assembly started working on 14th June 1993. The first act of the assembly was making. Prince Norodom Shehanouk, head of the state, nullifying coup-d-et al of 18th March 1970, giving the Prince full powers as head of the state. The next day Prince Shehanouk proposed the formation of an Interim Joint Administration with prince Runaridh and Hunsen as co-chairmen. The C.P.P softened its position the ceasation collapsed and the results of the election were recognized. UNTAC agreed to form a committee of enquiry in order to deal with alleged electoral irregularities. PDK also declared that it would accept the outcome of the elections. C.P.P., FUNCINPEC, and BLDP agreed to the proposal of Shehnouk to form GNPC and the list of the Cabinet ministers was submitted to the Constituent assembly by 24th June1993.

The Constituent assembly elected its president and two vice presidents and adopted the rules of procedure on 30th June 1993. Two permanent Committees were established for drafting the constitution and the rules of procedure. UNTAC provided logistical and operational assistance as well as technical advice to the assembly. A vote of confidence was held on 1st July 1993. The establishment of GNPC though not foreseen under the Paris Agreement, provided for a co-operative frame work between all parties in the constituent assembly. The existing three units of administration were fused. All the parties in the administration and PDK held tentative discussions for national reconciliation. Inspite of the fact that the main body of troops and civilian staff remained in Cambodia after the elections, a substantial number of the repatriation component and electoral component, their function coming to an end, had already been withdrawn by the end of June 1993. The withdrawl plan of the Secretary-General (S/26090) was approved by the Security Council. However the Secretary – General proposed that continued international assistance and support were still required as the country still faced enormous problems of security, stability, mine clearance, infrastructure improvement and general economic and S.O.Cial development. He wanted to establish Phnom Penh an integrated office headed by United Nations Representative to deal with a number of residual issues after the complete withdrawl of UNTAC. The Security Council in its Resolution

860 on 27th August 1993 approved UNTAC's withdrawl by 15th November, 1993. It, however, acting on the recommendations of the Secretary – General (S/26675), in its Resolution 880 of 4th November extended the period of withdrawl of mine clearance, and training units to 30th November 1993 and the military police and medical components too 31st December at the latest. As the security conditions deteriorated in Cambodia, a number of military police officers and members of medical units were needed for the safety and security of UNTAC personnel and equipment. Still in December the military police officers were reduced to thirty from seventy one and the medical unit to eight from ten.

The Constituent Assembly adopted the new constitution on 21st September 1993. The vote was One hundred and thirteen in favour and five against, with only two abstentions. Thus, UNTAC's mandate concluded on 24th September 1993. Prince Norodom Shehanouk formally promulgated the new constitution of the Kingdom of Cambodia making the country a constitutional monarchy, independent, sovereign, peaceful, neutral, and non aligned. The same day, prince Shehanouk was elected, the King of Cambodia by the royal council of the thrown. The constituent assembly was transformed into legislative assembly. The king appointed Prince Norodom Runriddh, leader of FUNCINPEC first prime minister in the new government and Hun Sen, leader of C.P.P. the second Prime Minister. The Special Representative left Cambodia on 26th September 1993. The Security Council expressed its satisfaction (S/26531) and the auspicious developments in Cambodia since the holding of the elections and stressed the importance of Continued support of international community to the consolidation of peace, democracy and promotion of development in Cambodia.

The first and second Prime Ministers of Cambodia, jointly requested the Secretary-General to consider the possibility of despatching twenty or thirty Unarmed united Nations military observes for a period of six months after UNTAC's mandate ended. As such their presence would strengthen the confidence of the people and also enhance the stability of Cambodia and its new Government at a critical time (S/ 26546). The Security Council accepted the request in principle and asked the Secretary-General to submit the detailed proposal on the matter. On the recommendations of the Secretary-General (S/26649) the military liaison team consisting of unarmed military officers headed by Colonel Mumiruz Zaman (Bangladesh) was set up in Phnom Penh on 15th November 1993. This would be distinct from the integrated united office intended by the Secretary-General. Australia, Belgium, China, France, India, Indonesia, Malaysia, New Zealand, Pakistan, Poland, Russian Federation, Thailand and Uruguway contributed the officers. Liaison was conducted at the ministerial executive and ambassadorial level by the CMLO while at the functional level by other officers. The U.N. Headquarters was regularly reported on security conditions and other developments. Mobile teams were also sent outside Phnom Penh at the request of the government, as well as when the CMLO deemed it necessary. The Secretary-General appointed Mr. Benny Widyono as his representative in Cambodia (S/994/ 389) on 29th March 1994. On May 2nd the Government requested an extension of the teams mandate for a further period. However, endorsing the Secretary-General's proposal three military advisers from Belgium, France and Malayasia were retained in Cambodia for this purpose following the teams departure on 15th May 1994. One military adviser was attached to the Representatives' office after April 1995 and extended his mandate through March 1996. The expenditure of UNAMIC and UNTAC amounted to $ 1,620, 963,300, repatriation and resettlement of refugees and displaced persons as were as rehabilitation assistance were funded by voluntary contributions.

The Indian participation in Cambodia was quite substantial. Indian army sent an Infantry Battalion, a field ambulance, a mine training team. Staff Officers and seventeen military observers. The area of responsibility of battalion group and field ambulance included political sensitive provinces of Kampong Cham, Svery Ring and Prey Veng. The tasks of the infantry battalion included (i) Disarmieting of armed factions. (ii) Providing a secure environment for registration of votes. (iii)Electoral security and (iv) Protection of U.N. Civilian members and property.

Infanty battalion which served in UNTAC consisted of one Assam Commanding Officer colonel A.K. Tiwari and four J.A.K. Rifles with colonel A.N. Bhargava as commanding officers. India also provided three military observers in the United Nations Military Liaison team of twenty unarmed military observers.

Subedar Rawal Singh was honoured with Kirtichakra. Colonel A.N.Bhargava, Major Rajpal Punia and Major Hareendar Paul Sood were rewarded with Yudh Seva Medals. Naib Subedar Surendar Singh and riflcman Sukhwinder Singh were awarded Seva medals. Major Vinod Pillai received U.N.Force Commander's citation. A few, Havaldar Vikraman Nair, Havaldar Madhava Chandra Raj, Sepoy Bupin Chandra Ray and Sepoy Bhupal Singh were posthumously awarded role of honour in the peace-keeping operations.

REFERENCES

1. *The World Book of Encyclopedia* (International), World Book in Corporation Ascott Setzer Company, p.176.
2. *Ibid.,* p.176a
3. *Ibid.,* p.176a
4. *Ibid.,* p.176a
5. *Ibid.,* p.176a
6. Dennis Duncanson, 'Who will govern Cambodia?' *The World Today,* June 1982, p.243.

7. *Op. cit.,* The World Book of Encyclopedia, p.176a.
8. The Blue Helmets, *A Review of United Nations Peace-keeping,* The United Nations Department of Public Information, New York, 1996, p.449.
9. Ozay Mehmet, Development in a War-torn Society: What Next in Cambodia, *Third World Quarterly,* Vol.No.18, pp.675, 676.
10. *Op. cit.,* The Blue Helmets, p.449.
11. Annapurna Nautiyal, 'Cambodia: A Problem of Peace and Stability', *India Quarterly,* Oct. Dec. 1992, p.44.
12. *Op. cit.,* The Blue Helmets, p.449.
13. Stephen J. Solars, 'Cambodia and the International Community', *Foreign Affairs,* Vol.69, No.2, 1990, pp.101, 102.
14. *Op. cit.,* The Blue Helmets, p.450.
15. *Ibid.,* p.450.
16. *Ibid.,* p.451.
17. See Appendix No.VII & VIII.
18. David Roberts, 'Cambodia: Problems of a U.N. Brokered Peace', *The World Today,* July 1992, p.129.
19. *Op. cit.,* The Blue Helmets, p.452.
20. *Ibid.,* p.453.
21. *Ibid.,* p.453.
22. *Ibid.,* p.454.
23. *Op cit.,* David Roberts, p.131.
24. *Op. cit.,* The Blue Helmets, p.454.
25. *Ibid.,* p.455.
26. *Ibid.,* p.455.
27. *Ibid.,* p.452.
28. *Ibid.,* p.455.
29. Ruth Bottomley, 'Balancing Risk: Village de-mining in Cambodia, *Third World Quarterly,* Vol. 24, No.5, 2003, pp.824, 825.
30. *Op cit.,* The Blue Helmets, p.456.
31. *Ibid.,* p.456.
32. *Ibid.,* p.456.
33. *Ibid.,* p.460.
34. *Ibid.,* p.460.
35. *Ibid.,* p.461.
36. *Ibid.,* p.461.

37. *Ibid.,* p.461.
38. *Ibid.,* p.461.
39. *Ibid.,* p.462.
40. *Ibid.,* p.463.

5

United Nations Protection Force (UNPROFOR) March 1992–Dec. 1995

The sight of families splitting up upsets people. Thus the same happens when states split-up. The Yugoslavian federation consisting of six federal republics: Bosnia and Herzegovina, Croatia, Macedonia, Montenegro, Serbia and Slovania and two autonomous provinces reintegrated into Serbia: Valvodina and Kosovo split up. It reached a critical stage with Croatia declaring independence.[1] It is like a divorce of partners with one partner not wanting to divorce and both partners poor and unreasonable owing a lot of money to each other and a lot to third parties as well. Inter-Republican relations reached the lowest ebb both economically and politically. The movement of goods and capital between republics was blocked by funding republican governments passing legislation — taxes on goods and on property owned by other republics, prohibitive taxes for running the representative offices of 'enemy' republics and confiscation of foreign property. The industrial production dipped in Kosovo, in Montenegro, in Croatia, in Macedonia, in Slovania, in Bosnia & Herzegovina. Unemployment was mounting. In Croatia alone 60 percent of workforce (about 900000 people) were not receiving the salaries but only coupons. The National Bank of Serbia granting Serbian banks

UNPROFOR Deployment as of March 1995

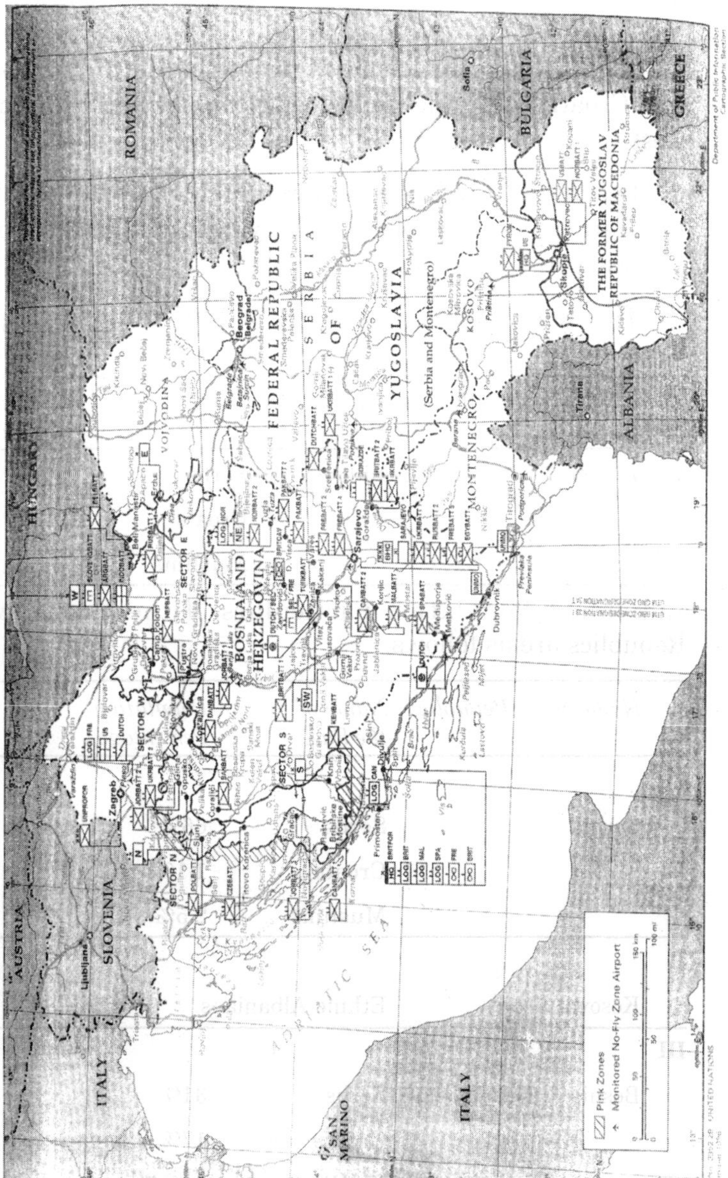

fifteen times more than the allowed ceiling resulted in the breakdown of monetary policy.[2] Since the declaration of independence by Croatia and Slovania they were thrown out of the monetary system of Yugoslavia. However Slovenia and Croatia were the richest and best connected with the west.[3]

Besides all this the ethnic composition of the republics too aggravated the problem, each trying to dominate the other politically.

The demographic particulars of 1991 census are given below.[1]

Name of the country	*Total population*	*Name of the Race*	*Population Percentage*
Yugoslavia	23.5 millions	Serbs	36%
		Croats	20%
		Muslims	10%

Individual Population particulars of the Yugoslavian Republics are as follows.

	Name of the Republic	*Name of the Race*	*Population Percentage*
I			
	Serbia	Serbs	66%
		Croats	1.1%
		Muslims	2.5%
II			
	Kosovo	Ethnic Albanians	81%
III			
	Bosnia & Herzegovina	Serbs	31%
		Croats	17%
		Muslims	44%

(Contd...)

	Name of the Republic	Name of the Race	Population Percentage
IV			
	Croatia	Serbs	12%
		Croats	78%
		Muslims	1% (or less than 1%)

President Josip Broz Tito laid the foundations to bring balance among the diversity of the population during his ruling. In July 1971, the president introduced a collective system of leadership to provide equal opportunities to all races in the country.[4] He also introduced regular rotation of the personnel among political posts. Likewise several innovative ideas were also incorporated in the policy at the time of making the constitution in 1974, such as, giving maximum autonomy to the republics, keeping the federal government responsible only for national defence, designing foreign policy, the single national market system etc.[5]

Afterwards in 1979, the principle of rotating leadership was also extended to the Secretaryship of the League of Communists of Yugoslavia (L C Y). Thus the collective state of Yugoslavia under his Presidency was founded by him, led by him and continued till his death in May 1980.[6] The LCY and the Collective Presidency took the responsibilities of the State after the demise of President Tito.

Unfortunately, the country was under constant crisis in 1980s. Economic and political crisis, social and nationalist unrests were increasing; ethnic tensions were high.[7] The Collective federal presidency and its six rotating presidents were unable to negotiate a revised national structure or to create effective ways to deal with the changing circumstances.[8]

Two referendums were made in Croatia and Slovenia and they both declared independence in June 1991. Accordingly, in September 1991 the republic of Macedonia also supported independence, after a referendum. The members in the assembly of Bosnia and Herzegovina also voted in favour of independence in October 1991 but it was not undisputed. The Muslim members and Croats supported the independence and the Bosnian Serb members protested it through their walk-out. The Republic of Serbia strongly opposed the declaration of independence. They expressed great concern to the welfare of Serbs residing in Croatia and Bosnia and Herzegovina. The circumstances became more serious and the Serbs living in Croatia started fighting against the declaration of independence in June 1991, with the support of the Yugoslavian National Army (JNA) dominated by Serbs.[9] The fighting lasted only one month and stopped in July 1991 when JNA withdrew its support after an agreement between JNA and the European Community (now the European Union).The European Community made several attempts to stop the hostility among the races and to restore peace in Croatia but its framework did not yield good results.

The Security Council meeting of the United Nations decided to intervene and on 25th September, 1991, passed a resolution 713 (1991), calling on all States to employ immediately a "general and complete embargo on all deliveries of weapons and military". This was the first step in the involvement of United Nations in former Yugoslavian matters.[10] The Council also applauded the efforts of the European Community, with the support of the States participating in the Conference on Security and Cooperation in Europe (CSCE) (the Organization for Security and Cooperation in Europe, OSCE), to restore peace and dialogue in Yugoslavia and invited the Secretary-General to offer his good offices. The Secretary-General Javier Perez De Cuellar started the operations. He appointed Mr. Cyrus Vance, the former United States Secretary of State, on 8th October 1991, as his personal envoy for Yugoslavia. Mr. Vance conducted a meeting in Geneva inviting Presidents of Serbia, and Croatia, the Secretary of State for National Defence of Yugoslavia and Lord Carrington, the Chairman of European Communities Conference in Yugoslavia. The meeting resolved to call for an immediate cease-fire and establish a United Nations Peace keeping operation. The impact was instant. The cease-fire occurred almost immediately.

Meanwhile Mr. Cyrus Vance released a statement that the deployment of the United Nations Peacekeeping Operations could not be envisaged without full compliance by all parties who attended the Geneva conference. Thus its resolution 721, passed on 27th November 1991, the Security Council endorsed the personal envoy's statement. The Secretary-General sent a plan for possible peace-keeping operations to the Security Council through a report and the Council approved it on 15th December through its resolution 724 (1991).[11] Accordingly a small group of military officers, civil police and United Nations secretariat staff members went to the areas to make preparations to implement the plan. In 1992 on 2nd March, Mr. Cyrus Vance convened a meeting in Sarajevo, between military representatives of the Republic of Croatia and the representatives of JNA. In the meeting the agreement for the unconditional cease-fire was signed. Meanwhile, General Boutros Boutros-Ghali from Peru was appointed as Secretary-General in the place of Perez De Cuellar. He sent a group of fifty military liaison officers to the highly sensitive areas to keep maintaining the cease-fire, in accordance with the United Nations peacekeeping operation strategies. The United Nations Protection Force (UNPROFOR) was established when the Security Council passed a resolution 743 on 21st February 1992, for an initial period of twelve months.[12] It was an interim arrangement to create conditions of peace and security required for the negotiation of an overall settlement of the crisis in Yugoslavia.

The mandate of the UNPROFOR was related to Croatia first, and it was extended to Bosnia and Herzegovina and later to Macedonia also.[13]

After its inception the UNPROFOR marked certain areas in Croatia as United Nations Protected Areas (UNPAS). For convenience sake the UNPAS areas were divided into four Sections. The East, North, South and West sections situated in the areas of Eastern Slovenia, Western Slovenia and Krajina. Some of these areas were thickly populated by Serbs and some had them in substantial minority of population. However, all those areas were filled with inter ethnic tensions and that sowed the seeds for armed conflict. The Security Council opined that some special interim arrangements were needed in those areas for the maintenance of the cease-fire status. The Security Council proposed (1). The demilitarization of all UNPAS areas along with the withdrawal of the J N A from Croatia. (2) The continuation of peace operations by the existing local authorities and police, on an interim basis under the supervision of United Nations till the achievement of an overall political solution to the catastrophe.

UNPROFOR's directive was to ensure that the UNPAS residents, lived in a safe environment and make them feel free from the fear of armed attacks. So the organization was authorized to control access to the UNPAS for the demilitarization and to monitor the activities of the local police to ensure nondiscrimination and to protect human rights. Besides its regular activities, UNPROFOR was also to help the other humanitarian agencies of the United Nations to facilitate the return of civilian displaced persons to their homes in UNPAS areas. UNPROFOR had three supporting forces in its operations — the military, police and civil authorities; twelve enlarged infantry battalions, military headquarters, logistics, and other supporting army branches had the personnel ranged up to 2480 ranks. The police wing had five thirty police personnel. Its headquarters was at top gear of operations and it had a strength of 8332 members including 7975 military personnel. The military force commander, an Indian Lieutenant General Satish Nambiar and his principal staff members reached Belgrade on 8th March 1992. They proceeded to Sarajevo after the initial consultations in Belgrade and Zagreb (The capital of Croatia). The active participation of the deployment by the force began in the middle of March when the advance teams arrived. The logistic bases were established in Belgrade and Zagreb.

Besides the UNPAS, the Security Council authorized UNPROFOR to monitor things in "pink zones "(the Areas in Croatia which were earlier controlled by JNA, largely populated by Serbs but situated outside the boundaries of UNPAS), through a resolution 762 on 30th March 1992.[14] It also recommended the establishment of a joint commission headed by UNPROFOR. According to the guidelines suggested, the joint commission should consist of representatives from the Government of Croatia and the local authorities in the region. To restore the authority of the Croatian government in 'pink zones', the commission had to monitor the operations with the participation and cooperation of the European Community Monitoring Mission. Immediately, on 7th August 1992, the Security Council by its resolution 769, again authorized the second enlargement of UNPROFOR`s strength and mandate to control the entry of civilians into the UNPAS and to perform immigration and customs functions at the UNPAS boarders by international frontiers. The third enlargement came on 6th October1992, through a resolution 779 authorizing UNPROFOR to monitor the demilitarization in the Prevlaka peninsula near Dubrovnik.[15] The same resolution also approved the Secretary-General's action to make certain the control of the UNPROFOR on the vitally important Peruca Dam, situated in one of the "Pink Zones".

On the one hand Lt. General Satish Nambiar was renewing the UNPROFOR attempt in creating a peaceful environment, on the other had the Croatian army launched an offensive, in many locations in the southern part of the UNPROFOR's controlled areas and the adjacent pink zones because of its impatience with the slow progress of negotiations in respect of various economic facilities in the areas. As a result of the attacks the Peruca Dam was damaged on 22nd January 1993. The local Serbs responded to the Croatian attacks and they broke into a number of United Nations ammunition stores and took away the arms including heavy weapons. UNPROFOR took it very serious and warned both Croatian government and the Serb authorities against further violations. The force started the remedial operations to limit the damage occurred and to prevent escalation and also to initiate the cease-fire. As the conditions did not improve the Security Council brought out another resolution 802 on 25th January 1993 through which it demanded not only an immediate stop to the hostile activities by the Croatian armed forces in the areas of UNPAS but also their withdrawal from those places.[16] Besides the UNPROFOR very strongly condemned the attacks of the Croatian Armd forces on the UNPROFOR's personnel. The other demands were: the return of all heavy weapons seized by Serbs from controlled storage areas, maintaining strict compliance by all parties and others concerned with the terms of cease-fire arrangements including the disbanding and demobilization of Serb territorial defence units or other units of similar functions, finally and lastly it called upon them to cooperate fully with the International Conference on the Former Yugoslavia (ICFY) and to desist from actions which might weaken the efforts aimed at reaching a political settlement. The Croatian government informed the force commander Satish Nambiar of UNPROFOR on 26th January 1993, that in accordance with the compliance from the Serbs side they would remove their military troops but not the police from the areas mentioned by the

UNPROFOR, and the government also informed the UNPROFOR that Croatia's situations must be restored to the positions prior to the 22nd January 1993, for the implementation of other aspects mentioned in the resolution.

On 6th April 1993, the representatives of the government of Croatia and the local Serb authorities signed an agreement regarding the implementation of the resolution 802. [17] The agreement was to come into force when the co-chairmen of the ICFY steering committee received from both the parties assurances regarding the stationing of the police force in the areas from which the Croatian governments armed forces were withdrawn, and their agreement that UNPROFOR should exclusively fulfill all police functions in those areas during an interim period. Croatian authorities orally gave that assurance required for approval of their 'Assembly'. The parties also agreed to begin talks, under the auspicious of the co chairmen of the steering committee within 15 days of the implementation of the agreement in order to resolve the outstanding obstacles in the implementation of the United Nations plan for Croatia. Lt. Gen. Satish Nambiar assessed the additional resources required to implement the agreement and recommended that UNPROFOR be augmented by two mechanized infantry battalions of some nine hundred of all ranks each, one engineering company of up to one hundred fifty troops of all ranks and fifty additional military observers. The Secretary-General recommended that, once the agreement entered into force, the Security Council approved the recommended changes to UNPROFOR's strength and mandate.

The success in ensuring the complete withdrawal of JNA from the territory of Croatia (including the Prevlka peninsula) was a remarkable achievement by the UNPROFOR in its first year operations. The presence of UNPROFOR also helped to put a stop to the recurrence of hostilities in the UNPAS and in "pink zones" until the end week of January 1993. But there were some shortcomings. The local Serb authorities were in a non cooperative mood and their attitude was a hindrance to the UNPROFOR to achieve the complete demilitarization in UNPAS and disarming of the Serb Territorial defence and other irregular forces. With these failures the first year experiences became the combination of success and failure. As a result the UNPROFOR could not establish the normal conditions of peace and security which would have welcomed the voluntary return of the displaced persons to their homes and the citizens who had gone out as refugees'. Besides this the UNPROFOR was not able to establish border controls. The first ten months of the mandate period was filled with an atmosphere of terror and coercion in many parts of the four sectors. The efforts made by the United Nations civilian police to prevent discrimination and human rights violations in the UNPAS were not successful. The maintenance of law and order was slowly advanced through the reorganization and redeployment of the local police. While the non cooperation of the local Serb authorities, seriously impeded the implementation of United Nations peace keeping plan, the Croatian offensive of January 1993 significantly altered the situation on the ground. Eventually Mr.Franzo Tudzman, the president of Croatia, declared the willingness of his government for the extension of the mandate period of the UNPROFOR depending on its progress in the aspects of (1) complete disarmament of all Parliamentary forces and militia in the UNPAs and in "Pink Zones", (2) Voluntary and unconditional return of all refugees and displaced persons to their homes in the UNPAs (3) destruction of the heavy weapons of the military forces (4) maintenance of tight controls in the border areas of the UNPAs which were recognized as international frontiers of Croatia and (5) the restoration of Croatian authority in pink zones. The president also persuaded the Security Council to grant an enforcement mandate to the UNPROFOR.

When things were going in favour of the UNPROFOR's mandate, the Serb leadership in the UNPAs felt insecure and thought that the UNPROFOR betrayed them. It had no faith in the Security operations by UNPROFOR and felt unprotected. So it was rearmed and remobilized its forces in response to the Croatian offensive. The substantial reinforcements of Serb fighters from other places in the former Yugoslavia also occurred instantly. The Serbs broke into the storage points where the heavy weapons were stored under the peace keeping plan, and took them away. The Serbs not only refused to enter into negotiations with Croats but also did not agree to return the heavy weapons, and they put a condition that unless the Croatian armed forces were sent back to their original places (the places where they were before the offensive.) from the occupied portions they would not comply with UNPROFOR. The Croatian authorities rejected the withdrawal right away. The peace keeping plan had been envisaged as an interim arrangement pending an overall political solution to the Yugoslav crisis. The government of Croatia claimed that there was no longer any "overall political solution" to negotiate. The only issue for them was the return of the UNPAs and the Pink Zones, to Croatian control. The Krazina Serb leadership in UNPAs, however, refused to consider these territories as a part of Croatia and rejected talks on that basis, recalling that the plan was explicitly not intended to prejudge a political solution to the Yugoslavian crisis. Further, the Krazina Serbs argued that the two parties to the original plan, the president of Serbia and the Federal Yugoslav military authorities in Belgrade, no longer had reorganized legal status in the areas where UNPROFOR was deployed. Therefore, the mandate and deployment of UNPROFOR needed to be reviewed with the authorities representing the so called "Republic of Serb Krazina". It was under this state of affairs the initial twelve months mandate period of UNPROFOR in Croatia was coming to a close. Against this stalemate the Secretary-General suggested three options for the UNPROFOR. (1) UNPROFOR could be withdrawn (2) the mandate could be modified or (3) the mandate could be renewed with no change. The consequences of the three possibilities were also observed. The withdrawal of UNPROFOR from the UNPAs would certainly result in the resumption of large scale hostilities, nullifying the political efforts which were made and the material resources which were already invested. The modification of the mandate could not be approved because any enforcement capability "would be a fundamental contradiction of the nature and purpose of UNPROFOR's deployment in Croatia, as a peace keeping force entrusted with the implementation of a plan agreed by all parties". The final option was the only possibility for consideration, but not without any hurdles. The difficulties which the Security Council faced in Croatia, had two principal factors behind them. They were (1) the inability to implement the peacekeeping plan and (2) the lack of an agreed settlement to the conflict between the Republic of Croatia and the Serb populations living in the UNPAs and the pink zones. Satish Nambiar opined that unless these two factors were addressed, a sound basis would not exist for renewing UNPROFOR's mandate in Croatia. The problems that arose from the Croatian offensive were to be resolved urgently and only then a basis could be established for completing the implementation of the peacekeeping operation plans and to agree on a framework for negotiating. The Secretary-General told the Security Council that he had asked the co-chairmen of the ICFY Steering committee to address these questions urgently with a view to establishing a basis on which, the recommendation for an extension of UNPROFOR's mandate would be possible. On 19 February 1993, the Security Council adopted resolution 807, by which it extended UNPROFOR's mandate for an interim period until 31 march 1993.[17] The Security Council demanded that the parties and others concerned comply fully with the United Nations peace keeping plan in Croatia and their other commitments, and refrain from positioning their forces near the UNPAS and in the "pink zones". It invited the Secretary-General to take all appropriate measures to strengthen the security of UNPROFOR, in particular by providing it with the necessary defensive means. The council urged the parties and others concerned to cooperate fully with the co-chairmen of the ICFY steering committee in the discussions under their auspicious. The co-chairmen held several rounds of talks in New York and Geneva with representatives of the government of Croatia and the Serb populations living in the UNPAS and the "pink zones". While some progress was made in these talks, fundamental differences remained between the two sides. The Secretary-General told the Security Council that more time would be needed to bring the negotiations to a meaningful conclusion. He therefore recommended the extension of UNPROFOR's mandate for a further interim period of three months. On 30th March 1993 the Security Council, by resolution 815, extended the mandate of UNPROFOR for an additional interim period until 30th June 1993.[18] It also reaffirmed its commitment to ensure respect for the sovereignty and territorial integrity of Croatia (as well as of the other republics where UNPROFOR was deployed).

The Council thus made it clear formally that the international community would not entertain the claim of the local Serb authorities to recognize as a sovereign entity. The Secretary-General later reported to the council that the local Serb authorities rejecting the resolution as prejudging the outcome of the political negotiations, and as such following its adoption, their resistance to any dialogue had intensified. The council also decided to reconsider within one month, or at any time at the request of the Secretary-General, UNPROFOR's mandate in the light of developments of ICFY and the situation on the ground. It requested the Secretary-

General to report to it on how the peace plan for Croatia could be effectively implemented. On 24th June 1993 the Secretary-General drew the attention of the Security Council to the failure of the parties to permit implementation of the United Nations Plan and, to co-operate in establishing a political process leading to an early settlement.[19] He noted, nevertheless, that the presence of UNPROFOR was indispensable for controlling the conflict, fostering a climate in which negotiations between the parties could be promoted, preventing the resumption or escalation of conflict, providing a breathing-space for the continued efforts of the peacemakers and for supporting the provision of essential humanitarian assistance. He also informed the council that the termination of UNPROFOR's mandate at that point would risk the resumption of a major conflict in the region and cause severe adverse conditions for humanitarian relief operations in Bosnia and Herzegovina. The Secretary-General recommended that the Security Council extended the mandate of UNPROFOR by a further three months, to September 1993. In doing so, by its resolution 847 of 30th June 1993, the Security Council also requested the Secretary-General to report within one month about the in implementation of the peacekeeping plan and all relevant Security Council resolutions.[20]

Following the outbreak of hostilities in Croatia, precipitated by the incursion into the UNPAs and "Pink Zones" on 22nd January 1993, Intensive efforts were made within the framework of the International conference. However, on 6th July 1993 new tensions arose following the decision of the Croatian government to take unilateral actions aimed at rebuilding and reopening the Maslenica bridge on 18th July 1993. On 15th and 16th July 1993, the Erdut and Zagreb agreements were concluded which required the withdrawal of Croatian armed force and police from the area of the Maslenica bridge by 31st July and the placing of the bridge under the exclusive control of UNPROFOR moved 2000 troops into the areas adjacent to those from which the Croatian forces were to withdraw. The UNPROFOR troops could not be deployed however, because the Croatian military would not allow UNPROFOR's full access to the areas concerned. Despite Croatian's failure to withdraw and the Serb shelling and the sinking of one of the pontoons of the Maslenica Bridge on 2nd August 1993 the Co-Chairmen nevertheless concluded that there was still enough common ground to continue negotiations.[21] The negotiation began in Geneva on 12th August 1993 on cease-fire which could include the elements of the original Erdut and Zagreb agreements. Despite intensive discussions in Geneva, Zagreb and Knin, an overall cease-fire agreement could not be achieved. On 9th September, after several days of grave incidents in the UNPAS and the 'Pink Zones", there were rising tensions and intensified bombardment on both sides of the confrontation line. The Croatian Army once again carried out a military attack in the area of Medak, where three Serb villages were seized. As a result the hostilities worsened on 10th and 11th September 1993. The parties finally agreed to a cease-fire in September 1993 when the Secretary-General's representative Mr.Yasushi Akashi and UNPROFOR's Commander Lt. Gen. Satish Nambiar intervened with a call from the Secretary-General. The UNPROFOR moved some five hundred to six hundred troops into the area to replace the Croatian armed forces which eventually withdrew to positions occupied before the incursion began. On 20th September 1993, the Secretary-General recommended that the Security Council should renew the mandate of UNPROFOR for a period of six more months. Referring to Croatia, the Secretary-General said that he had been "sorely tempted" to recommend the withdrawal of UNPROFOR because the key parts of the original United Nations peacekeeping plan, had been difficult, to implement, and had become more challenging since the recommencement of hostilities following the Croatian incursion of 22nd January

1993. The basic solution to the problem had to be sought through political dialogue. In this process, the principal objective of UNPROFOR could only be to keep the peace, thereby permitting negotiations to take place. To enhance the security of UNPROFOR, the Secretary-General requested the extension of air force support to the territory of Croatia because the Security Council had already authorized the Member States to take all necessary measures, through the use of air power, in support of UNPROFOR . So he requested the extension of close air force support not only in Croatia but also in Bosnia and Herzegovina. When The Council was going to take decision to extend UNPROFOR's mandate, the Secretary-General declared that he would give "favourable consideration" to a suggestion by the president of Croatia that:

UNPROFOR be Divided into Three Parts

1. United Nations Protected Force (Croatia). 2.Unprofor [Bosnia and Herzegovina] 3.Unprofor the former Yugoslavia (Republic of Macedonia) while retaining its integrated military, logistical and administrative structure under the command of one special representative of the Secretary-General and one theatre Force Commander. In the meantime, on 24 September 1993, the Security Council was informed by the Croatian Government that if the mandate of UNPROFOR was not amended to promote energetic implementation of the relevant resolutions of the Security Council, Croatia would be forced to request UNPROFOR to leave the country not later than 30th November 1993. UNPROFOR's mandate was set to expire on 30th September 1993. In the midst of intensive consultations the Security Council extended the mandate for 24 hours on 30th September and for four days on 1st October 1993. On 4th October, the Council, by its resolution 871 of 1993 extended the mandate for a period of six months, to 31st March 1994.[22] It took this

action under chapter VII of the charter, reiterating its determination to ensure the security of UNPROFOR and its freedom of movement. The Council reaffirmed the crucial importance of the full and prompt implementation of the United Nations peace-keeping plan for Croatia and called upon the signatories of the plan and all others concerned, in particular republic of Yugoslavia (Serbia and Montenegro), to co-operate in its full implementation. Declaring that continued non-co-operation in the implementation of relevant resolutions would have serious consequences, the council affirmed that full normalization of the International community's position towards those concerned would take into account their actions in implementing those resolutions, including those relating to the United Nations peace-keeping plan for Croatia. The Council called for an immediate cease-fire agreement between the Croatian Government and the local Serb authorities in the UNPAs mediated under the support of ICFY (International Conference on Former Yugoslavia). It urged all parties to cooperate with UNPROFOR in reaching and implementing an agreement on confidence building measures, including the restoration of electricity and water supply and rebuilding of communications in all regions of Croatia. Stressing the importance of restoring Croatian authority in the "Pink Zones", the council called for the revival of the Joint Commission established under the chairmanship of UNPROFOR. The Security Council decided to continue and to review urgently the extension of air force support to UNPROFOR in the territory of Croatia as recommended by the Secretary-General. It authorized UNPROFOR, in carrying out its mandate in Croatia, acting in self-defence, to take the necessary measures, including the use of force, to ensure its security and its freedom of movement.

As requested by Security Council resolution 871 of 1993, the Secretary-General reported to the Council on 1st December

1993.[23] In view of various initiatives under way, he could not recommend that the council reconsider the mandate of UNPROFOR in Croatia at that stage. Talks aimed at achieving a comprehensive cease-fire in and around the UNPAs in Croatia and initiating discussions on how to develop economic self-assurance within the framework of ICFY. On 17th December 1993, Croat representatives and local Serb authorities in Croatia signed a Christmas Truce Agreement, mediated by UNPROFOR. The two parties undertook to cease all armed hostilities along all the existing confrontation lines from midnight on 23rd December 1993 until midnight on 15th January 1994. They also agreed to implement certain confidence-building measures, and to open negotiations as soon as the truce took effect on a "general and lasting cease fire", with the separation of forces on both sides. Subsequently, the truce was extended beyond 15th January 1994, when both parties wanted to do so to establish complete peace.

On 29th March 1994 in Zagreb, representatives of the Government of Croatia and the local Serb authorities in UNPA accomplished a cease-fire agreement aiming to achieve the termination of hostilities. The agreement was prepared in the presence of the representatives of the Russian Federation and of the United States, and witnessed by the ICFY representatives and the Force Commander of UNPROFOR. In a letter on 30th March 1994 to the president of the Security Council, the Secretary-General reported that the implementation of the cease-fire agreement would involve inter alia, the interposition of UNPROFOR forces in a zone of separation of varying width, the establishment of additional control points, observation posts and patrols as well as the monitoring of the withdrawal of heavy weapons out of the range of the contact line. In order to enable UNPROFOR to perform the functions called for in the agreement, the Secretary-General recommended that the council increase the authorized strength of the force by four mechanized infantry companies (one mechanized infantry battalion of 1,000 of all ranks) and four engineering companies (600 of all ranks). In addition, a helicopter squadron of at least six helicopters with 200 of all ranks would be needed for effective monitoring of the cease-fire agreement. As the mandate period approached its expiration at the end of March 1994, the effectiveness of UNPROFOR was getting threats to the safety and security of United Nations personnel. The continuing failure of Member States to honour their financial obligations had led the Secretary-General to consider seriously whether the continuation of UNPROFOR constituted a worthwhile use of the limited peace-keeping resources of the United Nations. He told the Security Council on 16th March 1994 that the diversity and extent of the problems in the Yugoslavia required the increase of more military forces than contributed troops by nations. Nevertheless, UNPROFOR's operations made the international community to determine to help the parties to arrive at an overall political settlement. The Secretary-General therefore recommended its prolongation, adding that it was the responsibility of the parties to seize the opportunity to demonstrate that they were seriously committed to pursuing the path of peace.

On 31st March 1994, the Security Council, by its resolution 908 of 1994, extended the mandate of UNPROFOR for an additional six months period terminating on 30th September 1994. In relation to Croatia, the Council also decided that member states might take all necessary measures to extend strong Air force support to the territory of Croatia in defence of UNPROFOR personnel in the Performance of its mandate, under the authority of the council and subject to close co-ordination with the Secretary-General and UNPROFOR. UNPROFOR activities in Croatia focused on the monitoring of the general cease-fire agreement of 29th March 1994. By the end of May 1994, UNPROFOR reported almost total compliance, characterized by a general ending of hostilities, withdrawal of forces beyond fixed lines of separation and the placement of heavy weapons in agreed storage sites. UNPROFOR assumed exclusive control over the zone of separation, covering an area of over 1300 square kilometers. It was hoped that the parties would then begin comprehensive discussion on issues of mutual economic benefit.

However, during the months of April and May 1994, local Serb authorities issued a number of statements from their headquarters in Knin which appeared to close the door on political reconciliation. They announced their intention to pursue full integration with other Serb areas in the former Yugoslavia and fixed unrealistic preconditions for talks. It proved impossible to open negotiations at that stage. In another development, in early July, the association of displaced persons of Croatia, with the support of the Croatian authorities, imposed a blockade on all the crossing points into or within the UNPAs in order to draw attention to their plight and apply pressure on UNPROFOR to expedite their return to their homes in UNPAs. After a series of high level discussions between UNPROFOR and Croatian authorities, the agreement was made on 19th August 1994 to lift the blockade. In August 1994, following renewed mediation efforts by ICFY, senior officials from the Croatian Government and local Serb authorities were brought together for discussions in Knin. They committed to continue the negotiating process and so they agreed to establish eight expert groups to prepare for future negotiations on specific economic issues. Seventeen cross points were reopened out of nineteen by September 1994 but still tensions persisted on that issue.

The Security Council called for a review on the performance of the UNPROFOR during the six months period from 31st March 1994 to 30 th September 1994.The Secretary-

General reported to the Council that the UNPROFOR was doing well but the total success could not be achieved because, the conflicts between the races in former Yugoslavia were very closely interrelated and engrossed several factors. He also informed that in that context, the work of the contact group which had emerged in April 1994 and endorsed with five major powers, working with the co-chairmen of the ICFY Steering Committee, could be of great significance for UNPROFOR's future. With regard to UNPROFOR's mandate in Croatia, the Secretary-General outlined four problem areas:

1. The demilitarization of the UNPAs;
2. The restoration of Croatian authority in the pink zones;
3. The establishment of border controls; and
4. Assistance for the return of refugees and displaced persons to their homes.

The above four required either enforcement or the consent of both parties for their implementation. UN PROFOR had neither the means nor the mandate for enforcement action of this nature, and the cooperation of the parties was elusive. The successful implementation of the cease-fire agreement had nevertheless opened the possibility for progress, reduced dramatically the number of war causalities and allowed for increasing normalization of life. UNPROFOR however continued to be criticized by the Croatian Government and media for its instability to fulfill its entire mandate. It was also threatened continuously with unrealistic deadlines. While recriminations were related to the Croatian domestic political process, they also reflected certain incompatibilities in UNPROFOR's mandate. The resultant gap between Croatian expectations and what UNPROFOR was actually mandated to do and capable of achieving became increasingly difficult to bridge.

The Secretary-General stated that he remained alert to the possibility that the situation on the ground could be frozen in a stalemate in which UNPROFOR's continued presence contributed only to the maintenance of an unsatisfactory statuesque. It was of the greatest importance, however, to secure continued respect for the cease-fire agreement and at the same time further efforts would have to be made in order to create a basis for the reopening of negotiations. These tasks required the continued presence of UNPROFOR. On 30th September 1994, the Security Council, by resolution 947 extended UNPROFOR's mandate until 31st March 1995.

The March 1994 cease-fire agreement helped to create a climate conducive for negotiations pursued under ICFY auspicious as well as for follow-up measures undertaken by UNPROFOR. Another step towards confidence building and an eventual resolution of the conflict in Croatia was made on 2nd December 1994, when the Croatian sides concluded an agreement pertaining to economic issues. The agreement provided for the re-establishment of water and electricity services, the re-opening in Croatia, of the Zagreb-Belgrade highway and the reopening of the oil pipeline through the Karajina. In parallel with the economic negotiations, two ICFY negotiations Adrens and Edie together with the Ambassadors to Croatia, the Russian Federation and the United States the "Zagreb Four" worked on a plan for a political settlement of the conflict between the parties.

On 12th January 1995, the President of Croatia informed the Secretary-General of his Government's decision not to agree a further extension of UNPROFOR's mandate beyond 31st March. President Tudjman stated that "Croatia's overall experience during the past two years" had brought him to the conclusion that although UNPOFOR had played an important role in stopping violence and major conflicts in Croatia, it is an indisputable fact that the present charter of the UNPROFOR's mission does not provide conditions necessary for establishing lasting peace and order.

The Secretary-General expressed to the Security Council his hope that the Croatian Government would reconsider its position. He would however, undertake a detailed study of the practical consequences and financial implications of a withdrawal of UNPROFOR from Croatia. His principal concern was that the withdrawal would considerably increase the likelihood of a resumption of hostilities. He reiterated his conviction that the fundamental solution to the problem in Croatia could be sought only through political dialogue. On 17th January 1995, by a presidential statement, the Security Council reiterated its commitment to the sovereignty and territorial integrity of Croatia within its internationally recognized borders. The Council understood the concerns of the Croatian government about the lack of implementation of major provisions of the United Nations peace-keeping plan for Croatia, and would not accept the status quo becoming an indefinite situation. It believed, however, that UNPROFOR's continued presence in Croatia was of vital importance for regional peace and security and that the United Nations in general and UNPROFOR in particular had a positive role to play in achieving further implementation of the peace keeping plan and bringing about a political settlement. The Council hoped that discussions would lead Croatia to a re-examination of its position. Unfortunately the following months witnessed a significant escalation in military activity and tension. The climate of uncertainty was compounded by the decision of the self-proclaimed Serb assembly in Knin on 8th March 1995 to declare a state of 'immediate war alert'. Military preparations intensified on both sides. Neverthless, they both continued publicly to maintain their commitment to a peaceful resolution and to cooperate fully in implementing the economic agreement .On 8th February 1995, however the Serb assembly decided to postpone further negotiations and implementation except for continued cooperation regarding the Zagreb - Lipovac highway and the oil pipeline through UNPA sector North, until UNPROFOR's future presence in the protected areas was assured.

ICFY presented a "Draft agreement on the Krajina, Slavonia, Southern Baranja and Western Sirmium" to both sides on 30th January 1995. While the Croatian government accepted the plan as a basis for negotiation, the Serbs in Knin refused to receive it until the future presence of UNPROFOR was assured. Other international efforts intensified to find a compromise solution which would allow the continuing United Nations peace keeping presence in Croatia. Those efforts, led by the United States, resulted in a joint announcement on 12th March 1995 by the president of Croatia and the vice-President of the United States, which opened the way to a solution. The government of Croatia agreed, working with the United States Security Council and it's partners in the international community, to negotiate a new mandate for an international presence in Croatia. Pending the successful negotiation of such a mandate, the government of Croatia agreed that the existing international presence might continue to perform functions related to its mission in Bosnia and Herzegovina. It might also continue to perform functions essential to the continued implementation of the cease-fire agreement of 29th March 1994 and the economic agreement of 2nd December 1994. The Secretary-General instructed Mr.Thorvald Staltenberg, acting as his special envoy, to conduct negotiations with the parties to define the mandate of a future United Nations peacekeeping force, with which both sides would commit themselves to cooperate. As of mid March 1995, UNPROFOR in Croatia included 14,825 troops and military support personnel 256 military observers and 731 civilian police. The mandate of UNPROFOR had been authorized to continue until 31st March 1995.On 22nd March 1995, the Secretary-General informed the Security Council that in Croatia the retention of UNPROFOR in its existing form and with its existing mandate would not enjoy the consent of the government of Croatia. It was equally clear that the chapter VII option was not feasible either politically or in resource terms. At the same time, the total withdrawal of all United Nations peacekeeping forces from Croatia would result immediately in a grave threat to peace and security extending beyond the boarders of Croatia. Nor was it clear whether the peacekeeping operation in Bosnia and Herzegovina could be continued without a substantial United Nations presence and support facilities in Croatia the maintenance of a reduced force in Croatia under a new mandate seemed the only way to reduce the risks of a renewed major war, while permitting continued progress in implementing economic agreement and beginning political negotiations. The Secretary-General also noted, in reference to Mr.Thorvold Stoltenberg negotiations with the parties, that an agreement on the details of the new mandate and the modalities of the United Nations peace-keeping operations in Croatia required further work. The gulf between the positions of the government of Croatia and the Krajina Serb authorities on the role and functions of the new force remained wide, particularly with regard to the nature, size and functions of the force in the zone of separation and in the protected areas. Deployment patterns (e.g. fixed posts or mobile patrol or a combination of the two) and mode of functioning (e.g. monitor and report, as opposed to stop and search) of the United Nations force in the zone of separation and on the international borders also required further discussions.

The Secretary-General believed that the mandate of force should include support for implementation of the cease-fire agreement of 2nd December 1994, as well as implementation of those elements of the existing United Nations peace-keeping plan for Croatia that had been accepted by both parties as having continuing relevance. These would include, but not be limited to, maintenance of a United Nations presence on the international borders of the Republic of Croatia and confidence building and humanitarian tasks such as assistance to refugees and displaced persons, protection of ethnic minorities, mine-clearance and convey assistance. In addition the new force would continue to perform functions arising from the accord on the Prevlaka peninsula and from relevant resolutions of the Security Council, such as those dealing with the monitoring of the "no-fly-zone" and the extension of close air support in Croatia.

The Security Council restructured UNPROFOR in March 1995, Three separate but interlinked operations in Croatia, Bosnia and Herzegovena; Former Yugoslav republic of Macedonia with an extended mandate till 30th November 1995 known as United Nations Peace Forces (UNIF) replaced UNPROFOR. They were under the overall command and control of Special Representative of Secretary-General. Three force Commanders exercised overall command of military elements of the three operations. Each operation had its own civilian chief of mission.

The Security Council also established the United Nations confidence Restoration Operation in Croatia to be known as UNCRO. The Secretary-General was requested to take necessary measures for earlier deployment.

The peace force was mandated (a) to perform the functions envisaged in the cease-fire agreement of 29th March 1995 (b) to facilitate implementation of the economic agreement of 2nd December 1994 (c) to facilitate implementation of all relevant Security Council resolutions (d) to monitor, control and report the crossing of military personnel, equipment, supplies and weapons over the international borders between the federal republics (e) to facilitate the delivery of international humanitarian assistance to the republic of Bosnia and Herzegovenia through the republic of Croatia (f) to monitor, demilitarization of prevlaka paninusula. UNCRO was an interim arrangement for a negotiated settlement for the territorial integrity of Croatia guaranteeing the securely and rights of all communities. The member stats are to closely coordinate and extend close air support to the theatre force commander and security to UNCRO's personnel in the performance of its mandate.

UNCRO upheld the integrity of the zone of separation in spite of military tensions and Croatian's intention to recapture some areas. The conditions of minorities were well protected in all the sectors. It was also gradually withdrawing and repatriating all United Nations Military personnel from the former sectors closing the sector headquarters. United Nations military observers in Prevlaka and Dubrovnik areas helped to control tensions in the explosive regions. By mid November 1995 UNCRO's overall strength was 6581 troops and military support personnel 164 military observes, and 296 civilian police deployed in different sectors as per necessity.

The basic agreement on the region of Eastern Slavonia, Baranja and Western Sirimun, the Secretary-General was asked to make arrangements for transitional administration and transitional peace keeping force to implement the agreement. The mandate of UNCRO would terminate by 15th January 1996 (or) the deployment of the transitional peace keeping force which even was earlier. The Secretary-General submitted his report on 13th December 1995. The Security-Council was asked to mandate the forces to be deployed under Chapter – VII of the charter with the capacity to take necessary actions to maintain peace and security and defend itself in view of the fact that the parties never honoured their commitments to the agreements as well as the risk of differing interpretations of the precise nature of the basic agreement. He asked for a mechanized division of two brigades with combat capability, air support and a strong armed reserve comprising 9300 combat troops and 2000 logistic troops. The Security-Council concurred with the Secretary-General's proposals and adopted the resolution 1037 of January 1996 establishing United Nations peace-keeping operation for an initial period of twelve months. The United Nations transitional administration for Eastern Slovenia (UNTAES), Baranja and Sirimum along with the military component was also accepted. UNTAES supervision of facilitated demilitarization of the region and monitoring voluntary and safe return of refugees and displaced persons to their home of origin in cooperation with UNHCR besides maintaining peace and security.

The civilian component of UNTAES established temporary police force, defined its structure and size, developed a training programme and oversaw the implementation and monitoring treatment of offenders and prison system, undertook civilian administration, public services, organized elections and certified the results. Thus, the peace-keeping operations in the region successfully ended with the co-operation of international community.

The centrifugal forces ever present in the multinational federation produced spontaneous disintegration and destroyed the edifice of socialist Yugoslaviaian assiduously built by Tito of mixed Slovene - Croatian parentage, a national figure and a symbol of the brotherhood and unity of Yugoslav people. With his death, Tito himself, the political structure as well as the economic divide in republics, all are responsible for the disintegration besides the great ethnic divide especially between Croatians and Serbians.

The Chief offices concentrated in Tito were the president of the Republic, President of the League of Communists, and commander-in-chief of the armed forces as well as the Presidency of the federal republic. In 1971 after a series of amendments to the constitution, similarly to the league of communists consisted of twenty three-men collective presidium was slimmed to eight plus Tito giving only one representative to each republic and autonomous provinces. After Tito there was no one in Yugoslavia of his stature to stem the divisive force. The Titorist system of complicated collective rule, rotating chairmanships for all top parties and state bodies failed to deliver, after Tito. The political situation in Kosovo, local Albenians demanding that Kosovo be upgraded from a province of Serbia to the status of a full republic on par with Serbia, Croatia and other four built up a powerful national backlash in Yugosalvia's largest nation. Albenian were in league with each other working against Serbian interests. Appeals to ethnic nationalist Sentiments over the interests of the nation as a whole, was responsible for the confrontational declarations on the absolute right of republics to secede gave way to a more sophisticated recognition that ethnic unrest and unilateral faits accomplish exacerbated existing political and economic crisis. The dream of Tito that the League of Communists would bind socialist Yogoslavia together, shattered with the federal communist party disintegrating and non communist governments coming to power in four of the six republics. Tito's decentralized management system along with economic independence, superficially glossed over by Tito's immense personal authority was equally responsible for the disintegration of the republics.

Besides this constitutional crisis, the economic crisis emboldened the republics to assert their pound of flesh. The general European recession had its effects on Yugoslavia with the inflation rate running at a rate of thirty percent and unemployment at fifteen percent of the public sector work force of five millions. Economy flagging, tensions, between developed north and developing south posed a serious problem for collective leadership. Yugoslavia's chief financial heache was its large hard-currency debt which stood at $ 20.1 billions by the end of 1981. The Governments demand for a special law to appropriate the bulk of foreign currency provoked the federal republic of Slovenia. Slovenian politicians felt that Slovene firms and Slovenia itself were unjustly made to pay for the wreckless investment and borrowing policies of other enterprises and republics. The long term economic reforms programme collided with interests of the individual republics and provincial party organizations. Serbs felt illserved both politically and economically. The victory of the nationalist opposition groups in north-west republics forced Serbian leaders, increase their own nationalist rhetoric.

The U.N. and the international community stepped in at the right time and set up an internal law and order through its peacekeeping force and could persuade Croatians, Serbians, Slovenians to confine to their internationally agreed borders with enough protection to all ethnic minority communities and their welfare.

The ethnic bloodshed and break up of the former Republic of Yugoslavia has been regarded as perhaps the worst tragedy of the European continent since the World War II. The U.N. involved itself in September 1991 and put on embargo on the supply of arms to the various constituents who comprised of former Republics, namely Slovenia, Croatia, Bosnia, Herzegovina, Serbia and Macedonia.

The U.N. protection force (UNPROFOR) was established in Croatia as an interim arrangement to create the conditions of peace and security required for the negotiations of an overall settlement of Yugoslavia crisis. The UNPROFOR's mandate was to ensure that the three "United Nations Protected Areas" (UNPAs) in Croatia were demilitarized and protected from fear of armed attack. Lieutenant General Satish Nambiar, PVSM, AVSM, of India was appointed as the first head of the mission and force commander of UNPROFOR in April. This distinguished and brave General of the Indian Army executed this difficult mission with noteworthy depth of understanding and range of vision. He completed his assignment of one year with great distinction in one of the most complex cperations undertaken by the United Nations accompanied by Lt Col. Philip, as staff officer.

REFERENCES

1. Walter Consuelo Langsam Ph.D., *The World Since 1914,* The MacMillan Company 1940, pp.881, 882
2. K.F.CVIIC, Yugoslavia's double Crisis, *The World Today,* September 1982, pp.348, 349.
3. The Blue Helmets, *A Review of United Nations Peace-keeping.*
4. K.F.CVIIC, Yugoslavia's Moslem Problem, *The World Today,* March 1980, p.109, 110.
5. F.B.Sigleton, *Yugoslavia without Tito,* p.204.
6. *Op cit.,* The Blue Helmets, p.487.
7. *Ibid.,* p.487.
8. V.P.Gagnon, Jr., Yugoslavia, *Foreign Affairs,* Volume 70, No.3, 1991, p.18.
9. *Ibid.,* p.26.
10. Alan James, The U.N. in Croatia: an exercise in futility? *The World Today,* May 1993, p.93.
11. *Op. cit.,* The Blue Helmets: p.488.
12. See Appendix No.IX.
13. *Op cit.,* Alan James, p.93.
14. *Op cit.,* The Blue Helmets: p.514.
15. *Op cit.,* Alan James, p.180.
16. *Op cit.,* The Blue Helmets, p.514.
17. *Ibid.,* p.514.
18. *Ibid.,* p.516
19. *Ibid.,* p.516
20. *Op cit.,* The Blue Helmets, p.516
21. Croatia: the politics behind the War, *The World Today* – April 1993, p.62.
22. *Op cit.,* The Blue Helmets, p.518.
23. *Ibid.,* p.518.

6

United Nations Operation Mission in Mozambique (ONUMOZ)

December 1992–November 1994

Mozambique is an African country on the East Coast with Tanzania in the north, Malawi in the North West, Zambia in the West, Zimbabwe in the South West and with Swaziland in the South. It enjoyed the pride of possessing 2,500 kilometres of coast line of the Indian Ocean and became independent on 25th June 1975, after a ten-year guerilla struggle against Portuguese rule.[1] This was ruled by the Government of FRELIMO (Frente da Libertacao de Mocambique) with Joaquine Alberto Chissano as president of Mozambique.[2] The FRELIMO government was against apartheid policy of the minority governments around it. It closed its borders with Rhodesia (now Zimbabwe) on South West protesting the country white minority government. Fighting broke-out between the troops of Mozambique and Rhodesia. Several black Rhodesians fled to Mozambiaque and were encouraged to fight against Rhodesian white minority government. The blacks gained control and the country's name was changed to Zimbabwe.[3] Mozambique was equally critical of her southern neighbour, South Africa, a white minority government, following apartheid policy. The government of Mozambique minimized the number of its

ONUMOZ Military Deployment as of October 1994

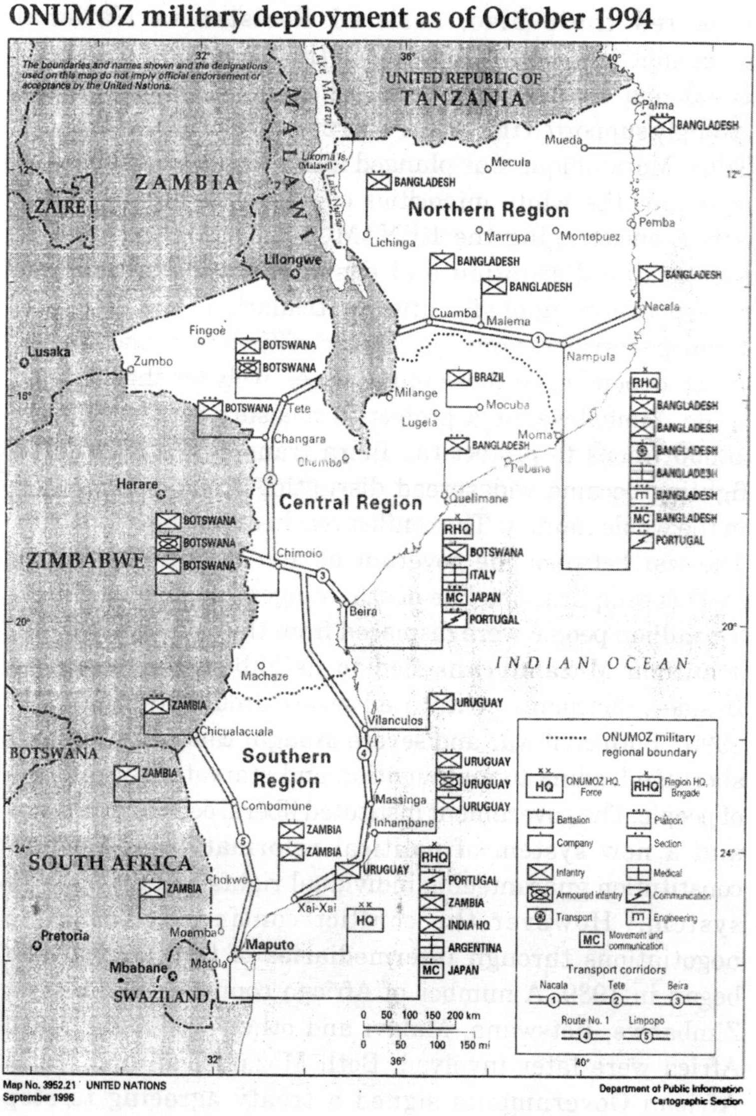

nationals working in South Africa, affecting the economy of that country. South Africa fearing that Zimbabwe might be repeated there also, assisted Resistencia National Mocambicana (RENAMO) under the leadership of Afonso Dhlakama. Both South Africa and other Western Countries strongly supported the rebels with men, material and money.[4] Thus, Mozambique was plunged into a long and debilitating civil war, the white minorities of Rhodesia, besides South Africa encouraging the RENAMO. RENAMO resorted to tactics like disruption and destruction of Mozambique transport and supply facilities particularly in the Beira and Limpopo corridors arousing concern of Zimbabwe and Malawi which depended on these routes excessively for their foreign trade. Zimbabwe, as a protective measure sent more than 10000 troops to protect the Beira transport corridor.[5] The fighting became widespread disrupting economic activities in the whole country. The conflict reached its zenith in 1980's. The war between the government and RENAMO resulted serious complications like death, hunger and disease. About 3.8 million people were displaced from the countryside. Half a million Mozambicans fled to neighbouring countries. Besides, the country witnessed severe drought during 1980-1990.[6] Both civil war and severe drought caused severe food shortage leading to malnutrition and starvation of millions of people. The government instituted liberal economic reforms and a new system of political reformation and a new constitution guaranteeing individual rights and multi-party system.[7] However the conflict continued. Tentative negotiations through intermediaries of Catholic Church began in 1989. A number of African countries like Kenya, Zimbabwe, Botswana, Malavi and others including South Africa were later involved. Both Mozambican and South African Governments signed a treaty agreeing to stop assistance to guerillas. The negotiations pickedup momentum and enjoyed support of western governments like Italy, Portugal and United Kingdom. After fourteen long years of devastating civil war Mr.Joquin Alberto Chissano, President of the Republic of Mozambique and Mr. Afonso Dhlakama president of RENAMO signed a cease-fire treaty in Rome (the capital of Italy) on 4th October 1992.[8] The General Peace Agreement was intended to establish the principles and modalities for achieving peace in Mozambique. The agreement further called for the United Nations participation in monitoring the implementation of the peace agreement as well as providing technical assistance. The conduct of free and fair general elections and monitoriug the elections.

The U.N. Secretary-General Boutros Boutros-Ghali submitted a report to the Security Council in October 1992. He proposed to the United Nations role in Mozambique. He recommended on immediate plan of action. He sought the approval of the council to appoint an interim Special Representative. The Security-Council adopted a resolution 782 on 13th October 1992.[9] Welcoming a signing of the General Peace Agreement and approving the appointment of a special representative Mr. Aldo Ajello of Italy was to be despatched along with a team of about twenty five military observes.

Mr. Aldo Ajello was asked to proceed to Mozambique in March 1993 and assist the parties in setting up the joint monitoring machinery to finalise the modalities and conditions for the military arrangements and to carryout other necessary arrangements. Aldo Ajello and a team of twenty one military observers arrived in Mozambique on 15th October 1992, the day General Peace Agreement came into force.[10] On 20th October two teams of military observers were deployed to the provincial capitals Nampura, Beira. Two additional outposts were later established to verify the withdrawal of foreign troops from Mozambique, an important element of the General Peace Agreement.

Both Mozambican parties committed themselves to effective specific action for a joint mechanism to monitor and verify its implementation, but no such action had been initiated. Mr. Aldo Ajello started extensive discussions with the parties for ensuring early start of the implementation of the agreement. Major violations of the cease-fire and complaints were lodged with a special representative. He urged the parties refrain from any type of military operation and to discuss and settle all disputes through negotiations. The Secretary General as well as the president of the Security Council was kept informed of the developments. The President expressed the council's deep concern about the reports of major violations of cease-fire. He called upon the parties to halt such violations immediately and to cooperate fully with the interim special representative. Both parties met on many occasions sending high level delegations both bilaterally and together with the special representative.

The implementation of the agreement was to be supervised and monitored by a commission chaired by United Nations representative. This supervisory and monitory commission was to be responsible for authentic interpretation of the General Peace Agreement. It should settle any dispute arising between the parties and guide and coordinate the activities of the subsidiary committees. The Supervisory and Monitory Commission (CSC) was initially composed of government and RENAMO delegates from Italy, the mediation party at the Rome talks, France, Portugal, the United Kingdom, the United States, which acted as observer in Rome, and the Organisation of African Unity (OAU).

The Principal Subsidiary Commission, the cease-fire commission held its first meeting on 4th November 1992. It consisted of Government and RENAMO delegations with representatives of Botswana, Egypt, France, Italy, Nizeria, Portugal, the U.K. and U.S. later joined by Germany in December chaired by the U.N. representative. The reintegration commission is composed of Government and RENAMO delegations with representatives of France,

Portugal, Denmark, the Netherlands, Germany, Italy, Norway, South Africa, Spain, Sweden, Switzerland, the United Kingdom the United States of America and the European Community chaired by U.N. representative. The Joint Commission for the formation of Mozambican Defence Force (C.C.F.A.D.M.) was comprised of Government and RENAMO delegates with representatives of France and United Kingdom chaired by the U.N. representative.

The Secretary-General submitted an exhaustive report with a detailed operational plan of the United Nations operation in Mozambique (ONUMOZ) on 3rd December 1992[11]. He described the difficulties of the operation such as the size of the country, devastated state of the infrastructure, the disruption of economy on account of war, drought, the limited capacity of the government to cope with the new tasks and complexity of the process envisaged in the agreement. He also referred to the wide responsibilities entrusted to the United Nations under the agreement. Boutros Boutros-Ghali further stated that he believed that the international community had to take a great risk, in the light of the recent experience elsewhere, but believed that risk was worth taking. The Security Council by a resolution 797 on 16th December 1992, approved the Secretary-General's report and decided to establish ONUMOZ with a time limit until 31st October 1993. Major General Lelio Goomcalves Rodrigues Da Silva of Brazil was appointed on 14th February 1993 and he assumed his duties as Force Commander of ONUMOZ.

The mandate of ONUMOZ, in accordance with the General Peace Agreement, included four elements namely Political, Military, Electoral and humanitarian. The operational concept was based on strong inter-relation between the four components requiring fully integrated approach and co-ordination. Aldo Ajello opined that without sufficient humanitarian aid, adequate military protection, sufficient progress in the security situation, the confidence required for disarmament and rehabilitation would suffer. The special Representative directed all activities of the U.N. in Mozambique. He became responsible for imparting political guidance of the peace process besides facilitating the implementation of the agreement by chairing the Supervisory and Monitoring Commission as well as its subsidiary commissions. He required about twenty international staff and any adequate number of locally recruited staff.

The political component called for the verification of the arrangments for the cease-fire and other military aspects in Mozambique. It was to be carried out by teams of U.N. military observers at forty nine assembly areas in three military regions and elsewhere in the field. Teams were also to be deployed at airports, ports, other critical areas, as well as RENAMO's head quarters. ONUMOZ was to monitor and verify the ceasefire, the separation and concentration of forces of the two parties, complete withdrawl of forces. It should also provide security in all the four transport corridors, disarming all private and irregular armed groups. It should also provide security arrangements for vital infrastructure and also for United Nations and other international activities in support of peace process.

The agreement provided for the withdrawl of foreign troops to be initiated with the cease-fire coming into force. Simultaneously the cease-fire commission should assume responsibility of verifying and ensuring security of strategic and trading routes, the important being the four transport corridors - Beira, Limpopo, Nampula and National High Way number-1 and also the security of the corridors to protect humanitarian convoys. The infantry battalions were thus to be judiciously deployed.

The military component required a head quarters company and a military Police Platoon: three hundred and fifty four military observers five logistically self-sufficient infantry battalions, each composed of about eight hundred and fifty four personnel, one engineering battalion with contracted assistance as needed, three logistic companies and air communication, medical and movement control support units. The Secretary-General also suggested the deployment of a civilian technical unit to support the logistic tasks relating to the demobilization programme in the assembly areas divided into segments in the entire country, with adequate resources. He also proposed to leave open the possibility of incorporating a police component too at the request of Mozambican parties. He deftly acquired the consent of both the parties for a police component of one hundred and twenty eight to monitor civil liberties and provide technical assistance.

Another important task of ONUMOZ was the conduct of elections for legislature and the presidential elections to be held simultaneously with in a year of the signing of the agreement. This might be extended as per the warranty of circumstances. The electoral division was to monitor and verify the electoral process organized by the National Election Commission. It should also provide direction and maintain contacts with the government, RENAMO, the National Election Commission and the main political parties. Mr.Aldo Ajello the special representative of the Secretary General was to coordinate technical assistance to the electoral process through the United Nations Development Programme, other existing mechanisms of the United Nations System and bilateral channels. He also recommended the inclusion of international electoral officers and staff consisting of 148 electoral officers and supporting staff for a systematic and impartial conduct of the elections. Nearly twelve hundred international observers were deployed during the period of the elections immediately proceeding and following also.

The humanitarian aspect of ONUMOZ mandate brought forth two objectives for international humanitarian assistance (1) to serve as an instrument of reconciliation and (2) to assist the return of people displaced on account of war and hunger including the refugees in the neighbouring countries or in provincial and district centres. The United Nations Office for the humanitarian assistance and coordination (U.N.O.H.A.C) was to be established as an integral component of ONUMOZ. The head office was to be in Maputo with sub-offices at the regional and provincial levels replacing the office of United Nations special coordinators for relief operations and humanitarian assistance programmes. The international community contributed directly seventy eight percent of approximately $ 650 million required to meet Mozambiques needs for humanitarian assistance during the period of ONUMOZ mandate. The United Nations system of organization and agencies, international public and Non-Governmental organizations (NGOs) as well as a number of Mozambican entities played a significant role in the design and implementation of both the individual and overall humanitarian programmes. The emphasis was on the restoration of essential services in rural areas. The humanitarian assistance programme was to respond effectively to their reintegration of all Mozambicans particularly the return of refugees and to resettle them in their original communities. The humanitarian assistance committees convened by UNOHAC's field officers in the provinces coordinated the efforts of all concerned parties. UNOHAC completed resettlement of nearly 4.5 million internally displaced persons, 1.5 million refugees and two hundred thousand former combatants and their dependents successfully.

ONUMOZ faced many difficulties from the beginning on account of various delays of administrative, as well as of logistic nature. Inspite of the fact the cease-fire was held largely, the time tables in the agreement had proved unrealistic. Continuing deep mistrust resulted in to beginning the demobilization and delay in the deployment of U.N.

military observers. RENAMO insisted on the deployment of 65 percent of ONUMOZ troops in Mozambique before the election process began on account of mistrust on FRELIMO. A number of logistic and legal problems surfaced in the absence of the status of these forces with the Mozambique government. Communicating these difficulties the Secretary-General communicated to the Security Council stressed the need to control the military situation for creating proper conditions for free and fair elections. Since it was evident that elections could not be held in October 1993, the Schedule had to be redrafted after discussions with the parties. The security council in its resolution 818 on 14TH April 1993.[12] Stressing on delays and difficulties in the peace process strongly urged the government and RENAMO to finalise the precise time table for the full implementation of the provisions of the agreement including separation, concentration and demobilization of the forces as well as for the elections. The council strongly urged both sides to comply with their commitments and cooperate with the secretary General and his special representative in the full and timely implementation of the mandate of OUNMOZ according to the provisions of the agreement.

The delay in the implementation of the mandate prolonged the miserable plight of the people. Hence the United Nations made a determined effort to implement the operational activities of ONUMOZ as per the peace Agreement. ONUMOZ was able to fully deploy its military infrastructure in all the three operational regions. Another positive achievement was the establishment of Voluntary Trust Fund (VTF) on 10th May 1993 to assist RENAMO to obtain office space, accommodation and equipment to establish itself as a political entity. The work of the Joint Commission also resumed. There was a massive international effort for humanitarian assistance due to sharp increasein the return of refuges and displaced persons. The withdrawal of foreign troops from Malawi and Zimbabwe, as provided in the agreement was successfully completed. After intensive negotiations, the status of forces agreement was signed between the government and United Nations on 14th May 1993 facilitating the entire range of work of ONUMOZ.

However concentration and demobilization of troops, formation of the new army, commissioning of state administration and establishment of National Election Commission remained pending. The Secretary General in his communication (ss/26034) of 30th June 1993 informed the Security Council that the implementation of the major provisions of the agreement was imperative for the future stability of the country and it brooks no delay in finalizing a new and realistic time table. He insisted that the confinement and demobilization process should be completed by early 994 and the training of a new Mozambican army should be initiated as soon as possible. He was willing to accede to the request of government and RENAMO on the understanding that it would not entertain any obligation on the part of the United Nations for training and establishing new armed forces. However, he formed joint commission for peace with the consent of the Security Council. The Government and RENAMO agreed for the formation of Mozambican Defence forces.

The Secretary-General presented the new time table. The resumption of the work of the Joint Commission would begin on 3rd June 1993 and would conclude with elections in October 1994. The concentration and demobilization of troops of both parties was expected to take eight or nine months in stages starting in September 1993. 50 percent of the soldiers would be demobilized by January 1994 and the process should be completed by May 1994. 30000 soldiers were expected to be inducted in the new army and the remaining would return to civilian life. Half of the new army would be operational by May 1994 and the rest would be completed by September

1994. Voters registration was expected to take three months scheduled from April – June 1994. The demobilized soldiers, the repatriated refugees and displaced persons and all the resettled population might register themselves in time for the elections. The Security Council welcomed the progress of the implementation of the agreement by its resolution 850 of 9th July 1993. It expressed concern over continuing delays and approved the Secretary-General's recommendations.

The Secretary-General's report of 30th August 1993 to the Security-Council was quite encouraging. The most significant development was the long overdue direct talks between the president of Mozambique Jaquin Albarto and the President of RENAMO Afanso Dhlakama. A significant progress was made in Key areas - the government explicitly and RENAMO implicitly agreed the dead line of October 1994 for holding the elections. The Special Representative Aldo Ajello was instructed to follow closely the revised time-table for the demobilization of forces, formation of the Unified Armed Forces, and of course, elections. He strongly urged both the parties also to continue their dialogue with an eye on action oriented process to bring the peace process to a successful conclusion. Two major agreements had been signed by both the presidents of government of Mozambique and RENAMO on 3rd September 1993.

The Government and RENAMO would integrate into the state administration and the areas under RENAMO control till then would be integrated into state administration. Both the parties agreed to request the United Nations to monitor all police activities in the country so that the impartiality of the National Police would be upheld. It should also monitor the rights and liberties of the citizens and provide technical support to the police commission (COMPOL) established under the agreement. The U.N. Police force would be responsible for verifying all police activities in the country in consistence with the agreement. The Secretary General in his letter to the Security Council on 10th September 1993 informed his plan to send a small survey team of experts to make recommendations with regard to the size of the police component. However he proposed to deploy, in the meanwhile, 128 ONUMOZ police observers as per the previous resolution. The Security Council by its resolution 863 of 13th September 1993 urged both the parties to strictly implement the agreement without need for further postponement. It further urged RENAMO immediate assembling of its forces and both parties to demobilize troops in accordance with the revised time table.

The Secretary-General took pains to visit Mozambique from 17-20th October 1993 to speed up the process. He met all the leaders of all political parties and the representatives of international community. He announced a major break through on 20th October 1993 after prolonged arguments. A consensus was reached for the assembling of the troops and their demobilization of both RENAMO and the government. Simultaneously disarmament of parliamentary forces, militia and irregular troops would also take place. There was also an agreement on establishment of local police commission's subcommittees to monitor the activities of Mozambique police, the composition of National Election Commission, Electoral Law and a time-table for all this. The revised time table for the implementation of the agreement was approved by the Supervisory and Monitoring Commission on 22nd October 1993.

The Security Council by its resolution 879 on 29th October 1993 decided to extend ONUMOZ's mandate for a short interim period initially and later renew it for every six months basing on the Secretary-General's report every ninety days. ONUMOZ carried out the task of extensive operational activities throughout Mozambique. The Security of the four transport corridors, Beira, Limpopo, Nampula as well as National High Way No.1 and main roads was ensured by regular road and aerial patrol as well as providing United Nations escort to vehicles on roads and trains. Security was also initiated for oil pumping stations, air ports, United Nations wear houses, ONUMOZ head quarters and temporary and permanent arms depots of both troops. ONUMOZ's military component provided humanitarian help also facilitating engineering and medical assistance. The Military Observers looked into allegations of cease-fire violations, supervised the confinement of troops in the cantonments and also assisted the establishment and preparation of assembly areas. Initially twenty of the forty nine assembly areas, twelve for the government and eight for RENAMO, were opened and the assembly of the troops began. Fifteen additional assembly areas were opened on 20th December 1993.

The ONUMOZ's, at the instance of U.N., created civilian police component. It was mandated to monitor all police activities in the country and verify if their actions were consistent with the agreements. It was also endowed with the duty of monitoring citizens' rights and civil liberties. It was to provide technical support to National Police Commission and verify the activities of private protection and Security agencies. It would also verify the strength and location of the Government Police forces and their material. The process of reorganization and retraining of the rapid action police including its activities, weapons and equipment was also its duty. Civil police, together with ONUMOZ's other components monitor the proper conduct of the election campaign and ensure that all political organizations respected the political rights of individuals and groups. It worked in tandem with the existing electoral, military, humanitarian and administrative components of ONUMOZ. It conducted its own investigations and recommended corrective actions as and when necessary.

The demobilization was initiated with a view to completing it by May 1994. The confinement of troops formally commenced on 30th November as a consequence of lengthy negotiation. The government troops assembled much in larger number than RENAMO forces in the initial stages. Both had to demobilize their troops from different parts of the country. They did not withdraw their troops properly because of mutually suspicion. After delays in the dismantling of governments paramilitary forces and militia scheduled to begin simultaneously with the assembly and demobilization of regular troops. The process eventually commenced on 12th January 1994.

The cease-fire commission in collaboration of with ONUMOZ dealt with the notification of alleged cease-fire violations. Gradually, the cease-fire violations were relatively very few and posed no serious threat to the peace process.

Formation of Mozambican Defence Force was one of the most important operational activities of ONUMOZ. France, Portugal and U.K. came up with a programme aimed at assisting the formation of a unified army. The training of instructors for the new Mozambican army consisting of five hundred and forty officers from both government and RENAMO began at Nyanga and Zimbabwe by United Kingdom. This was completed by 20th December 1993 and they were transported to Mozambique on 12th January 1994 to help in training infantry soldiers at the three defence forces training centres. France and Portugal also conducted training proramnes for different branches of National armed forces. The Joint Commission prepared documents pertaining to organization, operating procedures, uniforms, ranking symbols and training of united armed forces. This was done with a view to promoting integrity, patriotism, and unity among the groups. Another motive is to inculcate a desire to serve and save the country and to enhance the growth resources instead of devastations. This could only be achieved by the unity of all the parties. Apart from this FADM was instrumental in conducting elections peacefully.

The electoral process was also one of the operational activities of ONUMOZ. The Government came up with a draft electoral law and distributed it to RENAMO and other political parties on 26th March 1993. A multiparty consultative conference was convened on 27th April 1993. RENAMO declined to attend the meeting on account of paucity of time to study the text. Although smaller parties attended, they walked out for the same reason as RENAMO besides demanding material and financial support. The conference resumed its work on 2nd August 1993 with all parties including RENAMO. There was a deadlock on the composition of National Election Commission. The Secretary General's visit in 1993 October from 17-20th helped in breaking the deadlock. A consensus was finally reached on (a) voting rights for expatriate Mozambicans, (b) Composition of provincial and district election commission (c) composition of the technical secretariat for election administration and (d) establishment and composition of election tribunal on 26th November 1993, following a number of meetings between president Chissano and Dhlakama in the presence of special representatives. The electoral law was approved by the Mozambican National Assembly on 9th December 1993 after nine day delay. The law was promulgated by the president of Mozambique shortly and it came into force on 12th January 1994. The members of the National Election Commission were appointed on 1st January 1994.

The process of registration for elections began on 1st June but later was extended till 2nd September 1994. The initial estimate of 8.5 million eligible voters based on 1980 senses was inaccurate and the National Election Commission rejected it. Out of new estimate of 7,994,850 voters more than three quarters had been registered by 22nd August 1994. A trust fund was established to assist the political parties to organize themselves for active participation in the campaign to be commenced on 22nd September and also the elections. The

Secretary-General, in his report on 26th August, appraised the Security Council the difficulties encountered and how he overcame. He also pointed out to the considerable progress made in humanitarian programs contributing significantly to achieve national reconciliation. 76 percent of the displaced persons were resettled. There were still three hundred and forty two thousand refugees in the neighbouring countries expected to return by the end of 1994. Demining was also in good progress. Rioting among soldiers both inside and outside assembly areas increased till early August when demobilization was nearly completed. The level of criminal activity was also alarmingly high in rural and urban areas. ONUMOZ stepped up the patrolling of major routes reinforcing guarding units of United Nations property and key locations. The most significant role of the U.N. during September and October was technical preparations for the conduct of the elections and creating the conditions necessary for the holding of free and fair elections. It was also to create proper environment for a stable and peaceful transition to a democratically elected government. The Secretary-General was able to report to the Security-Council on 21st October 1994, the preparedness to hold the elections as per schedule. There had been no violations of cease-fire. Voters registration had ended in an orderly manner. The electoral campaign was also in an active and peaceful phase. The political situation too was normal with calm prevailing everywhere.

The Secretary-General noted the atmosphere during the electoral campaign to be tense and the armed ban treaty rampantly violated. Although 111,539 weapons had been surrendered from both the troops and 43,491 weapons from paramilitary forces, the continuing proliferation of weapons was a cause for anxiety. The public pronouncements by certain candidates cast a doubt over the acceptance of the election results. However, the Secretary-General opined that the obvious risk of rise and fall of political temperature before and after the poll was worth taking. Since the future of Mozambicans lay in the hands of its people and their leaders, caution and statesmanship were of utmost importance.

The Security Council too expressed its strong belief that necessary conditions for holding free and fair elections on 27th and or 8th October 1994 would be established under effective national and international monitoring. The council appealed to all concern to ensure calm election campaign and responsible conduct of voting. The authorities vested with the task of conducting polls should remain impartial and avoid violence or threat of violence during and after the elections. The council reminded all the parties and their delegations that they should all abide themselves to the results of the elections as per the agreement.

The international community arranged for the deployment of approximately two thousand three hundred electoral observers including some nine hundred from the United Nations, on the eve of the elections, to observe and verify the polling and the count of votes in all the provinces. A host of organizations as the organization of African Union (OAU), European UNION (E.U.), and the association of European Parliamentarians for South Africa sent their own teams. However the President of RENAMO made allegations against some irregularities in the election process and announced his decision to withdraw on 26th October 1994. The Security Council appealed to Mr.Dhlakama to reconsider his decision promising appropriate procedures to be put in place through the National Election Commission and all concerns of RENAMO would be addressed. He further emphasized that all parties should honour their commitments and the elections should be as per the plan agreed by all the parties. The Special Representative Mr. Aldo Ajello seriously pursued to resolve the situation contacting Mr.Dhlakama. His efforts were fully supported by the ambassadors of all member states of the Supervision Commission. The President of South Africa, Zimbabwe and a few outer countries of the region also urged Mr.Dhlakama to reconsider his decision.

All polling stations opened on 27th October 1994 and massive turnout for voting was reported by United Nations monitors. More than half of the registered voters caste their votes on the very first day. RENAMO's monitors were present at almost all the polling stations. No major irregularities at polling stations were reported. Mr.Dhlakama revised his position and decided to vote on 28th October 1994. The voting period was extended by one day to 29th October 1994 to facilitate all the registered voters to exercise their right. The UNO's decision to extend the voting period was laudable. The U.N's decision to go ahead with elections in a way compelled RENAMO to participate. To accommodate RENAMO's changed decision UNO had to extend the date. The uncompromising efforts of the U.N. Peacekeeping force and the importance given to the democratic values received the whole hearted participation of RENAMO's registered voters too. The National Election Commission, in close cooperation with ONUMAS, ensured that all complaints of irregularities either by RENAMO or by other parties were fully investigated. The enabled the Special Representative to pronounce that the elections should be conducted peacefully in a well organized manner without any major irregularities or incidents. In some provinces more than 90 percent of the electorate caste their votes. The credibility of the elections was ensured and stressed by the special Representative as well as United Nations observers. The counting of votes was completed under the strict vigilance of ONUMOZ and others concerned.

The incumbent president Mr. Chissano was declared elected on behalf of United Nations. It was further declared that the elections in Mozambique from 27th October to 29th October 1994 had been free and fair. The announcement of the results fifteen days later was endorsed by the Security

Council. The delay was felt necessitated to ensure absolute accuracy and transparency under the strict scrutiny of all political parties U.N. observers and election monitors.

Mr. Chissano won the presidential elections securing 2,633,740 votes amounting to 53.3 percent. The leader of RENAMO Mr.Dhlakama received 1,666,965 votes coming to nearly 33.7 percent while Wehia Ripua of the Partido Democratica De Mozambique secured 2.9 percent of votes. A total of 5,402,940 representing 87.9 percent of the registered voters participated in the presidential elections. Blank votes were only 5.8 percent while they invalid were only 2.8 percent. FRELIMO received the largest share of votes with 2,115,0795 i.e. 44.3 percent followed by RENAMO with 1,803,506; 37.8 percent and Union Democratic with 247,793; 5.2 percent in the elections for the legislature. The total of two hundred and fifty seats in the new parliament were apportioned one hundred and twenty nine for FRELIMO, one hundred and nine for RENAMO, and twelve for U.D.[13] The Secretary General's Special Representative declared that the electoral process had been characterized by impartiality, dedication and high professionalism of the electoral authorities. It had been distinguished by the strong commitment of the political players to let the principle of democracy prevail and the will of the Mozambican peoples to live in peace and harmony was confirmed.

The installation of the new government took place by 15th December 1994 following the publication of the final electoral results. The Secretary-General extended the mandate of the ONUMOZ which was scheduled to expire on 15th November 1994 till the formation of the new government. The Security Council by its resolution 957 of 1994 approved the extension and authorized ONUMOZ to complete residual operations prior to its complete withdrawal on or before 31st January 1995. The Council welcomed the peaceful manner, the elections had been conducted and reiterated its intention to endorse the results.

The U.N. role in the peacekeeping operations in Mozambique is Quite laudable. The U.N. Secretary-General's prompt and personal intervention visiting Mozambique when ever a problem arose helped a lot to make the government and RENAMO sit together and resolve all problems through discussions. The determined and consistent efforts of the Security Council as well as the Secretary-General are not least responsible for the proper conduct elections and installing a democratic government in Mozambique. The support of the people, tired of the 14 year war, and their appreciation of U.N. efforts at every stage cannot but be mentioned in the establishment of peace and a democratic government in Mozambique. RENAMO's realization of the pulse of the people and retracting its denial to participate in the elections taking advantage of the initiatives taken by U.N. Secretary General also went a long way in establishing a democratically elected government in Mozambique.

The Indian contribution to ONUMOZ was note worthy. Two engineering companies, one head quarter company, one logistic company, staff and military observers actively participated in the U.N. operations in Mozambique Colonel S.D. Avasti was the Indian National Senior and also Chief of the staff at ONUMOZ's Head Quarters. Colonel H.S. Lidder later replaced him. The then U.N.Secretary General, Boutros Boutros-Ghali acknowledged and complimented the untiring efforts and dedication of Indian Army officers and troops in an interview to B.B.C.

> "The Indian troops by virtue of their superior training and high standard of discipline and sense of responsibility have had a significant contribution in ensuring the early return of peace in Mozambique".

REFERENCES

1. J.Fitzpatrick. The Economy of Mozambique: Problems and Prospects, *Third World Quarterly — January 1981,* Volume -3, No.1, p.77

2. *The World Book of Encyclopedia,* World Book Incorporation Ascott Seizer Company, p.750.
3. *Ibid.,* p.750.
4. *Ibid.,* p.752.
5. *Ibid.,* p.752.
6. Ruth Jacobson, 'Complicating Complexity': integrating gender into the analysis of the Mozambican conflict', *Third World Quarterly,* Vol.20, No.1, 1999, pp.175, 187.
7. *Op cit.,* J.Fitzpatrik, pp.86,87.
8. The Blue Helmets, A Review of U.N. Peace-keeping operation, *The United Nations Department of Public Information,* New York, 1996, p.321.
9. *Ibid.,* p.322.
10. *Ibid.,* p. 322.
11. See Appendix No.XII.
12. *Ibid.,* p.325.
13. Alex Vines, Mozambique 'A people's peace', *The World Today,* January 2000.

7
Conclusion

The United Nations peacekeeping has developed into one of the key approaches to deal with multifaceted crises that pose a threat to international peace and security. Since the end of cold war the number of military, police and civilian personnel deployed in United Nations peace-keeping operations around the world has reached exceptional levels. Not only has United Nations peacekeeping grown in size but it has become increasingly complex. Beyond simply monitoring cease-fires, today's multi-dimensional peacekeeping operations are called upon to assist the political process through the promotion of national dialogue and reconciliation, protect civilians, assist in the disarmament, demobilization and reintegration of combatants, support the organization of elections, protect and promote human rights, and assist in restoring the rule of law. Time and again the United Nations has been called upon to prevent a dangerous situation from escalating into war and to convince the opposing parties to sort out their differences through conference rather than resort to arms. It is true that the United Nations had to frequently face setbacks, but still it has persisted with its efforts at peacekeeping,

Post-cold war United Nations peacekeeping operations seem to be free, fair, frank and fearless. They were free from cold war rivalries, one witnesses more fair and frank discussion and bold collective actions. The international community could act fearlessly with no fear of the veto power paralysing Security Council resolution. The nature of conflicts has lately become more and more complex and presents no 'cut and dry' solutions. India has been contributing substantially over a prolonged period and till date remains committed to its objective of sustainable peace and peace building.

There was a change in the nature of peacekeeping operations in the post cold war year. Traditional peacekeeping operations were aimed at maintaining peace in a conflict zone by verifying compliance with ceasefires, supervise troop withdrawals and patrol buffer zones. But post-cold war became multi-dimensional with peace building and even peace enforcement activities becoming a part of the mandate of the peacekeepers. Peacekeeping became more comprehensive dealing virtually with every aspect of human affairs. The functions can be categorized into nine different functions.

1. Supervision, ceasefire monitoring and military observation.
2. Demobilization and reintegration
3. Disarmament
4. Humanitarian assistance
5. Electoral assistance
6. Human rights
7. Civilian police
8. Mine clearance
9. Co-operation with regional organizations.

Hence the functions were enlarged. A study of the peacekeeping operations in the post-cold war taking one from each continent reflecting the nine different functions demonstrates United Nation's multi-dimensional and global characteristic.

The crisis in all the five cases ranged from inter-state to intra-state. The problem in the first case between Iran and Iraq was an inter-state problem, each claiming border areas. The duration of UNIIMOG was from 20th August 1988 to 28th February 1991. The functions included verification confirmation and supervision of the ceasefire and withdrawal of all force to the internationally recognized borders. Brigadier V.M.Patel from India was appointed as assistant Chief Military observer (Iraq). India contributed the second largest contingent besides Hungary. Secretary-General Javier Perez de Cuellar opined, "the Indian Military observers performed their tasks in difficult areas with admirable dedication, professionalism and impartiality".

The problem in El Salvador was an intra-state one. The country witnessed a decade long civil war. ONUSAL functioned from 26th July 1991 to 30 April 1995. Here it performed eight of the nine different functions such as the verifying of the implementation of all agreements, creation of a new police force, reforming the judicial and electoral system, human rights, land tenure and other economic and social issues. India provided four military observers for United Nations observer mission in El Salvador. The Secretary-General recognized India's role and paid rich tributes for their great success in restoring peace.

The problem in Cambodia an intra-state one, stoked by neighbouring countries and all the big nations involving themselves on opposite sides. The UNAMIC functioned from 16th October 1991 to May 1994. The UNAMIC assisted the four Combodian parties to maintain ceasefire and the mandate included a major training programme for Combodians in mine detection and clearance and resettlement of refugees. UNAMIC was later absorbed by UNTAC. As a part of the peacekeeping mission India sent an infantry battalion, a field ambulance a mine training team, staff officer and seventeen military observers. India also provided three military observers in the United Nations military liaision team of twenty unarmed military observers. Subedr Rawal Singh was honoured with Keerti Chakra (an award of gallantry given by the Indian Government). Colonel A.N. Bhargava, Major Rajpal Punia and Major Hareendar Paul Sood were the recipients of the Yudh Seva Medals, while Major Vinod Pillai received the United Nations Force Commander's citiation. Havaldars Vikram Nayar, Madhava Chandra Raj, Sepoys Bupen Chandra Ray and Bhupal Singh were posthumously awarded 'Role of Honour'. Naib Subedar Surendra Singh and rifleman Sukvindhar Singh were awarded Seva Medals.

The problem in Croatia was the result of breaking up of Yugoslavia resulting in ethnic minorities fighting for their rights. The UNCRO functioned from 31st March 1995 to 15th January 1996. This one year is taken into consideration for the simple reason that India participated during this period only. The main function was to help the peaceful integration of Croatia protecting the interests and human rights of all. Lieutenant General Satish Nambiar was appointed as the first head of the United Nations protection force accompanied by Lt.Col. Philip, as his staff officer.

The operation in Mozambique dealt with a civil war as a result of Zimbabwe's opposition to the white government and their apartheid problem. It was first an intra-state, white minority government encourage a group in Mozambique to rebel. The United Nations operation in Mozambique ranged from 16th December 1992 to 15th November 1994 implementing the General Peace Agreement signed on 4th October 1992 in Rome by President of the republic of Mozambia and the president of RENAMO with the help of the initiative of the United Nations. The mandate authorized impartial implementation of the agreement. The United Nations peace-keeping mission performed eight functions including humanitarian assistance operation, except cooperation with regional organization and the mission was formally liquidated at the end of January 1995. India sent two Engineering Companies, one Head Quarters Company, one Logistic Company, staff and military observers. Colonel S.D. Avasti was the Chief of staff at ONUMOZ's headquarters, who was later replaced by Col H.S. Lidder. The then United Nations Secretary-General Boutros Boutros-Ghali said in an interview to B.B.C. "The Indian troops by virtue of their superior training and high standard of discipline and sense of responsibility have had a significant contribution in ensuring the early return of peace in Mozambique".

Transparency in the activities, present in all the five cases was the cornerstone for the success. People's cooperation in cases which forced some of the leaders to change their track as in Mozambique was responsible for the smooth functioning of the peacekeeping force. Persistent and persuasive efforts of Secretary-General played a big role to bring round intransigence in some cases like Cambodia. The firmness and boldness in implementing the agreements is no mean contributor for the success of United Nations peacekeeping in all the five cases. The United Nations efforts for upholding the democratic and human rights of the people went a long way in the success of the peacekeeping missions in all the cases except in Iran-Iraq. A mention has to be made of the shortcomings in all these cases. There was an undue delay for United Nations peace-keeping force to enter in Iran and Iraq. Eventhough all the permanent members of the Security Council fully aware of the crisis brewing in middle east.

Though Cambodia is a intra-state conflict, the study revealed that because of intervention of other countries like United States of America, China, Union of Soviet Socialist Republics and Association of South East Asian Nations, the issue could not be contained. Had United Nations taken a stand and sent the peace-keeping force then may be the other big powers would not have found it so easy to interfere in the domestic crisis in Cambodia.

As seen in the five cases peacekeeping today is not elimination of war alone but to provide humanitarian assistance, medical care and restore normal civilian activities in strife-torn areas. Thus the meaning of peacekeeping acquired a multidimensional role namely, peacekeeping, peacemaking, peace building and preventive diplomacy.

India on her part has made due contribution in all the cases by providing military and civilian contingents. Right from the inception of peacekeeping India has given full support to the United Nations resolutions and operations aimed at ending international tensions. The Indian military contingents have on many occasions successfully performed the role of peacekeeping under the flag of the United Nations. India has always played its part in international peacekeeping operations in various parts of the world. Thus the Indian Foreign Policy, core principles of world peace, international cooperation, faith in peaceful means for the settlement of disputes, non-aggression, rejection of war restate the principles of the United Nations. As such active participation in the peacekeeping operations has been a fundamental principle of Indian Foreign Policy.

An overall understanding of peace-keeping today has to be judged in the light of the fact that human costs of a failed transition to a stable society are very high. It is important to develop clear sets of agreed norms and expectations among various groups in formulating coherent approaches to peace-keeping. Thus India has been advocating for a broad based peace-keeping approach. Keeping these changes in view, the researcher makes the following suggestions.

1. The United Nations to set up conflict management committees on region-wise basis.

2. Just as the third world countries look to India to lead the way, India should make her presence felt at the policy making level of the United Nations peace-keeping.
3. Because of the psychological strain these missions have on the peace-keeping soldiers it would be good if they were given leave after every six months periodically.
4. The procedure for the United Nations to initiate the debate on the deployment of peace-keeping forces seems bureaucratic and cumbersome. Instead the procedure can be cut short and the force deployed immediately. This might save thousands of lives and restore peace.
5. Some pictorial evidence or documentary film of other conflict zones in different regions focusing on the catastrophical consequences of delayed decisions may influence the policy makers to think and act quickly.
6. Establishment of an early warning office which should continuously monitor potential trouble sports around the world.
7. The former Indian Prime Minister, Narasimha Rao, suggested that 'international peace-keeping forces should be selected from regions and areas far removed from where they are to be sent for undertaking credible operations'. In line with this it is imperative for the ground soldiers to be familiar with the area and their local language, and terrain.
8. The Government of India should request the United Nations to institute a permanent training centre for Asia, Africa and South-East Asia peace-keepers. The fact that India has been contributing large contingents of peacekeepers since inception and has vast experience in peacekeeping, India should initiate this idea.

9. A permanent committee to recommend to the Security Council on the deployment of United Nations Peace-keeping force should be established India by virtue of her longstanding participation should head the committee.

APPENDIX - 1

Chapter 6
Pacific Settlement of Disputes

Article 33

1. The parties to any dispute, the continuance of which is likely to endanger the maintenance of international peace and security shall, first of all, seek a solution by negotiation, enquiry, mediation, conciliation, arbitration, judicial settlement, resort to regional agencies or arrangements, or other peaceful means of their own choice.
2. The Security Council shall, when it deems necessary, call upon the parties to settle their dispute by such means.

Article 34

The Security Council may investigate any dispute, or any situation which might lead to international friction or give rise to a dispute, in order to determine whether the continuance of the dispute or situation is likely to endanger the maintenance of international peace and security.

Article 35

1. Any Member of the United Nations may bring any dispute, or any situation of the nature referred to in Article 34, to the attention of the Security Council or of the General Assembly.
2. A state which is not a member of the United Nations may bring to the attention of the Security Council or the General Assembly any dispute to which it is a party if it accepts in advance, for the purposes of the dispute, the obligations of pacific settlement provided in the present Charter.

3. The proceedings of the General Assembly in respect of matters brought to its attention under this Article will be subject to the provisions of Articles 11 and 12.

Article 36

1. The Security Council may, at any stage of a dispute of the nature referred to in Article 33 or of a situation of like nature, recommend appropriate procedures or methods of adjustment.
2. The Security Council should take into consideration any procedures for the settlement of the dispute which have already been adopted by the parties.
3. In making recommendations under this Article the Security Council should also take into consideration that legal disputes should as a general rule be referred by the parties to the International Court of Justice in accordance with the provisions of the Statute of the Court.

Article 37

1. Should the parties to a dispute of the nature referred in Article 33 fail to settle it by the means indicated in that Article, they shall refer it to the Security Council.
2. If the Security Council deems that the continuance of the dispute is in fact likely to endanger the maintenance of international peace and security, it shall decide whether to take action under Article 36 or to recommend such terms of settlements as it may consider appropriate.

Article 38

Without prejudice to the provisions of the Article 33 to 37 the Security Council may, if all the parties to any dispute so request, make recommendations to the parties with a view to a pacific settlement of the dispute.

Action with Respect to threats to the Peace, Breaches of the Peace, and Acts of Aggression: UN Charter VII

Article 39

The Security Council shall determine the existence of any threat to the peace, breach of Peace, or act of aggression and shall make recommendations, or decide what measures shall be taken in accordance with Article 41 and 42 to maintain or restore international peace and security.

Article 40

In order to prevent an aggravation of the situation, the Security Council may, before making the recommendations or deciding upon the measures provided for in Article 39, call upon the parties concerned to comply with such provisional measures as it deems necessary or desirable. Such provisional measures shall be without prejudice to the rights, claims or position of the parties concerned, the Security Council shall duly take account of failure to comply with such provisional measures.

Article 41

The Security Council may decide what measures not involving the use of armed force are to be employed to give effect to its decisions and it may call upon the members of the United Nations to apply such measures. These may include complete or partial interruption of economic relations and of rail, sea, air, postal, telegraphic, radio and other means of communication are the severance of diplomatic relations.

Article 42

Should the Security Council consider that measures provided for in Article 41 would be inadequate or have proved to be inadequate, it may take such action by air. Sea, or land forces as may be necessary to maintain or restore international peace and security. Such action may include demonstrations, blockade and other operations by air, sea or land forces of Members of the United Nations.

Article 43

1. All members of the United Nations, in order to contribute to the maintenance of international peace and security, undertake to make available to the Security Council, on its call and in accordance with a special agreement of agreements, armed forces, assistance and facilities, including rights or passage, necessary for the purpose of maintaining international peace and security.
2. Such agreement or agreements shall govern the numbers and types of forces, their degree of readiness and general location and the nature of the facilities and assistance to be provided.
3. The agreement of agreements shall be negotiated as soon as possible on the initiative of the Security Council. They shall be concluded between the Security Council and Members and shall be subject to ratification by the signatory states in accordance with their receptive constitutional processes.

Article 44

When the Security Council has decided to use force it shall, before calling upon a member not represented on it to provide armed forces in fulfillment of the obligations assumed under Article 43, invite that member, if the member so desires, to participate in the decisions of the Security Council concerning the employment of contingents of that member's armed forces.

Article 45

In order to enable the United Nations to take urgent military measures, members shall hold immediately available national air force contingents for combined international enforcement action. The strength and degree of readiness of these contingents and plans for their combined action shall be determined, within the limits laid down in the special agreement or agreements referred to in Article 43, by the Security Council with the Assistance of the Military Staff Committee.

Article 46

Plans for the application of armed force shall be made by the Security Council with the assistance of the Military Staff Committee.

Article 47

1. There shall be established a Military Staff Committee to advise and assist the Security Council on all Questions relating to the Security Council's military requirements for the maintenance of international peace and security, the employment and command of forces placed as its disposal, the regulation of armaments, and possible disarmament.
2. The Military Staff Committee shall consist of the Chiefs of Staff of permanent members of the Security Council or their representatives. Any member of the United Nations not permanently represented on the committee shall be invited by the committee to be associated with it when the efficient discharge of the committee's responsibilities require the participation of that member in its work.
3. The Military Staff Committee shall be responsible under the Security Council for the strategic direction of any armed forces placed at the disposal of the Security Council. Questions relating to the command of such forces shall be worked out subsequently.

4. The Military Staff Committee, with the authorization of the Security Council and after consultation with appropriate regional agencies, may establish regional sub-committees.

Article 48

1. The action required to carry out the decision of the Security Council for the maintenance of international peace and security shall be taken by all the Members of the United Nations or by some of them, as the Security Council may determine.
2. Such decisions shall be carried out by the Members of the United Nations directly and through their action in the appropriate international agencies of which they are members.

Article 49

The Members of the United Nations shall join in affording mutual assistance in carryingout the measures decided upon by the Security Council.

Article 50

If preventive or enforcement measures against any state are taken by the Security Council, any other state, whether a Member or the United Nations or not, which finds itself confronted with special economic problems arising from the carrying out of those measures shall have the right to consult the Security Council with regard to a solution of those problems.

Article 51

Nothing in the present Charter shall impair the inherent right of individual or collective self-defence if an armed attack occurs against a Member of the United Nations, Until the Security Council has taken measures necessary to maintain international peace and security. Measures taken by Members in the exercise of this right of self-defence shall be immediately reported to the Security Council and shall not in any way, affect the authority and responsibility of the Security Council under the present Charter to take at any time such action as it deems necessary in order to maintain or restore international peace and security.

APPENDIX II

UN Resolution 377 (V)

3 November, 1950

Uniting For Peace

The General Assembly,

Recognising that the first two stated purposes of the United Nations are: "To maintain international peace and security, and to that ends to take effective collective measures for the prevention and removal of threats to the peace and for the suppression of acts of aggression or other breaches of the peace, and to bring about by peaceful means, and in conformity with the principles of justice and international law, adjustment or settlement of international disputes or situations which might lead to a breach of the peace", and "To develop friendly relations among nations based on respect for the principle of equal rights and self-determination of peoples, and to take other appropriate measures to strengthen universal peace".

Reafirming that it remain the primary duty of all Members of the United Nations, when involved in an international dispute, to seek settlement of such a dispute by peaceful means through the procedures laid down in Chapter VI of the Charter, and recalling the successful achievements of the United Nations in this regard on a number of previous occasions,

Finding that international tension exists on a dangerous scale, Recalling its resolution 290 (IV) entitled "Essential of Peace", which states that disregard of the Principles of the Charter of the United Nations is primarily responsible for the continuance of international tension, and desiring to contribute further to the objectives of that resolution.

Reaffirming that the initiative in negotiating the agreements for armed forces provided for in Article 43 of the Charter belongs to the Security Council and desiring to ensure that, pending the conclusion of such agreements, the United Nations has at its disposal means for maintaining international peace and security.

Conscious that Failure of the Security Council to discharge its responsibilities on behalf of all the Member States, Particularly those responsibilities referred to in the two preceding paragraphs, does not relieve Members State of their obligations or the United Nations of its responsibility under the Charter to maintain international peace and security.

Recognising in particular that such failure does not deprive the General Assembly of its rights or relieve it of its responsibilities uner the Charter in regard to the maintenance of international peace and security.

Recognising that discharge by the General Assembly of its responsibilities in these respects calls for possibilities of observation which would ascertain the facts and expose aggressors; for the existence of armed forces which could be used collectively; and for the possibility of timely recommendation by the General Assembly to Members of the United Nations for collective action which, to be effective, should be prompt.

1. Resolves that if the Security Council, because of lack of unanimity of he permanent members, fails to exercise its primary responsibility for the maintenance of international peace and security in any case where there appears to be a threat to the peace, breach of the peace, or set of aggression, the General Assembly shall consider the matter immediately with a view to making appropriate recommendations to Members for collective measures, including in the case of a breach of the peace

or act of aggression the use of armed force when necessary, to maintain or restore international peace and security. If not in session at the time, the General Assembly may meet in emergency special session within twenty-four hours of the request therefore. Such emergency special session shall be called if requested by the Security Council on the vote of any seven members, or by a majority of the Members of the United Nations;

2. Adopts for this purpose the amendments to its rules of procedure set forth in the annex to the present resolution;

3. Establishes a Peace Observation Commission which, for the calendar years 195 and 1952, shall be composed of fourteen Members, namely, China, Colombia, Czechoslovakia, France, India, Iraq, Israel, New Zealand, Pakistan, Sweden, the Union of Soviet Socialist Republics, the United Kingdom of Great Britain and Northern Ireland, the United States of America and Uruguay, and which could observe and report on the situation in any area here there exists international tension the continuance of which is likely to endanger the maintenance of international peace and security. Upon the invitation or with the consent of the State into whose territory the Commission would go, the General Assembly, or the Interim Committee when the Assembly is not in session, may utilize the Commission if the Security Council is not exercising the functions assigned to it by the Charter with respect to the matter in question. Decisions to utilize the Commission shall be made on the affirmative vote of two-thirds of the members present and voting. The Security Council may also utilize the Commission in accordance with its authority under the Charter;

4. Decides that the Commission shall have authority in its discretion to appoint sub-commissions and to utilize the services of observers to assist it in the performance of its functions;
5. Recommends to all governments and authorities that they co-operate with the Commission and assist it in the performance of its functions;
6. Requests the Secretary General to provide the necessary staff and facilities, utilizing, where directed by the Commission, the United Nations Panel of Field Observes envisaged in General Assembly resolution 297 B (IV);
7. Invites each Member of the United Nations to survey its resources in order to determine the nature and scope of the assistance it may be in a position to render in support of any recommendations of the Security Council or of the General Assembly for the restoration of international peace and security;
8. Recommends to the State Members of the United Nations that each Member maintain within its national armed forces elements so trained, organized and equipped that they could promptly be made available, in accordance with its constitutional processes, for service as a United Nations unit or units, upon recommendation by the Security Council or the General Assembly, without prejudice to the use of such elements in exercise of the right of individual or collective self-defence recognized in Article 51 of the Charter;
9. Invites the Members of the United Nations to inform the Collective Measures Committee provided for in paragraph 11 as soon as possible of the measures taken in implementation of the preceeding paragraph;
10. Requests the Secretary-General to appoint, with the approval of the Committee provided for in paragraph

11, a panel of military experts who could be made available, on request, to Member State wishing to obtain technical advice regarding the organization, training, and equipment for prompt service as United Nations units of the elements referred to in paragraph 8;

11. Establishes a Collective Measures Committee consisting of fourteen Members, namely; Australia, Belgium, Brazil, Burma, Canada, Egypt, France, Mexico, Philippines, Turkey, the United Kingdom of Great Britain and Northern Ireland, the United States of America, Venezuela and Yugoslavia, and directs the Committee, in consultation with the Secretary-General and with such Member States as the Committee finds appropriate, to study and make a report to the Security Council and the General Assembly, not later than 1 September 1951, on method, including those in section C of the present resolution, which might be used to maintain and strengthen international peace and security in accordance with the Purposes and Principles of the Charter, taking account of collective self-defence and regional arrangements (Articles 51 and 52 of the Charter);

12. Recommends to all Member States that they co-operate with the Committee and assist it in the performance of its functions;

13. Requests the Secretary-General to furnish the staff and facilities necessary for the effective accomplishment of the purposes set forth in sections C and D of the present resolution;

14. Is fully conscious that, in adopting the proposals set foth above, enduring peace will not be secured solely by collective security arrangements against breaches of international peace and acts of aggression, but that

a genuine and lasting peace depends also upon the observance of al the Principles and Purposes established in the Charter of the United Nations, upon the implementation of the resolutions of the Security Council, the General Assembly and other principal organs of the United Nations intended to achieve the maintenance of international peace and security, and especially upon respect for and observance of human rights and fundamental freedoms for all and on the establishment and maintenance of conditions of economic and social well-being in all countries; and accordingly.

15. Urges Member State to respect fully, and to intensify, joint action, in co-operation with the United Nations, to develop and stimulate universal respect for and observance of human rights and fundamental freedom, and to intensify individual and collective efforts to achieve conditions of economic stability and social progress, particularly through the development of underdeveloped countries and areas.

For the purpose of maintaining international peace and security, in accordance with the Charter of the United Nations, and, in particular, with Chapters V, VI and VII of the Charter,

The General Assembly

Recommends to the Security Council

That it should take the necessary steps to ensure that the action provided for under the Charter is taken with respect to threats to the peace, breaches of the peace or acts of aggression and with respect to the peaceful settlement of disputes or situations likely to endanger the maintenance of international peace and security.

That it should devise measures for the earliest application of Articles 43, 45, 46 and 47 of the Charter of the United Nations regarding the placing of armed force at the disposal of the Security Council by the States Members of the United Nations and the effective functioning of the Military Staff Committee;

The above dispositions should in no manner prevent the General Assembly from fulfilling its functions under resolution 377 A(V).

The General Assembly

Recognizing that the primary function of the United Nations Organization is to maintain and promote peace, security and justice among all nations, Recognizing the responsibility of all Member States to promote the cause of international peace in accordance with their obligations as provided in the Charter,

Recognizing that the Charter charges the Security Council with the primary responsibility for maintaining international peace and security. Reaffirming the importance of unanimity among the permanent members of the Security Council on all problems which are likely to threaten world peace, Recalling General Assembly resolution 190 (III) entitled "Appeal to the Great Powers to renew their efforts to compose their differences and establish a lasting peace",

Recommends to the permanent members of the Security Council that:

(a) They meet and discuss, collectively or otherwise, and, if necessary, with other States concerned, all problems which are likely to threaten international peace and hamper the activities of the United Nations, with a view to their resolving fundamental differences and reaching agreement in accordance with the spirit and letter of the Charter;

(b) They advise the General Assembly and, when it is not in session, the Members of the United Nations, as soon as appropriate, of the results of their consultations.

APPENDIX III

United Nations Observer Group in Central America (ONUCA)

Authorization	Security Council resolutions 644 (1989) of 7 November 1989650 (1990) of 27 March 1990653 (1990) of 20 April 1990654 (1990) of 4 May 1990656 (1990) of 8 June 1990675 (1990) of 5 November 1990691 (1991) of 6 May 1991719 (1991) of 6 November 1991730 (1992) of 16 January 1992
Function	Established to verify compliance by the Governments of Costa Rica, El Salvador, Guatemala, Honduras and Nicaragua with their undertakings to cease aid to irregular forces and insurrectionist movements in the region and not to allow their territory to be used for attacks on other States. In addition, ONUCA played a part in the voluntary demobilization of the Nicaraguan Resistance and monitored a cease-fire and the separation of forces agreed by the Nicaraguan parties as part of the demobilization process.
Location	Costa Rica, El Salvador, Guatemala, Honduras and Nicaragua
Headquarters:	Tegucigalpa, Honduras
Duration	7 November 1989 to 17 January 1992
Strength:	Initial authorization: 260 military observers; crews and support

	personnel for an air wing and naval unit. Additional authorization: Infantry battalion of approximately 800 all ranks. Maximum deployment (May/June 1990); 1,098 military personnel The mission was supported by a number of international and local civilian staff.
Fatalities	None
Financing	Method of financing: Assessments in respect of a Special Account Expenditures: $88,573,157 (net)

Personal Representative of the Secretary-General for the Central American Peace Process:

	Alvaro de Sota (Peru)	September 1989 - February 1992.
Chief Military Observers	Major-General gustin Quesada Gomez (Spain)	November 1989-December 1990
	Brigadier-General Lewis MacKenzie (Canada) (Acting)	December 1990 – May 1991
	Brigadier-General Victor Suanzes Pardo (Spain)	May 1991-January 1992.

Contributors	*Duration*	*Contribution*
Argentina	June 1990-January 1992	Naval Crew and Four Fast patrol boats
Brazil	April 1990-January 1992	Military Observers
Canada	December 1989-January 1992	Military Observers, Helicopter unit
Colombia	December 1989-January 1992	Military Observers

Ecuador	April 1990- November 1991	Military Observers
Germany, Federal Republic of	December 1989 – December 1991	Civilian Medical Personnel, Air Crew
India	May 1990- January 1992	Military Observers
Ireland	December 1989- January 1992	Military Observers
Spain	December 1989- January 1992	Military Observers
Sweden	May 1990 - January 1992	Military Observers
Venezuela	December 1989- January 1992 April – July 1990	Military Observers, Logistics Unit Infantry battalion

Voluntary Contributions

Germany, Federal Republic of (December 1989-November 1991: rental, equipment and maintenance of a fixed wing aircraft; basic salary of air crew and of civilian medical personnel); Switzerland (air ambulance service).

United Nationas Observer Mission in El Salvador (ONUSAL)

Authorization: Security Council resolutions

693 (1991) of 20 May 1991729 (1992) of 14 January 1992784 (1992) of 30 October 1992791 (1992) of 30 November 1992832 (1993) of 27 May 1993888 (1993) of 30 November 1993920 (1994) of 26 May 1994961 (1994) of 23 November 1994991 (1995) of 28 April 1995

Function: Established to verify the implementation of all agreements between the Government of El Salvador and Frente Farabundo Marti para la Liberacion Nacional aimed at ending a decade-long civil war. The agreement involved a cease-fire and related measures, reform and reduction of the armed forces, creation of a new police force, reform of the judicial and electoral systems, human rights, land tenure and other economic and social issues. After the armed conflict had been formally brought to an end in December 1992, ONUSAL verified elections which were carried out successfully in March and April 1994. After ONUSAL completed its mandate on 30 April 1995, a small group of United Nations civilian personnel – known as the United Nations Mission in El Salvador (MINUSAL) – remained in El Salvador to provide good offices to the parties, to verify implementation of the outstanding points of the agreements and to provide a continuing flow of accurate and reliable information.

Location: El Salvador
Headquarters: San Salvador
Duration: 26 July 1991 to 30 April 1995

Strength: Authorized maximum: 380 military observers; 8 medical officers; and 631 civilian police. Provision was also made for some 140 civilian international staff and 180 local staff Maximum deployment: 368 military observers (February 1992) and 315 civilian police (May 1992). The Electoral Division was augmented by some 900 electoral observers during the elections.

Fatalities 3 Civilian police 2 Local staff 5 total

Financing: Method of financing: Assessments in respect of a Special Account Expenditures: $ 107,003,650

Special Representatives of the Secretary-General and Chiefs of Mission:

Iqbal Riza (Pakistan)	July 1991-March 1993
Augusto Ramfrez-Ocampo (Colombia)	April 1993-March 1994
Enrique ter Horst (Venezuela)	1 April 1994-Sep. 1995*

* Mr. Horst continued as Special Representative of the Secretary-General after the termination of ONUSAL's mandate and served as Chief of Mission of MINUSAL until September 1995. He we succeeded by Mr.Ricardo Virgil (Peru) as the Secretary. General's Representative and Director of Mission.

Chief Brigadier-General

Military Observer:	Victor Suanzes Pardo (Spain)	January 1992— May 1993.
Police Commiss-ioners	General Homero Vaz Bresque (Uruguay)	March 1992-April 1994
	Comisario Principal Alfredo Carballo (Spain)	May 1994-March 1995.

Contributors	*Duration*	*Contribution*
Argentina	June 1992-November 1994	Medical Unit
Austria	February 1992-November 1994	Civilian Police
Brazil	July 1991-April 1995	Military Observers
	April-May 1992	Medical Unit
	June 1993-April 1995	Civilian Police
Canada	July 1991-August 1994	Military Observers
Chile	April 1992-April 1995	Civilian Police
Colombia	January 1992-November 1994	Military Observers
	May 1993-April 1995	Civilian Police
Ecuador	July 1991-March 1994	Military Observers
France	July 1991-November 1994	Civilian Police
Guyana	April 1992-April 1995	Civilian Police
India	January 1992-April 1994	Military Observers
Ireland	January 1992-June 1994	Military Observers

Italy	July 1991-April 1995	Civilian Police
Mexico	February 1992-April 1995	Civilian Police
Norway	January-February 1992	Military Observers
	February 1992-June 1993	Civilian Police
Spain	July 1991-April 1995	Military Observers
	July 1991-April 1995	Civilian Police
Sweden	January 1992-November 1994	Military Observers
	April 1992-November 1994	Civilian Police
Venezuela	July 1991-April 1995	Military Observers
Voluntary	Switzerland (Cash:$70,398)	
Contributions	As at 28 February 1995, voluntary contributions received in the Trust Fund for the Commission on the Truth amounted to $2,309,069.	

United Nations Advance Mission in Cambodia (UNAMIC)

Authorization: Security Council resolutions:717 (1991) of 16 October 1991728 (1992) of 8 January 1992

Function: Established to assist the four Cambodian Parties to maintain their cease-fire during the period prior to the establishment and deployment of the United Nations Transitional Authority in Cambodia, and to initiate mine-awareness training of civilian populations. Later, the mandate was enlarged to include a major training programme for Cambodians in mine-detection and mine-clearance and the mine-clearing of repatriation routes, reception centres and resettlement areas. UNAMIC was absorbed by UNTAC in March 1992.

Location:	Cambodia
Headquarters:	Phnom Penh
Duration:	16 October 1991-15 March 1992.
Strength:	Initial authorization: 116 military personnel (50 military liaison officers, 20 mine-awareness personnel, 40 military support personnel). There was also provision for approximately 75 International and 75 local civilian support staff. Subsequent authorization: 1,090 additional military personnel. Provision was also made for 34 additional civilian staff. Maximum deployment: 1,090 (March 1992)
Fatalities:	None
Financing:	(see UNTAC, below)

Chief Liaison Officer	A.H.S. Ataul Karim (Bangladesh)	November 1991-March 1992
Senior Military Liaison Officer:	Brigadier-General Michel Loridon (France)	November 1991-March 1992

Contributors	*Duration*	*Contribution*
Algeria	November 1991-February 1992	Military Observers
Argentina	November 1991-February 1992	Military Observers
Australia	November 1991-February 1992	Military Observers
Austria	November 1991-February 1992	Military Observers
Belgium	November 1991-February 1992	Military Observers
Canada	November 1991-February 1992	Military Observers
China	November 1991-February 1992	Military Observers
France	November 1991-February 1992 December 1991-February 1992	Military Observers Air Unit
Germany	November 1991-February 1992	Military Observers

Ghana	November 1991-February 1992	Military Observers
India	November 1991-February 1992	Military Observers
Indonesia	November 1991-February 1992	Military Observers
Ireland	November 1991-February 1992	Military Observers
Malaysia	November 1991-February 1992	Military Observers
New Zealand	November 1991-February 1992	Military Observers
Pakistan	November 1991-February 1992	Military Observers
Poland	November 1991-February 1992	Military Observers
Russian Federation (Soviet Union before 24 December 1991)	November 1991-February 1992	Military Observers
Senegal	November 1991-February 1992	Military Observers
Thailand	February 1992	Military Observers
Tunisia	November 1991-February 1992	Military Observers
United Kingdom	November 1991-February 1992	Military Observers
United States	November 1991-February 1992	Military Observers
Uruguay	November 1991-February 1992	Military Observers
Voluntary Contributions	Included in UNTAC; see below	

United Nations Tansitional Authority in Cambodia (UNTAC)

Authorization: Security Council resolutions:745 (1992) of 28 February 1992860 (1993) of 27 August 1992880 (1993) of 4 November 1993

Function Established to ensure the implementation of the Agreements on a Comprehensive Political Settlement of the Cambodia Conflict, signed in Paris on 23 October 1991. Under the Agreements, the Supreme National Council of Cambodia (SNC) was "the unique legitimate body and source of authority in which, throughout the transitional period, the sovereignty, independence and unity of Cambodia are enshrined". SNC, which was made up of the four Cambodian factions, delegated to the United Nations "all powers necessary" to ensure the implementation of the Agreements. The mandate given to UNTAC included aspects relating to human rights, the organization and conduct of free and fair general elections, military arrangements, civil administration, the maintenance of law and order, the repatriation and resettlement of the Cambodian refugees and displaced persons and the rehabilitation of essential Cambodian infrastructure during the transitional period. Upon becoming operational on 15 March 1992, UNTAC absorbed UNAMIC, which had been established immediately after the signing of the Agreements in October 1991. UNTAC'S mandate ended in September 1993 with the promulgation of the Constitution for the Kingdom of Cambodia and the formation of the new Government.

Location Cambodia

Headquarters: Phnom Penh

Duration: 28 February 1992-24 SEPTEMBER 1993

Strength: Maximum authorized: 15,547 troops, 893 military observers, and 3,500 civilian police, Provision included upto 1,149 international civilian staff, 465 United Nations Volunteers and 4,830 local staff, supplemented by international contractual staff and electoral personnel during the electoral period.

Fatalities 41 Military

4 Military observers

14 civilian police

5 international United Nations staff

14 local staff

78 total

Financing Method of financing Assessments in respect of a Special AccountExpenditures: $1,620,963,300 (UNAMIC and UNTAC combined)

Special Representative of the Secretary-Generaland Chief of Mission:

	Yasushi Akashi (Japan)	January 1992-September 1993
Force Commander	Lieutenant-General John Sanderson (Australia)	March 1992-September 1993
Police Commiss-ioners:	Brigadier-General Klaas Roos (Netherlands)	March 1992-August 1993
	Deputy Inspector General Shahudul Haque (Bangladesh) (Acting)	August-September 1993

Contributors	***Contribution***
Algeria	Civilian Police, Military Observers
Argentina	Military Observers
Australia	Civilian Police, Troops
Austria	Civilian Police, Troops, Military Observers
Bangladesh	Civilian Police, Troops, Military Observers
Belgium	Military Observers, Troops
Brunei Darussalam	Civilian Police, Troops, Military Observers
Bulgaria	Civilian Police, Troops, Military Observers
Cameroon	Civilian Police, Military Observers
Canada	Troops
Chile	Troops
China	Troops, Military Observers
Colombia	Civilian Police
Egypt	Civilian Police
Fiji	Civilian Police
France	Civilian Police, Troops, Air Unit, Military Observers
Germany	Civilian Police, Troops

Ghana	Civilian Police, Troops, Military Observers
Hungary	Civilian Police
India	Civilian Police, Troops, Military Observers
Indonesia	Civilian Police, Troops, Military Observers
Ireland	Civilian Police, Troops, Military Observers
Italy	Civilian Police
Japan	Civilian Police
Jordan	Civilian Police, Troops, Military Observers
Kenya	Civilian Police
Malaysia	Troops
Morocco	Civilian Police
Namibia	Troops, Military Observers
Nepal	Civilian Police
Netherlands	Civilian Police
New Zealand	Troops, Military Observers
Nigeria	Civilian Police
Norway	Civilian Police
Pakistan	Civilian Police, Troops, Military Observers
Philippines	Civilian Police, Troops
Poland	Troops, Military Observers
Russian Federation	Troops, Military Observers
Senegal	Military Observers
Singapore	Civilian Police, Troops
Sweden	Civilian Police
Thailand	Troops
Tunisia	Civilian Police, Troops, Military Observers
United Kingdom	Troops, Military Observers

United States	Troops, Military Observers
Uruguay	Troops, Military Observers

Voluntary Contributions in kind or in services:

Australia	Military Support Unit
France	Air Support Unit
Japan	Audio-visual equipment, health kits
Switzerland	Air ambulance services
United States	Ready-to-eat meals.

Voluntary Contribution in Cash

Japan ($2 million), Australia ($1 million), Netherlands ($2.2 million), Philippines ($100,000). United Kingdom ($1 million), United States of America ($2 million), Luxembourg ($26,054), New Zealand ($25,807), Japan ($1.1 million), Japan – advance ($2 million), private donation ($10,000).

Trust Fund for the Cambodian Peace Process: As at 31 October 1993, $8.7 million had been contributed by Australia, Bangladesh, Barbados, Denmark, Ireland, Italy, Luxembourg, New Zealand, Norway, Senegal, Singapore and Sweden as well as by a private institution.

Trust Fund for a Human Rights Education Programme in Cambodia: As at 31 October 1993, a total of $1.6 million had been contributed by Australia, Belgium, Canada, the Netherlands, New Zealand, Sweden, the United Kingdom and the United States.

Cambodia Trust Fund: As at 31 October 1993, $2.2 million had been contributed by Australia, Chile, Republic of Korea, the Netherlands, New Zealand and Norway.

Trust Fund for the De-Mining Programme in Cambodia: As at 31 October 1993, a total of $713,4000 had been contributed by New Zealand and the United States.

United Nations Protection Forece (UNPROFOR) (21 February 1992-31 March 1995)

Authorization: Security Council resolutions:743 (1992) of 21 February 1992749 (1992) of 7 April 1992758 (1992) of 8 June 1992761 (1992) of 29 June 1992762 (1992) of 30 June 1992764 (1992) of 13 July 1992769 (1992) of 7 August 1992776 (1992) of 14 September 1992779 (1992) of 6 October 1992781 (1992) of 9 October 1992786 (1992) of 10 November 1992795 (1992) of 11 December 1992807 (1993) of 19 February 1993815 (1993) of 30 March 1993819 (1993) of 16 April 1993824 (1993) of 6 May 1993836 (1993) of 4 June 1993842 (1993) of 18 June 1993844 (1993) of 18 June 1993847 (1993) of 30 June 1993869 (1993) of 30 September 1993870 (1993) of 1 October 1993871 (1993) of 4 October 1993900 (1994) of 4 March 1994908 (1994) of 31 March 1994914 (1994) of 27 April 1994947 (1994) of 30 September 1994982 (1995) OF 31 March 1995.

Function: Initially, established in Croatia as an interim arrangement to create the conditions of peace and security required for the negotiation of an overall Settlement of the yugoslav crisis. UNPROFOR's Mandate was to ensure That The Three "United Nations Protected Areas" (Unpas) in croatia were demilitarized and that all persons residing in them were protected from fear of armed attack. In The course of 1992, UNPROFOR's Mandate was enlarged to include monitoring functions in certain other areas of Croatia ("Pink Zones"); to enable the force to control the entry of civilians into the UNPAS and to perform immigration and customs functions at the UNPA borders at international frontiers; and to include monitoring of the demilitarization of the Prevlaka Peninsula and to ensure control of the Peruca Dam, situated in one of the "Pink Zones". In addition, UNPROFOR monitored implementation of a cease-fire agreement signed by the Croatian government and local Serb authorities in March 1994 following a flare-up of fighting in January and September 1993. In June 1992, as the conflict intensified and extended to Bosnia and Herzegovina, UNPROFOR'S mandate and strength were enlarged in order to ensure the security and functioning of the airport at Sarajevo, and the delivery of humanitarian assistance to that city and its environs. In September 1992, UNPROFOR's mandate was further enlarged to enable it to support efforts by the United Nations high commissioner for refugees to deliver humanitarian relief throughout Bosnia and Herzegovina, and to protect convoys of released civilian detainees if the international committee of the red cross so requested. In addition, the force monitored the "No-Fly" zone, banning all military flights in Bosnia and Herzegovina, and the United Nations "Safe Area" established by the Security Council around five Bosnian town and the city of Sarajevo. UNPROFOR was authorized to use force in self-defence. In reply to attacks against these areas, and to coordinate with the North Atlantic Treaty Organization (NATO) the use of air power in support of its activities. similar arrangements were subsequently extended to the territory of Croatia. UNPROFOR also monitored the implementation of a cease-fire agreement signed by the Bosnian Government and Bosnian Croat forces in February 1994. In addition. UNPROFOR monitored cease-fire arrangements negotiated between Bosnian Government and Bosnian Serbs Forces, which entered into force on 1 January 1995. In December 1992 UNPROFOR was also deployed in the former Yugoslav Republic of Macedonia, to monitor and report any developments in its border area which could undermine confidence and stability in that Republic and threaten its territory. On 31 March 1995, the Security Council decided to restructure UNPROFOR, replacing it with three separate but interlinked peace-keeping operations (see UNPF below).

Location: Bosnia and Herzegovina, Croatia, the Federal Republic of Yugoslavia (Serbia and Montenegro) and the former Yugoslav Republic of Macedonia.

Headquarters: Initially Sarajevo; Later Zagreb

Strength: Authorized: 4,870 all ranks there was also provision for almost 1,000 international civilian staff, 1,500 international contractual personnel and more than 3,000 local staff Maximum (30 September 1994): 39,922, including 38,614 troops, 637 military observers and 671 civilian police. At 31 March 1995: 38,848, including 37,421 troops, 677 military observers and 750 civilian

Fatalities:	3	Military Observers
	159	Other Military Personnel
	1	Civilian Police
	2	International United Nations Staff
	2	Local Staff
	167	(total, UNPROFOR unit 31 March 1995)

Financing: Method of Financing: Assessments in respect of a Special Account Expenditures: (See UNPF below)

Personal Envoy of the Secretary-General

Cyrus Vance (United States)	October 1991-April 1993.

Special Representatives of the Secretary-General and Heads of Mission of UNPROFOR:

	Thorvald Stoltenberg (Norway)	May 1993-December 1994
	Yasushi Akashi (Japan)	January 1994-[see UNPF below)
Forces Commanders	Lieutenant-General Satish Nambiar (India)	March 1992-March 1993
	Lieutenant-General Lars-Eric Wahlgren (Sweden)	March-June 1993
	Lieutenant-General Jean Cot (France)	Jue 1993-March 1994
	General Bertrand de Lapresle (France)	March 1994-February 1995
	General Bernard Janvier (France)	March 1995-[See UNPF below)
Police Commissioners	Chief Superintendent Kjell Johnsen (Norway)	1992-1993

	Chief Superintendent (Canada)	Mike O' Reilly	1993-1994
	Chief Superintendent (Denmark)	Sven Frederiksen	1994-1995 (see UNPF below)

Contributors	*Duration*	*Contribution*
Argentina	April 1992-March 1995	Civilian police
	April 1992 – March 1995	Troops
	April 1992 – March 1995	Military observers
Australia	April 1992 – November 1993	Military observers
Bangladesh	April 1992-March 1995	Civilian Police
	September 1994-March 1995	Troops
	April 1992-March 1995	Military observers
Belgium	April 1992-March 1995	Troops
	April 1992-March 1995	Military observers
Brazil	September 1993-March 1995	Civilian police
	August 1992-March 1995	Military observers
Canada	April 1992-March 1995	Civilian police
	April 1992 – March 1995	Troops
	April 1992 – March 1995	Military observers
Colombia	April 1992-March 1995	Civilian police
	April 1992 – May 1994	Military observers
Czech Republic	April 1992-March 1995	Troops
(Czecho-slovakia before 31 December 1992)	April 1992 – March 1995	Military observers
Denmark	April 1992-March 1995	Civilian Police
	April 1992 – March 1995	Troops
	April 1992 – March 1995	Military observers
Egypt	April 1992-July 1994	Civilian police
	December 1994-March 1995	
	April 1992 – March 1995	Troops
	April 1992 – March 1995	Military observers

Finland	July 1994-March 1995	Civilian police
	April 1992-March 1995	Troops
	April 1992 – March 1995	Military observers
France	April 1992-March 1995	Civilian police
	April 1992 – March 1995	Troops
	April 1992 – March 1995	Military observers
Ghana	April 1992 – March 1995	Military observers
India	April 1992-March 1995	Military Observers
Indonesia	October 1994-March 1995	Civilian police
	September 1994-March 1995	Troops
	October 1993-March 1995	Military observers
Ireland	April 1992-March 1995	Civilian Police
	April 1992-March 1995	Military observers
Jordan	April 1992 - March 1995	Civilian police
	April 1992 – March 1995	Troops
	April 1992 – March 1995	Military observers
Kenya	April 1992 - March 1995	Civilian police
	April 1992 – March 1995	Troops
	April 1992 – March 1995	Military observers
Lithuania	November 1994-March 1995	Troops
Luxembourg	April 1992-July 1993	Troops
Malaysia	October 1994-March 1995	Civilian police
	October 1993-March 1995	Troops
	September 1993-March 1995	Military observers
Nepal	April 1992 - March 1995	Civilian police
	April 1992 – March 1995	Troops
	April 1992 – March 1995	Military observers
Netherlands	November 1993-March 1995	Civilian police
	April 1992-March 1995	Troops
	April 1992-March 1995	Military observers
New Zealand	September 1994-March 1995	Troops
	April 1992-March 1995	Military observers
Nigeria	April 1992 - March 1995	Civilian police
	April 1992 – March 1995	Troops
	April 1992 – March 1995	Military observers

Norway	April 1992 - March 1995	Civilian police
	April 1992 – March 1995	Troops
	April 1992 – March 1995	Military observers
Pakistan	October 1994-March 1995	Civilian police
	June 1994-March 1995	Troops
	September 1993-March 1995	Military observers
Poland	April 1992 - March 1995	Civilian police
	April 1992 – March 1995	Troops
	April 1992 – March 1995	Military observers
Portugal	April 1992-March 1995	Civilian Police
	January 1993-October 1994	Troops
	April 1992 – March 1995	Military
Russian Federation	April 1992 - March 1995	Civilian police
	April 1992 – March 1995	Troops
	April 1992 – March 1995	Military observers
Senegal	January-March 1995	Civilian police
Slovak Republic (Czechoslovakia before 31 December 1992)	April 1992-March 1995	Troops
Spain	November 1992-March 1995	Troops
	October 1992 – March 1995	Military observers
Sweden	April 1992 - March 1995	Civilian police
	April 1992 – March 1995	Troops
	April 1992 – March 1995	Military observers
Switzerland	July 1993 – March 1995	Civilian police
	April 1994-September 1994	Troops
	May 1992-March 1995	Military observers
Thailand	April 1992	Military observers
Tunisia	August 1992-March 1995	Civilian police
Turkey	June 1994-March 1995	Troops
Ukraine	May 1994-March 1995	Civilian police
	August 1992-March 1995	Troops
	July 1994-March 1995	Military observers
United Kingdom	April 1992-March 1995	Troops
	April 1992 – March 1995	Military Observers

United States	November 1992-March 1995	Troops
Venezuela	April 1992-November 1994	Military observers

Voluntary Contributions: [See UNPF below]

United Nations Protection Force (UNPROFOR)

(31 March – 20 December1995)

Authorization: Security Council Resolutions:982 (1995) of 31 March 1995998 (1995) OF 16 June 19951026 (1995) of 30 November 1995

Function After the restructuring of UNPROFOR on 31 March 1995, the Force continued to perform the functions envisaged in SECURITY Council resolutions relevant to the situation in Bosnia and Herzegovina. In November 1995, a United States initiative led to the Peace Agreement initialled and subsequently signed, in December 1995, by the leaders of Bosnia and Herzegovina, Croatia and the Federal Republic of Yugoslavia (Serbia and Montenegro). As requested by the Agreement, the Security Council authorized Member States to establish a NATO-led multinational Implementation Force (IFOR) to help ensure compliance with the provisions of the Agreement. After IFOR took over from UNPROFOR ON 20 December 1995, the latter's mandate was terminated.

Location Bosnia Herzegovina

Headquarters Zagreb

Strength Maximum strength (31 August 1995): 30,869, including 30,74 troops, 278 military observers and 17 civilian police At withdrawal: 2,675, including 2,433 troops, 156 military observers and 86 civilian police (31 DECEMBER 1995)

Fatalities: 31 March 1995-20 December 199538 Military personnel1 civilian police1 local staff40 totalGrand total UNPROFOR (21 FEBRUARY 1992-20 DECEMBER 1995)167 21 February 1992-31 March 1995) (see above)40 (31 March 1995-20 December 1995) (see above)207 grand total

Financing: Methods of financing and expenditures: (see UNPF above)

Head of Mission:	Antonio Pedauye (Spain)	March-December 1995
Military Co Commander:	Lieutenant-General Rupert Smith (United Kingdom) March-December 1995(From 31 March to 20 December 1995, Overall command and control of UNPROFOR was exercised from UNPF Headquarters in Zagreb by the Secretary-General's Special Representatives, Mr.Yasushi Akashi (from 31 March to 31 October 1995) and subsequently Mr.Kofi Annan (from 1 November to 20 December 1995), and the Theatre Force Commander, Lieutenant-General Bernard Janvier (from 31 March to 20 December 1995)]	

Contributors	*Duration*	*Contribution*
Argentina	April 1995	Troops
	April 1995	Military Observation
	October – December 1995	
Bangladesh	April – May 1995	Civilian police
	November – December 1995	
	April-December 1995	Troops
	April-December 1995	Military observers
Belgium	April-December 1995	Troops
	April-December 1995	Military observers
Brazil	April-December 1995	Civilian police
	April-December 1995	Military observers
Canada	April-May 1995	Civilian police
	April-December 1995	Troops
	April-December 1995	Military observers
Colombia	April – May 1995	Civilian Police
Czech Republic	April – December 1995	Military observers
Denmark	April-August 1995	Civilian Police
	December 1995	
	April-December 1995	Troops
	April-December 1995	Military observers
Egypt	April – July 1995	Civilian police
	November-December 1995	
	April-December 1995	Troops
	April-December 1995	Military observers

Finland	April-December 1995	Civilian Police
	April-December 1995	Military observers
France	April-December 1995	Civilian Police
	April-December 1995	Troops
	April-December 1995	Military observers
Germany	August-October 1995	Troops
Ghana	April-December 1995	Military Observers
Indonesia	April 1994 – June 1995	Civilian Police
	August – December 1995	Troops
	April – December 1995	Military observers
Ireland	April-December 1995	Civilian Police
	April-December 1995	Military observers
Jordan	April – May 1995	Civilian Police
	November-December 1995	
	April-December 1995	Troops
	April-December 1995	Military Observers
Kenya	April-May 995	Civilian Police
	December 1995	
	April-December 1995	Military Observers
Malaysia	April – May 1995	Civilian Police
	April – December 1995	Troops
	April – June 1995	Military Observers
Nepal	April – May 1995	Civilian Police
	April – December 1995	Military Observers
Netherlands	April-December 1995	Civilian Police
	April-December 1995	Troops
	April-December 1995	Military observers
New Zealand	April-December 1995	Troops
	April-December 1995	Military Observers
Nigeria	April-May 1995	Civilian Police
	April-December 1995	Military Observers
Norway	April-December 1995	Civilian Police
	April-December 1995	Troops
	April-December 1995	Military observers
Pakistan	April – May 1995	Civilian Police
	April-December 1995	Troops
	April-December 1995	Military Observers

Poland	April-December 1995	Civilian Police
	April – May 1995	Troops
	April-December 1995	Military observers
Portugal	April-December 1995	Civilian Police
	April-December 1995	Military Observers
Russian	April-December 1995	Civilian Police
Federation	April-December 1995	Troops
	April-December 1995	Military observers
Senegal	January-December 1995	Civilian Police
Spain	April-December 1995	Troops
	April-December 1995	Military observers
Sweden	April-December 1995	Civilian Police
	April-December 1995	Troops
	April-December 1995	Military observers
Switzerland	April – May 1995	Civilian Police
	April – December 1995	Military observers
Tunisia	April – May 1995	Civilian police
Turkey	April-December 1995	Troops
Ukraine	April-December 1995	Civilian Police
	April-December 1995	Troops
	April-December 1995	Military Observers
United	April-December 1995	Troops
Kingdom	April-December 1995	Military Observers
United States	April-December 1995	Troops

Voluntary contributions: (see UNPF above)

United Nations Confidence Restoration Operation in Croatia (UNCRO)

Authorization Security Council resolutions:981 (1995) of 31 March 1995990 (1995) of 28 April 1995994 (1995) of 17 May 19951025 (1995) of 30 November 1995.

Function: To perform the functions envisaged in the cease-fire agreement of 29 March 1994; facilitate implementation of the economic agreement of 2 December 1994; facilitate implementation of all relevant Security Council resolutions; assist in controlling, by monitoring and reporting, the crossing of military personnel, equipment, supplies and weapons, over the international borders between Croatia and Bosnia and Herzegovina, and Croatia and the FEDERAL republic of Yugoslavia (Serbia and Montenegro) at the border crossings; facilitate the delivery of international humanitarian assistance to Bosnia and Herzegovina through the territory of Croatia; and monitor the demilitarization of the Prevlaka peninsula. After Croatia's reintegration by force of Western Slavonia and the Krajina region in May and August 1995, the need for United Nations troops in those areas was effectively eliminated. However, in Eastern Slavonia – the last Serb-controlled territory in Croatia – the mandate of UNCRO remained essentially unchanged. The Government of Croatia and the Croatian Serb leadership agreed to resolve the issue of Eastern Slavonia through negotiation. United Nations- Sponsored talks concluded with the signing of the Basic Agreement on the Region of Eastern Slavonia, Baranja and Western Sirmium on 12 November. The Agreement provided for the peaceful integration into Croatia of that region and requested the Security Council to establish a transitional administration to govern the region during the transitional period. Following the establishment of the United Nations administration, the mandate of UNCRO was terminated.

Location	Croatia
Headquarters	Zagreb
Duration:	31 March 1995-15 January 1996
Strength:	Maximum (31 May 1995); 15,522, including 14,663 troops, 328 military observers and 531 civilian police At withdrawal: 3,376, including 3,110 troops, 98 military observers and 168 civilian police.
Fatalities	16 military personnel
Financing:	Method of financing and expenditures: (see UNPF above)
Head of Mission	Byung Suk Min (Republic of Korea) March 1995-January 1996

Military Commander	Major-General Eid Kamal Al-Rodan (Jordan) March-December 1995(Overall command and control of UNCRO was exercised from UNPF Headquarters in Zagreb by the Secretary-General's Special Representatives, Mr.Yasushi Akashi and subsequently Mr. Kofi Annan, and the Theatre Force Commander, Lieutenant-General Bernard Janvier)

Contributors	*Duration*	*Contribution*
Argentina	April 1995-January 1996	Troops
	october 1995-January 1996	Military Observers
Bangladesh	May 1995-January 1996	Civilian police
	June 1995-January 1996	Troops
	May 1995 – January 1996	Military Observers
Belgium	April 1995 – January 1996	Troops
	May 1995 – January 1996	Military observers
Brazil	May 1995-January 1996	Civilian Police
	May 1995 – January 1996	Military observers
Canada	May – July 1995	Civilian Police
	April 1995 – January 1996	Troops
	May 1995-January 1996	Military Observers
Czech Republic	April 1995-January 1996	Troops
	May 1995 – January 1996	Military Observers
Denmark	May 1995-January 1996	Civilian police
	April 1995-January 1996	Troops
	May 1995 – January 1996	Military Observers
Egypt	May 1995-January 1996	Civilian police
	June 1995-January 1996	Troops
	May 1995 – January 1996	Military Observers
Estonia	April – November 1995	Troops
Finland	May 1995-January 1996	Civilian police
	April 1995-January 1996	Troops
	May 1995 – January 1996	Military Observers
France	May 1995-January 1996	Civilian police
	April 1995-January 1996	Troops
	May 1995 – January 1996	Military Observers
Germany	September1995-January 1996	Troops

Ghana	May 1995 – January 1996	Military Observers
Indonesia	May – November 1995	Civilian police
	April 1995-January 1996	Troops
	May 1995 – January 1996	Military Observers
Ireland	May 1995-January 1996	Civilian police
	May 1995 – January 1996	Military Observers
Jordan	May 1995-January 1996	Civilian police
	April – December 1995	Troops
	May 1995 – January 1996	Military Observers
Kenya	May 1995-January 1996	Civilian police
	April 1995-January 1996	Troops
	May 1995 – January 1996	Military Observers
Lithuania	April – November 1995	Troops
Malaysia	May – September 1995	Civilian police
	Jun 1995 – January 1996	Troops
	May-Junc 1995	Military Observers
Nepal	May-August 1995	Civilian police
	April-December 1995	Troops
	May 1995-January 1996	Military Observers
Netherlands	May 1995-January 1996	Civilian police
	April 1995-January 1996	Troops
	May 1995 – January 1996	Military Observers
New Zealand	June 1995-January 1996	Troops
	May 1995 – January 1996	Military Observers
Nigeria	July – December 1995	Civilian Police
	July 1995 – January 1996	Military Observers
Norway	May 1995-January 1996	Civilian police
	April 1995-January 1996	Troops
	May 1995 – January 1996	Military Observers
Pakistan	May-November 1995	Civilian police
	June 1995-January 1996	Troops
	May 1995-January 1996	Military Observers
Poland	May 1995-January 1996	Civilian police
	April 1995-January 1996	Troops
	May 1995 – January 1996	Military Observers
Portugal	May 1995-January 1996	Civilian Police
	May 1995 – January 1996.	Military Observers

Russian Federation	May 1995-January 1996	Civilian police
	April 1995-January 1996	Troops
	May 1995 – January 1996	Military Observers
Senegal	May 1995-January 1996	Civilian Police
Slovak Republic	April 1995-January 1996	Troops
Spain	July 1995-January 1996	Troops
	May 1995-January 1996	Military
Sweden	May 1995-January 1996	Civilian police
	April 1995-January 1996	Troops
	May 1995 – January 1996	Military Observers
Switzerland	July 1995 – January 1996	Military observers
Tunisia	May – October 1995	Civilian police
Turkey	June-October 1995	Troops
Ukraine	May 1995-January 1996	Civilian police
	April 1995-January 1996	Troops
	May 1995 – January 1996	Military Observers
United Kingdom	June 1995-January 1996	Troops
	May 1995-January 1996	Military observers
United States	April – December 1995	Troops

Voluntary Contributions: (See UNPF above)

United Nations Operation in Mozambique (ONUMOZ)

Authorization: Security Council resolutions:797 (1992) of 16 December 1992850 (1993) of 9 July 1993879 (1993) of 29 October 1993882 (1993) of 5 November 1993898 (1994) of 23 February 1994916 (1994) of 5 May 1994957 (1994) of 15 November 1994

Function: Established to help implement the General Peace Agreement, signed on 4 October 1992 in Rome by the President of the Republic of Mozajmbique and the President of the Resistencia Nacional Mocambicana (RENAMO). The mandate of ONUMOZ was: to facilitate impartially the implementation of the Agreement; to monitor and verify the ceasefire, the separation and concentration of forces, their demobilization and the collection, storage and destruction of weapons; to monitor and verify the complete withdrawal of foreign forces and to provide security in the transport corridors; to monitor and verify the disbanding of private and irregular armed groups; to authorize security arrangements for vital infrastructures; and to provide security for United Nations and other international activities in support of the peace process; to provide technical assistance and monitor the entire electoral process; to coordinate and monitor humanitarian assistance operations, in particular those relating to refugees, internally displaced persons, demobilized military personnel and the affected local population. After successful presidential and legislative elections in October 1994, and the installation of Mozambique's new Parliament and the inauguration of the President of Mozambique in early December, ONUMOZ's mandate formally came to an end at midnight on 9 December 1994. The Mission was formally liquidated at the end of January 1995.

Location	Mozambique
Headquarters	Maputo
Duration	16 December 1992–9 December 1994.
Strength	Authorized: 6,625 troops and military support personnel, 354 military observers and 1,144 civilian police; there were also some 355 international staff and 506 local staff; in addition, during the polling, ONUMOZ deployed approximately 900 electoral observers Miximum strength of military component (30 November 199): 6,576 all ranks Maximum strength of civilian police component (31 October 1994): 1,087 At withdrawal (30 November 1994): 3,941 troops and military support personnel, 204 military observers and 918 civilian police.
Fatalities:	21 military personnel 2 civilian police 1 international United Nations staff——24 total——
Financing	Method of financing: Assessments in respect of a Special Account Expenditures: From inception to 15 November 1994: \$471,199,200 In addition, for the liquidation period from 16 November 1994 to 31 March 1995, the General Assembly appropriated \$ 39,053,300

Special Representative of the Secretary-General and Chief of Mission Aldo Ajello (Italy) October 1992-December 1994

Force Commanders	Major-General Lelio Goncalves Rodrigues da Silva (Brazil)	February 1993-February 1994
	Major-General Mohammad abdus Salam (Bangladesh)	March-December 1994
Police Commissioner:	Brigadier-General Ali Mahmoud (Egypt)	March-December 1994

Contributors	*Duration*	*Contribution*
Argentina	April 1993-December 1994	Troops
	April 1993-December 1994	Military observers
Australia	March-December 1994	Civilian PoliceTroops
	August-December 1994	
Austria	July-December 1994	Civilian Police
Bangladesh	January-December 1994	Civilian Police
	February 1993–December 1994	Troops
	February 1993–December 1994	Military Observers
Bolivia	July-November 1994	Civilian Police
Botswana	May-December 1994	Civilian Police
	February 1993-December 1994	Troops
	June 1993-December 1994	Military Observers
Brazil	January-December 1994	Civilian Police
	February 1993-March 1994	Troops
	June – December 1994	
Canada	February 1993-December 1994	Military Observers
Cape Verde	February 1993-December 1994	Military Observers
China	July 1993-December 1994	Military Observers
Czech Republic	June 1993 – June 1994	Military Observers
Egypt	March-December 1994	Civilian Police
	February 1993-December 1994	Military Observers
Finland	May-November 1994	Civilian Police

Ghana	July – December 1994	Civilian Police
Guinea-Bissau	January-December 1994 February 1993-December 1994	Civilian Police Military Observers
Guyana	November-December 1994	Monitors
Hungary	January-December 1994 February 1993-December 1994	Civilian Police Military Observers
India	June-December 1994 March 1993-December 1994 April 1993-April 1994	Civilian Police Troops Military observers
Indonesia	June-December 1994	Civilian Police
Ireland	March-November 1994	Civilian Police
Italy	January 1993-December 1994	Troops
Japan	May 1993-December 1994	Troops
Jordan	March-December 1994	Civilian Police
Malaysia	January-December 1994 January 1993 –December 1994	Civilian Police Military observers
Nepal	June-December 1994	Civilian Police
Netherlands	December 1993-December 1994	Military observers
New Zealand	March-December 1994	Troops
Nigeria	September-December 1994	Civilian Police
Norway	March-November 1994	Civilian Police
Pakistan	May-December 1994	Civilian Police
Portugal	February-December 1994 March 1993-December 1994 November 1993-December 1994	Civilian Police Troops Military Observers
Russian Federation	May 1993-December 1994	Military Observers
Spain	January-December 1994 February 1993-December 1994	Civilian Police Military Observers
Sri Lanka	May-December 1994	Civilian Police
Sweden	January-December 1994 January 1993 -December 1994	Civilian Police Military Observers

Switzerland	March-October 1994	Civilian Police
Togo	July-December 1994	Civilian Police
United States	March-December 1994	Troops
Uruguay	May-December 1994 February 1993-December 1994	Civilian Police Troops
Zambia	September-December 1994 February 1993-December 1994 August 1993-November 1994	Civilian Police Troops Military Observers

Voluntary Contributions: Italy (1993-1994 – air component: 8 helicopters, 3 fixed- wing aircraft, some 110 personnel [The air component was used by the Italian military forces in the mission area, and all associated costs were borne by the Government of Italy. However, these air resources were available to the United Nations in emergency situations]Trust Fund for the Implementation of the Peace Process in Mozambique (total: $17,710,806):Denmark ($500,000), France ($232,143), Italy ($11,447,486), Luxembourg ($42,156), Namibia ($1,000), Netherlands ($988,992), Norway ($107,150), Portugal ($300,000), South Africa ($290,000), Sweden ($367,454), Switzerland ($209,775), United Kingdom ($743,250), United States ($1,000,000), The Commission of the European Communities ($987,600)Trust Fund for Assistance to Registered Political Parties in Mozambique (total: $3,050,000):Canada ($ 163,666), Italy ($1,898,734), The Commission of the European Communities ($1,481,400).

Bibliography

U.N.Publications

Basic Facts About the United Nations, New York: United Nations, Department of Public Information, 1995.

Charter of the United Nations and Statute of the International Court of Justice, New York, United Nations, Department of Public Information, 1994.

Coordination of Economic and Social Activities, 1948., ISBN.0-313-20329-6 CESA.

Consultation Between the United Nations and Non-Governmental Organization, 1949, ISBN 0.3.3-2003 30X

Field Administration in the United Nations System. The Conduct of International Economic and Social Programs, 1961 by Walter Rice Sharp.

Ghali, Boutros, Boutros, *An Agenda for Peace,* New York, United Nations, Department of Public Information, 1992.

Latin America in the United Nations, 1956 by John A.Houston ISBN 0-313-20335-0 HOLU.

Noble Peace Prize 1988 award to U.N. Peacekeeping Forces", *U.N. Chronicle,* Volume – XXV, Number 4 December 1988.

"Peace Keeping: A Whole New Range of Responsibilities", *U.N.Chronicle*, Dec. 1993.

"Peace Mission: Speeding UP the process", *United Nations Chronicle,* Volume – XXXIII, November 4, 1996.

"Peace Path: Reports on United Nations Efforts to Preserve and Enhance Peace", *United Nations Chronicle,* Volume XXXIII November 3, 1996.

"Summit of Peace Makers", *U.N. Chronicle,* Volume XXXIII, November 2, 1996.

The Blu Helmets – A Review of United Nations Peace-Keeping, New York, United Nations Department of Public Information, 1990, 1996.

The Budget of the United Nations 1947, ISBN 0-313-20328-8, BUNN.

The General Assembly of the United Nations, A Study of Procedure and Practice, 1964 by Sydney Dawson Bailey, ISBN 0-313-20336-9 BAGA.

The International Court of Justice: Its role in the maintenance of International Peace and Security, 1951 by Oliver James, Lissitzyn, ISBN 0-313-203334. licj.

The Political Role of the General Assembly, 1951 by Henry Field Haviland, ISBN 0-313-20334-2 HAPG.

The Secretariat of the United Nations, 1964 by Sydney Dawson Bailey.

The United Nations and Cambodia 1991-1995, New York; United Nations, Department of Public Information, 1996.

The United Nations Secretariat 1950 ISBN 0-313-203318-8, *UNNS.*

United Nations Peace-Keeping, New York, United Nations, Department of Public Information, 1996.

United Nations Peace keeping - Information Notes: New York, United Nations, Department of Public Information, 1995.

United Nations – Peacekeeping operations, Information Notes: New York U.N.D.P.I. – 1993.

Voting and Handling of Disputes in the Security Council, 1950, by Edvardo Jiminez de Arechaga, ISBN 0-313-20332-6 ARVH.

Books and Articles

A. Appadorai, *National Interest and India's Foreign Policy*, Kalinga Publications, Delhi, 1992.

Adam Curle, *Making Peace,* Tavistock Publications, 1971.

Alan James, *Peacekeeping in International Politics,* MacMillan in associated with the I.I. for Strategic Studies (IISS). P.1990, V.199 (ZQ) 'N8 No. AC: 180982.

Albert Legault, *Peacekeeping Operations Bibliography,* International Information Centre.

Albright Madelcinc, K. "Building a consensus on International Peace-Keeping", *U.S.Department of State Despatch,* November 15, 1993, Volume 4, Number 46.

Andrew Boyd: "Fifteen Men on a Powder Keg". *A History of the U.N. Security Council,* Methum & Co. Ltd., 1971.

Anthony Parsons Micael Joseph, *From Cold war to Hot Peace,* London 1995, pp. 244-260.

Anne – Marie Smith, *Advances in Understanding International Peacemaking*, United States Institute of Peace.

Bailey, Sydney, D "The United Nations and the termination of Armed conflict, 1946-64", *International Affairs,* Volume 58, Number 1, Summer, 1982.

Banarjee, Arun Kumar: "From peace keeper to blood letting" The travels of the U.N., India quarterly, *A journal of International Affairs,* Volume LI, Numbers 2,3 April/ Sept., 1995, New Delhi.

Basu, Rumki, The United Nations – *Structure and Functions of an International Organisation,* New Delhi: Sterling Publishers Private Ltd., 1993.

Bellows, Thomas, J., Erikson, Stanley and Winter, Herbert, J., *Political Science: Introductory Essays and Readings,* Bemont: Wadsworth Publishing Company, Inc. 1971.

Bennet, Douglas: "Peace- keeping and multilateral relations in U.S. Foreign Policy", *D.S.Department of State Despatch,* December 5, 1994, Volume 5, Number 49.

Berridge, G.R.: "Diplomacy and the Angola/ Namibia Accords", *International Affairs,* Volume 65, Number 3, Summer, 1989.

Betts, Richard, K., "Delusions of Impartiality – The United Nations and Interventions", *Current,* Feb., 1995.

Bid Well, Shelford, "The Theory and Practice of Peace-Keeping", *International Affairs",* Volume 54, Number 4 Oct, 1978.

Bilgrami, S.J.R., *International Organisation – A View from Within*, New Delhi: Vikas Publishing House Private Limited, 1983.

Bingham, J.B., U. Thaunt: *The Search of Peace,* V. Golannez, London, 1966.

Bloomfield, L.P., "International Military Forces" *The Question of Peace keeping in Armed and Disarmed World,* Little Brown, Boston, 1969.

Blue Helmets and Empty Guns, *The New York Times Magazine*, January 2, 1994.

Bolton, John, R., "Wrong turn in Somalia", *Foreign Affairs,* Jan/Feb 1994, Volume 73, Number 1.

Boutros, Boutros – Ghali: Agenda for Peace 1995, (Second Edition) United Nations, New York, 1995.

Boyd, Andrew, "The United Nations, Thirty Years on", *International Affairs*, Volume 52, Number 1, January 1976.

Boyd, J.M., *United Nations Peace-Keeping, A Military and Political Appraisal,* Praeger, New York and London, 1971.

Building Peace and Development 1994, *Annual Report of the Work of the Organization.*

Burns, E.L. and Heathcote, *Peace-Keeping* by *United Nations Forces*, London 1963.

Burns, E.L.M., *Between Arab and Israeli*, Harap, London 1962, Obolensky – New York, 1963.

Carnegie Endowment for International Peace, United Nations Studies, *UNSS.*

Carolana Cosgrove and Kenneth J. Twitchett Edited by: "The New International Actors", *The United Nations and the European Economic Community.* MacMillan, St. Martin's Press, First Published in 1970.

Chander, Prakash and Arora, Prem, *International Relations,* New Delhi, Cosmos Bookhive Private Ltd., 1989.

Charles A.Becker (ED): *Problems of World Disarmament.*

Charters, David. A., *Peace-Keeping and the Challenge of Civil Conflict Resolution,* Centre for Conflict studies, University of New Brunsulick, 1994.

Chester Bowles, *The New Dimensions of Peace,* Harper & Brothers Publishers, New York, 1955.

Chhabra, Hari, Sharan, "Indian Peace-keeping forces in Somalia, *World Focus* W.F. October 1994.

Chris Brown, *Understanding International Relations,* MacMillan Press Ltd., 1997.

Claesson, Paul and Findlay, Trevor, "Case studies on Peace-Keeping: U.N.Som II, UNTAC and UNPROFOR" *Sipri Year Book,* 1994 Stockholm: Oxford University Press, 1994.

Clarke, Walter and Herbert, Jeffrey, "Somalia and the Future of Humanitarin Intervention", *Foreign Affairs*, March/April 1996.

Clerk M. Eicherlberger: *U.N.The First Twenty Years.*

Colonel A.K.Baradlal, Changing security scenario, Implication for UN Peacekeeping, Knowledge World, New Delhi.

Cox, Arthur M, *Prospects for Peace-Keeping*, Brookings Institutions, Washington D.C., 1967.

Crocker, Chester, A., "The Lessons of Somalia – Not everything went wrong", *Foreign Affairs,* May/June, 1995, Vol.74, Number 3.

Crossette, Barbara,"The Task of Peace-Keeping", The *Hindu,* Dec. 9, 1994.

David M. Malone (Ed.), "The U.N.Security Council" "*From the Could War to the 21st Century,* L.R.Publishers, 2004.

David S. Sorenson and Pia Christina Wood, *The Politics of Peacekeeping in the Post Cold War Era.*

David Steele, *The Reform of the United Nations.*

Daniel C. Thomas, and Michael T.K. Lare (Ed.), *Peace and World Order Studies,* 1989, West View Press, U.S.A.

Dhiraj R. Chambling, *India and the United Nations 1946-52.* Associated Publishing House, New Delhi, Second Ed. 1978.

Diehl, Paul, f.: "Peace-keeping operations and the quest for Peace", *Political Science Quality,* Volume 103, Number, 1988.

Dobbie, Charles, *A Concept for Post cold war Peace-Keeping*, Survival, Vol. 36, Number 3, Autumn, 1994.

Donald C.F. Daniel and Bradd C. Hayes, *Beyond Traditional Peacekeeping* MacMillan Press Ltd., 1995.

Dr. M.R.Kazimi, "Financing the U.N.Peace Keeping Opeations". "Capital Publishing House 1988, Delhi – 110 006.

Dr. Subhas C.Khare, LL.D. "Use of force under U.N. Charter" Metropolitan Book Co. (P) Ltd., New Delhi, *India,* 1985.

Dr.Surendra Bhutani, *The United Nations and The Arab-Israeli Conflict.* The Academic Press, 1977.

Durch William, J., Blechman, Barry, M., *Keeping the Peace: The United Nations in the Emerging World Order,* Report No.2, Washington D.C. The Henry L. Stimson Centre, 1992.

Edwin Tetlow, *The United Nations, The First 25 Years,* Peter Owen Ltd.: London, 1970.

Elise Boul Ding (Ed.), *New Agendas for Peace Research,* Rienner Publishers, Boulder & London 1992 V.1:19, (3Q)...N2.

Evan Luard: *The United Nations How it works and what it Does?* The MacMillan Press Ltd., 1979

Fabian, Larry L., *Soldiers without Enemies: Preparing the United Nations for Peace-Keeping,* Brooking Institutions, Washington, 1971.

Findlay, Trevor, "Armed Conflict Prevention, Management and Resolution" *SIPRI,* Stockholm International Peace Research Institute) *Year Book,* 1995, Stockholm: Oxford University Press, 1995.

Francis Parakatil, *India and United Nations Peace Keeping Operations,* S. Chand & Co., 1975.

Frid Mirbagheri, *Cyprus and International Peace Making,* C Hurst and Co. 1998.

Foreign Affairs, Sep./ Oct., 1996, Vol.75, Number 5.

Frydenberg, (ed.) *Peace-Keeping: Experience and Evaluation*, Norwegian Institute of International Affairs, *OSLO*, 1964.

Frye, William R: "A United Nations Peace Force", Ocena Public for Carnegie Endowment for International Peace, New York, 1957.

Ghan Shyam Pardesi, *Contemporary Peace Research*, Radiant Publishers, 1982.

G.R. Berridge, *International Politics States, Power and Conflict Since 1945*. Wheatsheaf Books, Sussex St Martin's Press, New York, 1987.

George, Aurelia: "Japan's participation in U.N. Peace keeping Operations", *Asian Survey*, June 1993, Volume XXXIII, Number 6.

Gerlach, Jeffrey, R., "A U.N. Army for the New World Order", *Orbis, A Journal of World Affairs*, Vol.37, Number 2, Spring, 1993.

Ghai, U.R., *International Politics, Theory and Practice*, Jalandhar: New Academic Publishing Company, 1980.

Ghali, Boutros, Boutros, "Peace-keeping Hazards", *World Focus*, October, 1994.

Good Speed, Stephen, S., *The Nature and Function of International Organisation*, New York, Oxford University Press, 1967.

Goodrich, L.M. and Hambro E., *Charter of the United Nations*, Boston, World Peace Foundation.

Goodrich, L.M. and Hambro, E., *Charter of the United Nations: Commentary and Documents* (Rev. Ed.). World Peace Foundation, Boston,1949.

Goodrich, Leland, M., *The United Nations*, New York: Thomas Y.Crowell Company, 1959.

Gordon Feller, Sherle R. Schwenninger, Diane Singerman, *Peace and World Order Studies,* 1981, Transnational Academic Program Institute for World Order.: V.1;19 (3Q) N8 M1.

Goulding, Marrack, "The Evolution of United Nations Peace Keeping", *International Affairs,* Volume 69, Number 1, Jan., 1993.

Groom, A.J.R., "Peace keeping: Perspectives and Progress", *International Affair,* Volume 47, Number 1, Oct 1974.

Gupta, Alka , *India and U.N.Peacekeeping Activities: A Case Study of Korea 1947-53.* Radiant Publishers, 1977.

Gupta, Anirudha, "The Angolan Crisis and Foreign Intervention", *Foreign Affairm Reports,* Vol. xxv, Number 2, Feb. 1976.

Gupta, M.G., *International Relations Since 1945,* Allahabad, Chaitanya Publishing House, 1986.

H.G.Nicholas, *The United Nations as a Political Institution,* Oxford University Press, 1952.

Habibulllah, V., In Search of World Peace, *Kurnool,* Zyboon Publishing House.

Hammar SK Jold D., *The Servant of Peace: A Selection of Speeches and Statements* edited by Wilder Foote and the bodily Head, London 1962.

Hanna Bokor-szego, "The Role of the United Nations in International Legislation".

Harbottle, Michael, "The October middle East war Lessons for U.N. Peacekeeping", *International Affairs*, Volume 50, Number 4, October 1974.

Harbottle, M., *The Blue Berets*, Cooper, London, 1975.

Hartmann, Frederick, H., *The Relation of Nations*, New York, The MacMillan Company, 1960.

Helms, Jesse, *Saving the U.N. – A Challenge to the Next* Secretary-*General*.

Hershey, Burnet, *Soldier of Peace: Dag-Hammarksjold,* Britanica Books, Chicago, 1961.

Higgins, R., United Nations Peace Keeping, *1946-67 Documents and Commentary* Vol.I, The Middle East, Oxford University Press, New York, London, 1970.

Higgins, Rosalyn, "The New United Nations and Former Yugoslavia", *International Affairs,* Vol. 69, Number 1, January 1993.

Hill, Roger: "Preventive Diplomacy, Peace-making, and Peace-keeping, *SIPRI year book,* 1993, Stockholm: Oxford University Press, 1993.

Hillen III, John, F., "Peacekeeping is hell – America Unlearns the lessons of Vietnam", *Policy Review,* fall 1993, Number 66.

Ho-Won Jeong by Pub. Peace building in Post conflict Societies, *Strategy & Process*, Viva Books Private Limited.

Ho-Wonjeong (Ed.), *The New Agenda for Peace Research,* Ashgate Publishing Company 1999. V1:19 (3Q)N9.

Hugh Hanning (Ed.), Peacekeeping and technology, *Concepts for the Future*.

Indar Jit Rikhye , *The Theory and Practice of Peacekeeping* International Academy by C.Hurst & Co. Ltd., London, 1984.

Inis L. Claude, Jr., "Swords into Plowshares", *The Problems and Progress of International Organisation*, Random House, New York, 1956.

Inis L. Claude, Jr., *The Changing United Nations*, Random House, New York, 1967.

Into the Valleys of Death: *U.S.News and World Report,* June 2, 1993.

James, A, *The Politics of Peace-Keeping,* Chatto & Windus London and Prager, New York, 1969.

James, Alan, "The U.N. Force in Cyprus, *International Affairs*, Volume 65, Number 3, Summer, 1989.

James M.Boyd, United Nations Peace-Keeping, Operations: *A Military and Political Appraisal.*

Jean K. Krasno, *The United Nations (Confronting the Challenges of Global Society, 2005,* Lynne Rienner Publishers Inc. Boulder, CO80301, U.S.A.

Jha, C.S., "U.N's Peace-Keeping", *World Focus,* Oct 1994.

Jim Whitman, *Peace Keeping and the U.N. Agencies,* Frank Cass, London. Portland, 1999.

J.N. Dixit, *India's Foreign Policy 1947-2003,* 1998, Picus Books, C-30, West End. New Delhi.

John MacKinlay, *The Peacekeepers An Assessment of Peacekeeping Operations at the Arab-Israel Interference,* London, Unwin, Hyman Boston, Sydney, Wellington. 1989.

John G. Stoessinger, *The United Nations and the Super Powers,* Random House, N.Y., 1965.

John W. Halderman "The Political Role of the United Nations", *Advancing the World Community*, 1981 Praeger 1981.

John, Marcum, A., "Lessons of Angola", *Foreign Affairs,* Vol.54, Number 3, April 1976.

Judit Balazs and Wliberg (Ed.), Peace Research for the 1990s 1993, Akodemiai Kiado, Budapest.

Juyal, Shreesh and Ramesh Babu, B. (eds): *The United Nations and World Peace,* Sterling Publishers Private Ltd., 1990.

K.P.Saksena, *Reforming the United Nations, The Challenge of Relevance*, Sage Publications, New Delhi 1998.

Karen A. Mingst, *Essentials of International Relations*, W.W. North and Company, New York, London.

Kasturchand M. Jhabak, *The Emerging role of Security Council As an Instrument of International Peace,* Printed in India at Jayashree Printers, Secunderabad 1987.

Kennedy, Paul and Russett, Bruce, "Reforming the United Nations", *Foreign Affairs,* September/October 1995.

Kenneth J. Twitchett, *The Evolving United Nations, A Prospect for Peace?* Europa Publications, London

Keswani, K.B., *International Relations in Modern World (1900-1988),* Bombay: Himalaya Publishing House, 1990.

Kitson Frank, *Low Intensity Operations Subversion of Insurgency & Peacekeeping,* Faber & Faber, London, 1971.

Krishnan, N., "United Nations at Cross roads", *World Focus,* New Delhi 'Aug. 1996.

Kurt Waldheim, "The Challenge of Peace", George Weidenfeld and Nicolson Ltd., 1980, London, SW4.

Lauterpacht, Eli: *The United Nations Emergency Force: Basic Documents,* London, 1960.

Lefever, Ernest W.: Uncertain mandate: *Politics of the U.N. Congo Operations*, John Hoprins Press, 1967.

Lefever, E.W., *In certatian Mandate, Politics of the U.N. Cooperations*.

Leon Cordnker, *The United Nations in International Politics,* Princeton University Press, 1971.

Lt.Gen. Depinder Singh PVSM VSM , *Indian Peacekeeping Force in Srilanka 1987-89,* Natraj Publishers, Dehradun, 2001.

Lt. Gen. M.R. Kochhar, *United Nations Peacekeeping and Operations in Somalia,* Dipika Kochhar, 4507, Sector 23-23A, HUDA, Gurgaon, Haryana (India).

Lever, Ernest, W., *Reigning in the U.N Foreign Affairs,* Summer, 1993, Volume, 72, Number 3.

Lie, Trygve: *In the Cause of Peace,* MacMillan, London/New York 1954.

Linda B.Miller, "World order and local Disorder", *The United Nations and Inter and Conflicts,* Princeton, New Jersey, Princeton University Press, 1967.

Luard, E., (ed) *The Evaluation of International Organisations,* Thames and Hudson, London, 1966.

Luc. Reychier & Thana Paffenholz, *Peace-Building (A.field guide),* Lynne Rienner, Boulder, London, 2001.

M.J.Peterson, "The General Assembly in World Politics", Allen & Unwin Inc., Mass, USA. 1986.

M.S.Rajan, *United Nations and World Politics,* Har-Anand Publications, New Delhi, 1995.

Magenthau, Hans J., *Politics among Nations,* A. Knopf, New York, 1960.

Mahajan, V.D., *International Relations Since 1945,* Allahabad, Chaitanya Publishing House, 1986.

Mahdi Elmandira, *The United Nations System an Analysis* Faber and Faber Limited, London, 1973.

Mangone, G.J., *A Short History of International Organisation,* McGraw Hill, New York, 1954.

Martin Hill, *The United Nations System,* Cambridge University Press, Cambridge, 1978.

Martin Paul, "Peace-keeping and the United Nations", *International Affairs* Volume – 40, Number 2, April 1964.

Martin, Pierre–Marie, *Introduction to International Relations,* edited by J.C.Johari, New Delhi: Sterling Publishers Pvt. Ltd., 1986.

Masland, Tom, with Barry, John in Washington, *The Pitfalls of Peace Keeping*, News Week, July 26, 1993.

Massannat, George S., and Abcarian Gilbert (eds), *International Politics – Introductory Readings,* New York, Charles Scribner's Sons., 1970.

Max Jakobson, "The United Nations in the 1990s" a Second Chance? *A twentieth Century Fund Book,* 'UNITAR'.

Melkote, Rama, S. and Rao, Narasimha, A., *International Relations,* New Delhi, Sterling Publishers Private Ltd., 1992.

Michaels, Marguerite, "Blue-Helmet Blues", *Time,* Nov. 15, 1993.

Military adviser to the Secretary – General by Indarjit Rikhye *U.N.Peacekeeping and the Corgo Crises,* Pub. Hurst & Co., London St. Martin's Press, New York.

Miller, Richard A., *Dag Hammarksjoeld and Crisis Diplomacy*, Oceana Publications, 1961.

M.L. Sondhi, Shrikant Paranjee, A peace Agenda for Indian *Foreign Policy,* Har Ananad Pub.

M.S. Rajan, World order and the United Nations (Essays from a Nonaligned Perspective)

Morgenthau, Hans, J., *Politics Among Nations – The Struggle for Power and Peace*, Calcutta: Scientific Book Agencies, 1969.

Muhammad Rajul Haq, *The Third world War and World Peace* 1980, 6 Feb. Sinigda Afsan Haq Shanta in English 1ST Edition : March 1982.

Mukhaerjee, Sakti, Mukherjee, Indrani, *International Organisation,* Calcutta, The World Press Private Ltd., 1979.

Mukesh *Kumar Kayathwal,* The United Nations (Retrospect and Prospect), Pointer Publishers, Jaipur, India, 1997.

Nambiar, Satish, "India and U.N. Peacekeeping", *World Focus,* Oct/Nov/Dec 1997, Vol.18, November 10-11-12.

Narasimhan, C.V., *The United Nations – An Inside View,* UNITIAR in association with Vikas Publishing House Pvt Ltd., New Delhi, 1988.

Nicholas, H.G., *The United Nations as a Patitical Institutions*, Oxford University Press, London.

Niranjan Bhuinya, *United Nations, Problems and Prospects*, K.P. Bagchi & Company, Calcutta, 1980.

Peacekeeping, Challenges for the Future, Edtd. By Hugh Smith Australia Defence Studies, A. Deference for Academy of Canbera, 1993.

Philip Alston (Ed.), *The United Nations and Human Rights,* 1992, Clarendon Press, Oxford.

Poonam Mann, *India's Foreign Policy in the Post Cold war era.*

Portfolio for Peace: Excerpts from the Writings and Speeches of U. Thant, Sec. Gen. of U.N. on major world issues – 1961-70. Office of Public Information, *United Nations,* New York, October 1970.

Prem Arora, *The United Nations, A Study of International Organisation*, Cosmos Bookhive (P) Ltd.

Rajesh M. Basrur, *India's External Relations: A Theortical Anaiysis,* 2000, Ajay Varma.

Richard M. Price and Mark W. Zacher (Ed.), *The United Nations and Global Security,* Palgrave MacMillan 2004.

Rorden Wilkinson and Steve Hughes (Ed.) *Global Governance. Critical Perspectives,* Routledge, London 2002.

Rosalyn Higgins, *United Nations Peace Keeping – 1946-67.*

Rosner, Gabriella, *The United Nations Emergency Force,* Colombia University Press, London/New York, 1963.

Ruth B. Russel, *United Nations Experience with Military Forces: Political and Legal Aspects.*

S. Subba Rao, *U.N. Peace Keeping Force, Military Operations,* R.S.341.13, S94, C.R.R. Law College, Eluru.

Satish Kumar, *The United Nations at 50 An Indian View.*

Shirley Hazzard – "defeat of an ideal" *A Study of the Self – Destruction of U.N.* – MacMillan Limited", London 1973.

Steven R., "The New U.N. Peacekeeping" Building Peace in lands of conflict after the colwars Ratner, St.Martin's Press, New York, 1995.

Subir Goswami, *Politics in Law Making, A Study of International Law Commission of the UN.* Ashish Publishing House' New Delhi, 1986.

Susan Willet, Participatory monitoring of humanitarian mine action: Giving voice to citizens of *NICARAGUA,* Mozambique and Cambodia, 2003.

Sydney D. Bailey and Samdaws, *The United Nations: A Concise Political Guide,* Great Britan, MacMillan Press Ltd., 1963.

Sydney D. Bailey: "Peaceful settlement of Disputes: Ideas and Proposals for research. *A Unitar Study,* First Published – 1969 by Sydney D.Bailey and Unitar.

Sydney D.Bailey: *The UN Security Council and Human Rights*, The MacMillan Press Ltd., 1994.

Synopsis of United Nations Cases in the field of Peace and Security 1964-65. Carnegie Endowment for International Peace, New York, 1966.

Thant, U, *Toward World Peace,* Yoseloff, New York, 1964.

Thant, U, *View from the U.N.*" First Published in the U.S.A. by Doubleday & Company Inc.

The Challenges of Peace Keeping and peace support into the 21 century peacekeeping 2015 – A perspective, United Service Institution of India, Centre for United Nations Peacekeeping.

The Indian Army' United Nations Peacekeeping operations 341.5840954 Ind. 40923;

Thomas W. Britt and Amy, B. Adler, *The Psychology of the Peacekeeper*, 2003, Praeger Publishers, USA.

Todor Zhivkov, *Peace and Security for the People,* Sofia Press 1985; V.1:19 (3Q) N8 M51:2, G-103060.

T.T. Poulose, *United Nations and Nuclear Proliferation,* B.R. Publishing Corporation, Delhi, 1988.

Volker Rittberger, (Ed.), *Global Governance and the United Nations System. The U.N.System in the 21st Century*, The United Nations University Press, 2001.

Wain House, David W., *International Peace Observation: A History and Forecast,* John Hopkins Press, Baltimore, 1966.

William R. Frye, *A United Nations Peace Force,* Acena Publications INC, New York City, 1957.

Wolfram. F. Hanrieder (Ed.), "Global Peace and Security" Trend and Challenges, Westview, USA Press Boulder and London, 1987, V.1:19 (ZQ) 'N8 M71 – 162081.

Young Seek Choue, "Proposal for Peace", Kyung Hee University Press, 1986, V.1;19 (3q) N8 M6 G-74672 Complied by: I.I.P.S.

Young Seek Cho, *Peace in the Global Village,* The Institute of International Peace Studies, 1987 Kyung Hee University Press V.1:19 (3Q) 'N8 M7 G-101344.

Young Seek Choue. Ph.D., "White Paper on World Peace", Chouean Irenology, 1991, Kyung Hee University Press V:1:19 (3a) 'N8 NI G-121129.

List of Journals

1. In Praise of Chauvinism: rhetorics of nationalism in Yugoslav politics, of John B Allock, *Third World Quarterly October,* 1989.
2. Dick A LeurdiK, Before and after Dayton: The U.N. and NATO in the Former Yugoslavia, *Third World Quarterly,* Vol.No.18, No.3, 1997.
3. Ex-Yugoslavia's neighbours: Who wants what? Written by Franz – Lothar Altmann, *The World Today,* August-September 1992.
4. Mozambique – Development Assistance, Bridging the gap of Mark Malloch Brown, The World Today, June 2000.
5. The case for Power sharing in 'EL Salvador' – Piero Gleijesses, *Foreign Affairs,* Spring 1983.
6. Cambodia" Will the Loser taken take all? *The World Today,* March 1995.
7. The Cambodian Famine – *The World Today* 1979.
8. 'The Cambodia alert' – *The World Today* July 1990.

List of Paper Clippings

The following clippings from various News Papers out of two dozens and half clippings were of great help to me not only to find information but to analyse the cases.

- U.N.realities – Times of India 17 May 2005.
- Towards 'larger freedom' by Kofi Annan.
- Global threats and U.N. reforms – Hindu (Madras) 24th March 2005.
- For a real U.N. Commission on Human Rights. *International Herald Tribune*. 27th April 2005.
- U.N. Reform: Annan sets the Agenda.
- Act Boldly: Annan Unveils his ambitious U.N.Overhaul Plan: The Kofi Annan Blue Print – *Times of India* 22 March 2005.
- Overhaul the U.N's human rights body – *International Herald Tribune* 18th January 2005.
- Indo, U.S. Panel on peacekeeping – *National Herald,* New Delhi.
- Shasi Tharoor, The U.N. at 60 – Another SAN Francisco Moment, Indian Expres, New Delhi 26th June 2005.
- Suhas Chakma, The story of U.N's failure, *The Pioneer,* New Delhi 27th May 2003.
- India roots for peace, *Tribune* 4 Feb. 2003.
- A recipe in self-defence, *United Nations and World Peace* by Punyapriya.
- "We need a new way to prevent conflicts" A job for the U.N.: by Jose Manuel Durao Barraso and Joaquim Chissano in *International Herald Tribune* 2008, May 2004.

- When the U.N. fails, we all do unless the U.N. Cooperation with the U.S., there can be no realistic reform, only fantasy. U.N. Peacekeeping duties need fundamental rethinking by Fareed Zakaria.
- Challenges Before the U.N. The Way to ensure human survival by Sampooran Singh, Tribune, Chandigarh, 10 December 1999)
- Back Annan's Call for a new human rights body (Annan's call to overhaul the U.N. human rights system must be needed by Loubna Freigh and Joanna Wescler, *International Herald Tribune,* 9th April 2005.

Index

A

ARENA, 74
Arora, Prem, 19
ASEAN, 84, 90

B

Baathist government, 30
Bhargava, A.N., 171
Boutros-Ghali, Boutros, 11, 20, 67, 92, 119, 149, 166, 172

C

Cambodia,
location, 81
Chissano, Joquin Alberto, 149
COMPOL, 157
COPAZ, 67, 69, 77
Cordier, Andrew W., 20
CSC, 150
Cuellar, Javier Porez de, 57

D

Doyle, Michael W., 21
Dureh, William J, 17

F

FADM, 160
FMLN, 56, 58, 60, 61, 63, 65, 66, 67, 69, 70
FRLIMO, 146
FUNCINPEC, 83, 85, 87, 105, 107, 109

G

General Peace Agreement, 149, 171
Goulding, Marrack, 67
Greind, Gunther G., 18

H

Ho-Won Jeong, 19

I

ICFY, 122, 123, 131, 132, 135

J

Jakobson, Max, 20
James, Alan M., 19
James, Alan, 17, 18
JNA, 118
Jooah, James OC, 19

K

Khmer Rouge, 83
Khomeni, Ayathulla, 32
Kje Skjelsback, 18
KPNLF, 83, 85, 87

L

Lahmann, Ingsid A., 17
LCY, 117
League of Communists, 142, 143
League of Nations, 2

M

Martin, Pierre Maria, 19
Mills, Susan R., 19
MINUSAL, 77
Moxon, Edward, 21
Mozambique, 146

N

NADK, 99, 102, 103
Nambiar, Satish, 121
National Academy for Public Security, 66, 77
National Police Commission, 159
Nehru, Jawaharlal, 1, 2, 9

O

OAU, 150, 163
ONUCA, 78, 191, 193
ONUSL, 193

P

Pacific Settlement of Disputes, 176
Palme, Olof, 33
PAT, 64
PDK, 87, 93, 97, 99, 100
Peacekeeping operation,
  basic features of, 11-12
  function of, 169
Pink Zones, 128, 129
PNC, 64, 66
Present study (the)
  conclusion, 168-175
  introduction, 1
  methodology, 15
  need for, 13
  objectives of, 14
  review of literature, 17
  scope of, 14

R

Ratner, Daniel, 21
RENAMO, 148, 149, 153, 156, 157, 158, 159, 161, 163, 164, 165
Rikhye, Indarjit, 18, 22

S

Saksena, K.P., 20
Second Paris Conference, 89
Social reconstruction, 83
SOFA, 7
Suez Crisis, 7
Supreme Electoral Tribunal of El Salvador, 70, 71

T

Tudzman, Franzo, 124

U

U. Thant, 20
UN Resolution 377(V), 183
UNAMIC, 196
UNCRO, 140, 141, 171
UNDP, 153
UNEP, 7, 18
UNHCR, 142
UNIF, 140

United Nations Advanced Mission in Cambodia (UNAMIC), 81-113
United Nations Charter, 1, 3, 8, 13
United Nations Iran-Iraq Military Observer Group (UNIIMOG), 30-53
United Nations Observer Mission in El Salvador (ONUSAL), 54-80
United Nations Operation Mission in Mozambique (ONUMOZ), 146-167
United Nations Protection Force (UNPROFOR), 114-145
  division in three parts, 130
UNO, 3
UNOHAC, 155
UNPAs, 120, 121, 122, 123, 127, 131, 134, 135
UNTAC, 90, 91, 92, 94, 95, 96, 97, 99, 100, 101, 102, 107, 111, 198
UNTAES, 142
UNTSO, 6, 34, 36, 37

V

Vance, Cyrus, 119
VTF, 155

W

Waldheim, Kurt, 33
Woodhouse, Tom, 21
World War II, 81

Z

Zagreb Four, 136

■■■